THE MEMOIRS

OF

RAYMOND POINCARÉ

THE MEMOIRS

OF

RAYMOND POINCARÉ

1914

TRANSLATED BY

SIR GEORGE ARTHUR

GARDEN CITY   NEW YORK
DOUBLEDAY, DORAN & COMPANY
1929

First published 1929

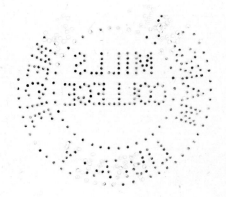

Printed in Great Britain by R. & R. CLARK, LIMITED, *Edinburgh*.

FOREWORD

THE two preceding volumes of the English edition of *The Memoirs of M. Raymond Poincaré* represented the first four volumes of the French edition of M. Poincaré's work : considerable compression had to be used in translating and adapting these. This third volume is a translation of Monsieur Poincaré's fifth volume, to which he has given the title *L'Invasion*. The French text has here been faithfully followed ; there has been no question of adaptation.

The numbers and dates of the telegrams from which the President of the French Republic derived much of his information are to be found in *L'Invasion*, as are also figures fully exhibiting the sad shortage of munitions in France at the outbreak of the war.

CONTENTS

CHAPTER I

CHAPTER II

CHAPTER III

CHAPTER IV

CHAPTER V

vii

CHAPTER VI

CHAPTER VII

CHAPTER VIII

CHAPTER IX

CHAPTER X

CHAPTER XI

CHAPTER I

Mobilisation completed—Concentration of troops begins—Plan No. 17—
Belgium invaded—Declarations of neutrality—M. Georges Clemenceau
—American overtures—The French in Alsace—Italy holds her hand—
Japan—Germans in the East.

FOR a few hours sleep brings forgetfulness of the catastrophe
which has befallen Europe and, awaking with the dawn, I ask
myself : " Can it be true that war has been declared upon
us ? " War ! Forty-four years have sped since my childish
eyes were horror-struck with the sight of it. The country
where I was born knew not only the terror of invasion but
was called upon to endure a foreign occupation, and my
schoolboy recollections are darkened by the vision of a long
defile of German helmets. Like myself, the people among
whom I grew up have preserved a bitter memory of these
mournful years. However hateful to see provinces torn
from the side of France, they have never wanted to see the
day when France would take up arms to seek a revenge : they
knew too well not only the risks which would be incurred, but
that on these provinces, more than any others, would fall
the largest penalty.

The same spirit of caution, perhaps less acute farther
away from the frontier, inspired more or less the French nation
at large. If our bond with Russia had from the beginning
found favour here, it was simply because it served to furnish
something like a permanent guarantee against threats or
provocations which might emanate from the already constituted Triple Alliance. The Triple Entente, in its turn, only
enjoyed popularity in France because it constituted a still
more efficacious instrument against an obviously growing
danger.

And now, in spite of forty-four years of prudence and care,

the great evil with which we always had to reckon has descended upon us. Can it really be so ? And what has the future in store for us ? I cannot rid myself of serious apprehensions. From the point of view of diplomacy our situation has never been better. Although our political systems are as the poles apart, France and Russia have accustomed themselves to harmonise the doings of their respective Chanceries without many blunders. Neither the differences of national temperaments, nor the contrast between the two Constitutions, nor the too frequent opposition of certain vested interests, nor the " touchiness " of certain Russian diplomats have served to throw cold water on the alliance. Our *entente cordiale* with England has been stretched since 1904 far enough to take stock of the various international problems, and we can now, after the halts and hesitations of the first few days, be sure that on land and sea Great Britain will be alongside Belgium and ourselves. But is not Germany far, far ahead of us in the matter of preparedness for war ? Our Three Years' Service has done something, but by no manner of means everything, to remedy what was our pronounced inferiority in men. But in material we indeed lag behind. Criticism in the Senate has not been beside the mark : we are badly off for heavy artillery ; the Parliamentary delay in voting special credits put back the reconstitution of our military plant ; we have over 4000 field guns, those excellent 75's which have proved their worth in the Balkans, but their flat trajectory does not enable them, like the German howitzers, to rake ground out of view of the men serving the guns. The Germans, on the other hand, are said to have 5000 77's, 1500 light howitzers, 2000 heavy howitzers and guns of other types.

No doubt this powerful material will have to meet the requirements of two distinct theatres of war—France and Russia, but nevertheless German superiority in heavy artillery, as compared to our own, must be a source of great anxiety for us. We can of course borrow some good siege guns from points which are not threatened, and as our Channel and ocean coasts are protected by the British Fleet, we can draw on our marine batteries. But when all is said

and done, we cannot put up against the enemy anything like
the guns and munitions which he will bring to bear against us.
How far will the worth of our units and the training of our
men balance our shortage in armaments ? The Minister of
War in Council began by saying that he was wholly confident
and so forth : then, overcome by emotion, he stopped, buried
his head in his hands and began to sob out loud. He quickly
recovered himself and repeated that victory was a certainty
for us. The General Staff is most reassuring, but at this
moment which of us knows the innermost thoughts of his
neighbour ? If I have any doubts of my own, ought I to
admit them to myself, and anyhow, ought I to let others
guess them ? I feel in my innermost self I must do nothing
by word or sign which in the slightest degree might daunt
the spirits either of the splendid young fellows who are
setting out to face death or of their families who will not
let sadness tinge their good-byes ; but one's mind is a good
deal less optimistic than one's will, and one must await
with some anxiety news as to the first brush with the
enemy.

Just twenty years ago Jules Simon, representing France
at the International Congress, convened to deal with the
labour question at Berlin, addressed an article to the Emperor
which ended :

" We are told that our army as reconstituted has become
invincible, but people forget that Germany has been no less busy
than ourselves and that it is no longer a question of heroic, but
of scientific, warfare. Glory which formerly depended on courage
can now only be gained by sheer numbers and by war plant."
And, " I say that each of the two peoples is liable to be beaten to
the ground. I have my fears even as to victory itself ; for the
victor will be swept into the cataclysm as surely as the van-
quished."

How true these words have proved themselves. Germany
has become nothing less than a great military workshop and,
as compared to hers, our military efforts have been poor and
languid. We have on our side national courage and we have
our quarrel just ; will this suffice ?

Happily, on this Wednesday, 5th August, implicit confidence prevails. Germany's declaration of war has resulted here in a magnificent outburst of patriotism. Never in all her annals of history has France shown herself of finer stuff than in this hour which is now striking. Mobilisation begun on the 2nd August is being completed to-day with a smoothness, a keenness and a sense of discipline which has compelled the admiration alike of Ministers and of Generals. There will be afoot more than 3,780,000 men, of whom 77,000 are native soldiers. It is a question now of concentrating for action these regular, reserve and territorial divisions. From to-day until the 12th, 2500 trains will be conveying the regulars, and the following week no less than 4500 trains will be required for the reserve and the territorials. Up till now everything on our railroads is going like clockwork, as if in obedience to one sovereign will.

The plan of campaign assigned to our armies is the Seventeenth, which has been drawn up since 1875, in other words, since the first alarm which Germany gave us after our defeat. It was adopted in April 1913 at a military council, and with the idea of strengthening the reserve formations, the Generals in Council decided to eliminate the brigade of reservists in each of the mobilised corps and to bestow on each regular division a double battalion regiment of reservists. It was thought advisable to create a 21st Army Corps and to carry out, in time of peace, the defence works—which had been far too long deferred—in the regions of Toul and Nancy. It was then unanimously decided to draw up a new plan with these dispositions : four armies, comprising eighteen corps and eight reserve divisions, should concentrate in first line between Mézières and Belfort ; a fifth army, comprising three corps, should be in second line from Ste. Menehould to Commercy, ready to pass up into the front line if necessary. The wings would operate, the right in Lorraine and the left to the north of the line from Verdun to Metz, while intervening forces, posted both on the Hauts de Meuse and in the Woëvre, would be detailed to keep contact between the armies responsible for the two combined attacks. Agreeably with this plan of campaign our troops will march towards the east and north-east. Has it occurred to anyone that Germany might

violate Belgium so as to invade France from the right bank
of the Meuse ?   In 1911 another plan, drawn up by General
Michel, hypothecated a much larger enveloping movement
on the part of the enemy, but our General Staff declined the
suggestion, which involved so insolent a violation of the right
of nations.   A bad mistake on our part, but a mistake born of
honesty.   What we did not know then, what we shall soon
learn to our cost, is that a fine contempt for Belgian neutrality has coloured all German military designs since Count
Schlieffen in 1891 replaced Waldersee at the head of the
German Military Staff.   General von Moltke who succeeded
Schlieffen in 1906, seems to have followed the dominant con-
ception of his predecessor, and we may well be obliged, in our
utter need, to modify in these coming days our chief military
dispositions.

For the moment everything is going well.   In no section
of the Press is any discordant note sounded.   Martial law has
been proclaimed and a censorship has been established, but
amid the general enthusiasm neither of these exceptional
measures is really necessary to ensure the nation speaking
with one voice.   The Ministers are spontaneous in their
desire to show that although many of them were recently
political adversaries they are now in complete sympathy
with the President.   It is arranged that we shall meet daily,
either as a Ministerial Council or as a Council of National
Defence.

The Austro - Hungarian monarchy — in whose interest
Germany has declared war, first with Russia and then
with France—maintains a position which offers something
of a paradox :   so far she has not broken off diplomatic
relations either with France or Russia.   But she has begun
to bombard Belgrade anew and to demonstrate towards
Priboja in the Sanjak, while the story runs that she is
sending to our frontiers the 14th Innsbruck Corps and
Slav regiments in exchange for Bavarian or Alsatian troops.
Count Berchtold is complaining to our Ambassador that
Austro-Hungarian subjects had been deported from Paris
under harsh conditions, and this just at the moment when
Count Szecsen has called to thank M. Doumergue for the

kindness which we are showing to his compatriots. Count Berchtold has, notwithstanding, assured M. Dumaine that there can be no question of clash of arms between French and Austrian forces. What is the real truth ? Our Ambassador is sure that Vienna wants to avoid breaking off relations with Russia and France at the same time, because the transport of Austrian troops to Galicia is still going on. Still uncertain as to Germany's strength and plans, it is decided to bring the 19th Algerian Corps to Paris. The *Vergniaud* and the *Condorcet* cannot form part of their escort across the Mediterranean, as they must look for the *Goeben* and the *Breslau,* of which we have heard so much these last months, and whose goings and comings now seem very suspicious. Yesterday the two German cruisers were signalled as being on the Algerian coast, having bombarded, with many casualties, Bône and Philippeville.

While our army is being methodically concentrated, Germany, who has deliberately hurried on the declaration of war, is already able to take the field, and at 6 P.M. on this 5th of August begins her attack on Liége. Yesterday morning she pushed towards the town six brigades and three cavalry divisions, while to-day the forts on the right bank of the Meuse have been bombarded, a column of infantry has crossed the river and there have been some sharp fights. The 7th German Corps has been pushed back and punished severely, but fighting has begun again in the southern sector, where the 10th German Corps has come up after a forced march of forty kilometres.

Our Minister at Brussels tells us that King Albert will take supreme command of the army, and he reckons the forces invading his country at 120,000 to 150,000 men, with heavy artillery, field and machine guns. If only we were on the same footing ! From Liége and Brussels there come cries for assistance, and in the Wallonian city the inhabitants and the garrison look for the near approach of French troops. The " Marseillaise " is acclaimed, the local General Staff have told the people that our army is marching to their rescue, General Joffre is entreated to send troops to Liége, and our consul begs us with all urgency to respond to the cry for help. Despite the overwhelming numerical superiority of the enemy the Belgians are holding out heroically. How can we be otherwise than heart-stirred by the cries of distress from our old friends, Latin in race and tongue and traditions, when Germany is seizing them by the throat ? We would like our reply to take the form of sending a large contingent to help, and the War Minister and I ask General Joffre if this could be done. The Generalissimo entirely appreciates that both from the moral and political point of view a relief force ought to be sent. But he cannot let our concentration be interfered with, and all that it is possible for him to do is to instruct General Mangin and General Sordet to take a brigade of infantry and three divisions of cavalry and try to check the march of the Germans across Belgium. The General Staff thinks it is impossible for us to give any help in the matter of defending Liége ; deeply grieved as Viviani and I are, we cannot override a purely military decision, and we must submit to the inevitable.

So in the first hours of the war the premeditation of the German General Staff is abundantly evident in the start which they have gained over our Allies and ourselves. Early in July they called upon the Reservists for a period which normally should have begun on the 1st August, and on the 26th July all leave was cancelled. What we do not know is that the Reservists belonging to the corps which are to take the field all rejoined the colours yesterday. The Landwehr men will have rejoined the colours the day after to-morrow, and the Landstürm men will be all in their place about the 15th August ; there will then follow the young soldiers of the special reserve. Germany is there-fore ready long before us, and is even going to throw into the first line the reserve troops, while at the moment when she is penetrating the Belgian frontiers we are powerless to defend Belgium's neutrality, although we have guaranteed it.

Anyhow, Belgium can now be sure that England, like ourselves, will be at her side to avenge her and to expel the enemy from the soil he has invaded. The Foreign

Office has published this evening a Note which leaves no room for doubt.

" Owing to the summary rejection by the German Government of the request made by His Majesty's Government for assurances that the neutrality of Belgium will be respected, His Majesty's Ambassador at Berlin has received his passports and His Majesty's Government have declared to the German Government that a state of war exists between Great Britain and Germany as from 11 P.M. on 4th of August."

Enthusiasm runs as high in England as it does in France ; the Royal Family are receiving extraordinary ovations, and everywhere there are signs of intense patriotism. The Central Empires have attracted to themselves the burning indignation alike of the French, English and Belgian people. But we ask ourselves anxiously what part the other Powers—little and great, near and far—will play in the conflict which has just broken out. Will they draw the sword, or will they tread the cool path of neutrality ? Japan, as Great Britain's Ally, will surely come in with the Triple Entente if (1) the British Government ask them to do so, and (2) if the results of the war will be reflected in the Far East. The Scandinavian countries do not seem to be in mutual agreement. Denmark quite reasonably feels herself at the mercy of a huge neighbour who has once grievously mutilated her. Norway has pronounced sympathies for the Triple Entente and hastens to tell us that, whatever happens, she will remain neutral. But what about Sweden ? Have Viviani and I smoothed away the ill-feeling which Sweden has lately shown towards Russia ? There is the lurking fear that the Swedes might actually side with the Germans. Happily the Swedish Foreign Minister, M. Wallenberg, is a wise and cool-headed man, and, moreover, he is greatly gratified by the British Government having spontaneously undertaken to respect the independence and integrity of Sweden so long as his country is merely neutral. We have at once identified ourselves with this move on the part of England, and we have begged Russia to do the same, and thus strengthen M. Wallenberg's hands in resisting any pressure either from within or without.

At Berne the Federal Council has drafted a Note, practically a replica of the 1870 declaration of neutrality: Switzerland reserves expressly the right of occupying, if necessary, the neutralised part of Savoy. No doubt the President of the Confederation has told our Ambassador that the clause is purely formal, but, however hypothetical, this claim on the part of our neighbours must be objectionable to the Savoyards who are devoted to France. During the day there comes to hand an inopportune Russian proposal as to promising Trentino and Vallona to Italy if she will take up arms against Austria. However tempting it may be to detach Italy from the Triple Alliance, such a guarantee would be extremely ill-advised, as, when victory is secured, it might be a question of setting Italian claims before the restitution to France of the provinces which have been torn from her. Until war was declared we have submitted in silence to the robbery of which we have been victims, but to-day the Imperial Government has by its aggression torn up the Treaty of Frankfort, and there cannot be a single Frenchman who does not thirst to prosecute the war until the events of the past have been completely repaired. We cannot therefore agree to the Russian suggestion except under the implicit condition that it should be " without prejudice to our national claims ". M. Sazonoff also proposes to guarantee the integrity of Roumania if she remains neutral. But, for some unknown reason, he asks us to tack on to the promise a threat in the event of Roumania clasping Austria's hand. This would be an extremely high-handed action towards a country which is now on excellent terms with Russia, and has always been on excellent terms with ourselves ; Doumergue therefore agrees as to the promise, but declines the threat.

The hours pass slowly, and in the course of the afternoon I receive the Ambassadors, Ministers and representatives of the Paris Press, the last of whom one can heartily thank for their support at this crisis ; the War Minister adds a few words of information as to the mobilisation and concentration of our armies. The journalists have come in their numbers, and represent every political school of thought, although for the moment France seems to be the only thought in their minds. M. Ernest Judet is there, but says no word ; [1] M. Almeyreda, the director of the *Bonnet Rouge*, the journal which has played so strange a part these last years, keeps apart from the others, and wears a very odd and mysterious look.

The great Catholic orator, Count Albert de Mun, comes a little later to tell me that although his infirmities will prevent his ever again mounting the tribune, his pen is always at the service of the national cause. He is full of congratulations as to the text and tone of my Address, and I can tell him that our alliances have been cultivated and strengthened by successive Republican Governments, and that to-day we are reaping the fruit of a sustained effort.

M. Aristide Briand and M. Millerand are insistent that at a moment so serious as this Viviani's Cabinet ought to be broadened ; I cordially agree and would like to see constituted a real Ministry of the Union Sacrée, a Coalition Government in which all political parties would be represented. " But if I were to open the door like this," Viviani pleads, " far too many candidates would try and make their way in, and I should be swamped." It is remarkable how many men quite honestly believe that they are for the moment indispensable to the country, and one scarcely knows whether they are prompted by a spirit of adventure, or by a sense of duty and self-sacrifice, or by ambition and self-conceit. The motives may be different, but the methods are the same, and each one pushes his way to Viviani with the one desire for office.

During the night of 5th to 6th August important telegrams come from London. The Cabinet has asked us to send over at once to London an officer who will explain our military dispositions, so that the best arrangements can be made as how to employ the British Expeditionary Force. So at last the King's Government has decided to land troops and join forces.

[1] Formerly director of *L'Éclair* ; an opponent of the *entente cordiale*.

Thursday, 6th August.—This morning Viviani, Doumergue and other Ministers discuss with me the point raised by Briand and Millerand that the Cabinet ought to be enlarged. Viviani still dreads anything like a Ministerial crisis ; the Minister of the Interior, who is gravely concerned as to the question of supplies for the civil population and of helping the families of the men who have been mobilised, is drawing up a scheme by which the existing services will be controlled and extended. A Commission will be appointed, on which Briand, Delcassé, Ribot and Léon Bourgeois will sit. But will so modest an employment of activities assuage the thirst of ambition ? Under the storm which we are riding, most of the passengers want to be at the helm, and certainly this is the case with George Clemenceau. I have received him once since I came to the Élysée, but the short interview was not followed up. Yesterday, however, so charming a note appeared in the *Homme Libre* that I can do no less than let him know how happy I shall be to have a chat with him, and he has at once come to see me.

Despite his seventy-three years, this old man is younger and more energetic than ever, and much more amenable than he was some months ago.

We spoke of Germany, which he does not like, and England, which he holds in high esteem, of Austria, which he detests and despises, and of Italy, which he wants to win over to our cause at once. At one moment when he mentioned the word Alsace, recollections of 1870 brought tears to his eyes, and when, after an hour's talk, he left me, I could say : " Whatever happens, when two Frenchmen have been stirred by the same deep feelings there must remain a link which will not be broken ". During the interview he once, as if mechanically, called me, as he used to do, " Cher ami ", but afterwards he studiously maintained a perfectly courteous but rather distant manner. To M. Thomson who had suggested to him to come and see me, he had said : " Willingly, but we must not speak of the past and I must keep a free hand for the future ". The past was my election to the Presidency, the future is the unknown. Clemenceau thus offers me a truce and nothing more. But in face of the enemy a truce between him and me

is not to be despised ; his brain and his pluck may some day
be not only useful, but necessary for the country.   It is with
Austria that Clemenceau seems to have his chief quarrel.   He
is surprised that Count Szecsen sits tight in Paris as if war had
not broken out.   This attitude of the Ambassador is the more
remarkable since—according to M. Dumaine—he is treating
his Government to stories about France which are pure
calumny,—that the Austrian shops are being looted, that
the Paris hotel-keepers are turning the Austrians out of doors,
that the police are folding their arms and doing nothing, and
that the Austrian Embassy is full of refugees.   Is Austria
trying to pile up pretexts to break with us when she thinks
the moment has come ?   Certainly there is in Paris no ani-
mosity against the Austrians and Hungarians, and no one
dreams of molesting them.

On the other hand, what blind hatred Germany has
shown to our Ambassador at Berlin.   He telegraphs us to-day
that he asked to travel home through Switzerland or Holland,
but was ordered to go through Denmark.   In the course of
the journey the officer detailed to look after him told him
that unless he paid out 3611 marks for the expenses of the
journey his train could not proceed to the Danish frontier.
The Ambassador offered a cheque for the amount claimed,
which was refused, and he had to scrape together, with the help
of his travelling companions, the required amount in gold.
The French representative at Berne tells us that our acting
consul at Mannheim has been grossly ill-treated on his way
to Switzerland and has been locked up in a luggage van,
while our Minister in Bavaria has had almost as unpleasant
an experience as M. Cambon, and has found at Zurich compatriots who have been insulted and struck on their journey
from Bavaria.   The news from Russia is fairly cheerful.   The
Grand Duke Nicholas in supreme command has decided to
take the offensive at once, and as a token of our alliance is
flying a French flag alongside his own.   The Czar has not
minced his words, and has said to Paléologue that he will
sacrifice his last soldier to secure victory, and that so long as
there remains a single German soldier on Russian soil he
will never sign peace.   " As soon as mobilisation is com-

pleted ", he added, " I will order a forward move. My troops
are as keen as possible and the Grand Duke is a great hustler."
All this is very nice, but unhappily it is only Germany who
can really take the offensive, and she is doing so with a smoothness and swiftness which are in marked contrast to Russian
delays. Luxemburg is invaded by the 8th Corps and a
cavalry division, and according to our General Staff there
are five German army corps and four mounted divisions in
Belgium. The cavalry would be marching to the north and
south of Liége from one side towards Wanemme and from the
other in the direction of Huy. The forts have been repeatedly
attacked, and while information is even more vague than
yesterday, we hear that a column of motor cars rushed into
the town, and having seized the military station, were subsequently turned out by the garrison. Despite the violence of
the assaults so far no fort has been taken, and the German
General Staff has taken refuge in one of them. M. Klobukowski says that the general objective of the German army
seems to be Maubeuge, and, unless he is much mistaken, we
are very far from Plan 17. Nor does our enemy spare any
effort to obtain the compliance of other nations. Our Ambassador at Constantinople reports that Turkey has already
decided to mobilise and affects to fear a Bulgarian movement
on Adrianople and a Russian movement on the Narrows.

"It would be well ", he telegraphs, "for the British Government to recall their Naval Mission during the war, so as to leave
the Turks no excuse for keeping the German Military Mission.
The German officers constitute a veritable danger as to keeping
Turkey neutral, for they leave nothing undone to stir up incidents
between Russia and Turkey and no fable is too false for them to
invent with which to frighten Turkey with regard to the Narrows."

Under injunctions from Berlin, Denmark has been
obliged to close the Belts with mines,[1] and the German fleet
can thus go as they please from the Baltic to the North Sea,

---

[1] Cf. *Erinnerungen* of Admiral von Tirpitz, who speaks of an agreement between him and the Danish Government at the beginning of the war.
In a long report presented to the Danish Army Commission in 1919, the
Danish Minister for Defence explains that the Germans had begun to lay
mines and would have completed the barrage themselves if Denmark had
not consented to establish it. The Danish military authorities were even
afraid of an occupation of Copenhagen.

and reciprocally, by the great Kiel Canal, where the Kaiser a few weeks ago heard of the Serajevo murder. On the other hand, the Russian fleets have no longer any way by which to communicate with the fleets of France and England. While Germany is thus making all her arrangements, England, who wanted war no more than ourselves and is even less ready for it, is arming herself as rapidly as possible. Mr. Asquith has handed over the War Office to Lord Kitchener, who, in 1870, fought with Chanzy's army against Prussia, and who received a year ago the war medal for that campaign. In a life of extraordinary activity Lord Kitchener has rendered incomparable and imperishable services to the British Empire. He has made his mark in Zanzibar, in the Valley of the Nile, in South Africa, in India, in Australia, in New Zealand. As Sirdar, he fought the Khalifa at Omdurman, crushed Mahdism, occupied the Bahr - el - Ghazal, and at Fashoda came in contact with Commandant Marchand. There was then no thought of the *entente cordiale*, but the French officers may well have congratulated themselves on the exquisite courtesy of Lord Kitchener, who, like Marchand, could only obey the behest of his Government. The new Cabinet Minister is known to be as valiant a soldier as he is an administrator of outstanding merit. He was on the point of starting for Egypt when he was recalled to replace Mr. Asquith, and his first step after receiving the Seals of Office was to tell Paul Cambon that he had at once given orders for the transport of the first troops to France. In the midst of all this war worry the United States Ambassador, Mr. Herrick, makes his way to the Élysée and hands me a short Note from President Wilson, which runs : [1]

" I consider that it is at once my privilege and my duty agreeably with Article 3 of The Hague Convention to tell you, in the most friendly spirit, how willingly I would act in the interests of European peace either now or at a time which might appear more suitable. . . ."

This is of course a well-meant proposal if a little timidly couched, and President Wilson must appreciate that, after all

[1] Papers relating to the foreign relations of the United States, 1914. Supplement : " The World War ".

that has happened at Liége, it is a little belated.   In thanking
the Ambassador I can only say that it is for the Powers who
have declared war to say if they are ready, in the event of
mediation, to withdraw their troops from the territory they
have invaded, and that anyhow we can decide nothing without the consent of our Allies.   We are of course very grateful
to President Wilson for his kind thought, which we will
remember if a propitious occasion occurs.   The Ambassador
having expressed his personal wishes that France might meet
with speedy success, I drafted a telegram to the President in
which I reminded him that France had always tried to maintain peace, and in order to do so had made every sacrifice
compatible with her honour ; that despite repeated provocations and violations of territory she had refused to be an
aggressor, but had herself been attacked at the moment when
the territory of a neutral country had been violated.   The
President has made the same overtures at Berlin, Vienna,
St. Petersburg and London, with no apparent effect, except
that Austria has replied by declaring war this evening on
Russia.   If only Germany, after having mobilised, had delayed her own declaration of war, peace might have been
saved.   But what is the use of " ifs " when the conflagration
is spreading ?   Yesterday Joffre, in view of the German
pressure on Belgium, thought it only prudent to send the
37th and 38th Divisions, landed from Africa, to support his
left wing at Laon.   Should the capture of Liége clear the way,
the Germans will cross the Meuse, head westwards and try to
envelop our left ; should Liége hold out for a while and they
are unable to manœuvre by their right, they will perhaps try
to pivot on Metz so as to pass our frontier by moving up the
Valley of the Meuse again.   Our Commander-in-Chief has no
idea which of these two things will happen, and as he is obliged to wait on German movements, our own initiative runs
the risk of being paralysed by a prolonged delay.

     7th August.—Clemenceau comes to see me again and
brings Count Sabini, the Italian commercial attaché, who
has something to say.   He tells me—and he is able to speak
officially without committing anybody—that Italy cannot
actually throw off her neutrality.   " It is too soon ", he

says without any circumlocution, " to make war on Allies of yesterday. The moment may well come, but just now it is a matter of securing neutrality itself and for this Italy must naturally be promised something."   He then reels out a series of rather vague suggestions, such as economical agreements, collaboration in Asia Minor, and so forth. To my great surprise Clemenceau does not bounce up, but listens with patience and something like sympathy. He, however, quite approves my saying that Italy has formally announced herself as neutral, and as such has no right to compensation, and that, moreover, as one of the Signatories to the 1902 agreement, she cannot, without renouncing that agreement, take side with our enemies. Doumergue will tell our Ambassador in Rome of this little conversation, but, like myself, he says it is impossible to promise Italy anything unless she actually throws in her lot with our own. England has, however, consented to the Russian proposal with regard to Trentino and Vallona if Italy comes in. This division of spoils before the fight seems to be rather illusory and a little ridiculous. The first thing which we and Belgium have got to do is to defend ourselves. King Albert, on hearing that Joffre has decided—even before our own concentration—to send him infantry and cavalry, telegraphs to me in warmest terms of gratitude, and in my reply I can announce that the Government has conferred the Cross of the Legion of Honour on the town of Liége. " Liége ", the King replies, " the country and the whole army will never cease to do their duty."   But on this very day the heroic city has been defiled by the enemy. The German troops have made their way into the town, seized the citadel and taken the bishop, the burgomaster and the senators as hostages. The Military Governor has been ordered to capitulate and has refused. He has told the third division which garrison the town to rejoin the Belgian army, but in order to give his own country and France further time for concentration of their armies, he has enjoined on the Forts to resist to the last and has himself retired to the Lonçin redoubt, whence he will control and stimulate the other eleven points of defence.

These details are unknown in Paris, and so sketchy is

our information that Philippe Berthelot has been instructed to proceed to Brussels and Louvain, where he will see the Belgian Chief of the Staff, ask for an audience with King Albert and bring us back more precise information. From afar the news is even more clouded and our ignorance of what is going on increases our anxiety We do know, however, that Sazonoff proposes to offer Roumania, besides guaranteeing her territorial integrity, the larger part of Transylvania and Bukovina, and to promise Ferdinand of Bulgaria some of the districts of Macedonia. I still think that these conditional gifts are as risky as they are puerile. Although Austria has declared war on Russia, Count Szecsen still remains comfortably in the Rue de Varenne and tells his dentist, " The Commune will save us ". But the Commune is the sequel of defeat, and, no thank you, my dear Ambassador, we are not there yet.

We have had something of a success to-day, as the 7th Corps has squeezed itself into Haute Alsace by the Belfort loophole, which since 1871 has been the opening on to our lost provinces ; the little town Altkirch, which Louis XIV. once gave to Cardinal Mazarin, has been carried at the point of the bayonet and the population has greeted the French troops with shouts of joy. At the same time our 41st Division has penetrated the Valley of the Thur, and although there is no question of a general offensive, General Dubail has been ordered to use one of his Corps de Couverture for action in Haute Alsace, perhaps from a moral or sentimental, rather than a purely military point of view. The first objective would be Thann-Mulhouse, whence an attempt would be made to reach the Rhine and then march towards Colmar. French soldiers in Alsace ! And this forty-four years after one of the greatest acts of rapine in the annals of history. Was not Gambetta right when he reckoned on justice being done in the near future.

8th August.—As we hear from Berne that Austrian troops are still moving towards our frontiers, and especially towards Alsace, Doumergue asks Count Szecsen to come and see him, and reminds him that these movements conflict with the assurances given by Count Berchtold. To the question whether the Austrian Government has changed its mind the Ambassador replies, " I do not know, but I will ask ". Doumergue telegraphs to Paul Cambon that it is impossible to let Austria go ahead against us while we are soothed by soft words, and begs him to remind the Cabinet of what is happening. Perhaps Austria's game is to force Italy's hand. In delaying as she did at first to pronounce herself hostile to Russia, and in withholding—as she is now doing—a decision as regards ourselves, Austria doubtless hopes to drive us into taking the initiative of declaring war. The Central Empires might thereby find a pretext to represent that, by virtue of the Triple Alliance, Italy must come to the help of the Power attacked. Conversely we do not want until now to break with Vienna, although the Dual Monarchy has declared war on Russia, and although the terms of our Convention make it incumbent on us to back Russia against two enemies. The situation becomes more and more abnormal. Austria is free to send her troops and her guns where she pleases, to stiffen the German army with her own, and in combination to paralyse Russian movements, while we look on without lifting a finger. Count Szecsen remains in Paris, and public opinion is a little bewildered by conditions which are neither war nor peace.

The news from Liége is very uncomfortable, and Berthelot, who has arrived at Brussels, tells us that three army corps are in front of the beleaguered city ; the town is occupied by the enemy, but the forts still hold out, and are prepared to repulse further assaults. A force of 80,000 men are covering Brussels and preparing to speak with the enemy. Baron de Brocqueville—who is at once Prime Minister and War Minister—has told Berthelot that the lines of the Meuse will hold out no less stubbornly than the Liége fortifications, that every able-bodied man is to be asked to enlist and that Belgium will fight to the last gasp. This was confirmed by King Albert, who has received Berthelot at a little château near Louvain, and who said that Belgium was fighting for her very existence, that she would fight to the last man against Germany, and that if necessary he would take a rifle in hand himself.

Our War Minister is delighted with the Belgian resistance, which enables us to complete the urgently necessary works at Maubeuge. Over and over again the Governor asked for money to carry this out, but the General Staff very naturally gave preference to defence works on the Est. To-day, however, it is the Nord which is the more seriously threatened, and at least a fortnight is necessary to put Maubeuge in a state of defence. Will the Germans allow us time to do it ?

In order to check the enemy's sweeping movement towards Flanders, Joffre, whose headquarters are at Vitry-le-François, has ordered the Passes of Bussang, Schlucht, Bonhomme, Ste. Marie et Saales to be occupied, and has pushed the troops from Altkirch and Thann to Mulhouse. We have now taken without bloodshed the beloved town who so delighted in giving herself to France in 1798, and where the Kaiser, since his accession, has never ventured to show his face. Delightful as this is, a voluntary German retreat is suspicious, and reports here are in rather gloomy contrast with the high hopes of our General Staff. There is, moreover, the disturbing news that the *Goeben* and the *Breslau* are pursuing their sinister courses and that after having bombarded our Algerian coasts they proceeded to coal at Messina, whence they have moved eastward. As the British Admiralty tells us that the Mediterranean Fleet is not able by itself to close the entrance to the Adriatic, it would seem that if we were to declare war on Austria it might be an incitement to attack the English ships, and perhaps force them to retire. The Admiralty says that as soon as our fleet can support the British there would be no further objection to breaking off relations with Vienna. Augagneur assures me to-day that our transport of troops is now sufficiently advanced to allow us to co-operate at sea with the English, and as the conditions of our Ally are thus fulfilled we can emerge from this curious position in which we have been placed in the face of Austrian threats.

An ugly note has been sounded at Sofia. Russia, with a halter in one hand and a corn bin in the other, has asked Ferdinand what are his intentions. The King has sheltered himself behind his Government, to which, as a rule, he does not pay much attention, and the Prime Minister in his turn has sheltered himself behind the King.   Ferdinand and his acolytes are the same as ever, and no doubt they have many tricks in store for us.   The telegrams from Russia are, however, more favourable.   The Czar has opened the special session of the Duma and stated that he will prosecute war until victory is complete ;   he is leaving for Moscow in a day or two, and has asked the British and French Ambassadors to accompany him and take part in the religious ceremony at the Kremlin.   From London comes some encouragement, as Cambon tells us that five out of the six divisions which compose the Expeditionary Force are to be sent overseas forthwith.   This evening comes a letter from Clemenceau which begins abruptly :

"Count Sabini has paid me a visit, accompanied by the Italian Military Attaché, who read me a despatch from his Government which indicated that Italy might at once take up arms against Austria.   My two visitors both seemed much excited by the happenings at Liége and by all the facts in our favour.   M. Doumergue will probably see the despatch, and it would be interesting to know if the conclusions have been modified.   The two gentlemen asked me if it were true that the British and the French were sending men to the number of hundreds of thousands to Namur.   I replied that I knew nothing whatever about it, and if I did I should not say.   They asked me if we had made good our delay in mobilisation, and I replied that we had done so to a great extent.   They were particularly anxious to know if I was entirely confident, and I completely assured them on this point.   It is curious that the same man who stated yesterday that Italy could not possibly come in at the moment now says the exact opposite. The explanation may not be far to seek.   G. CLEMENCEAU.

"P.S.—I was careful to say over and over again that the keenness and thoroughness with which England had thrown herself in with us was beyond anything we had hoped for."

I at once tell Doumergue about this Note and beg him to get into touch with Rome, as I am quite unaware as to what influence Sabini and the Military Attaché exercise over the Italian Government ; the Italian Ambassador, who was on a cruise when war was declared, has not yet come

back to Paris. Clemenceau's impetuous optimism, inspired
by his fervent love of France, is in happy contrast to the
rather sour pessimism which he displayed only in July at
the Senate.

The day closes without any light being thrown as to how
the German is going to manœuvre. In his General Order just
issued Joffre seems to think we shall still have to make our
chief effort in the Est. The First Army, based on the Vosges,
and supported on its right by the 7th Corps, will take the
offensive, together with the Second Army on its left round
Nancy. The two will attack together the German left, which is
supposed to comprise only six corps, whereas we can bring up
eight. Our Fourth and Fifth Armies, in front of the German
centre, where the Germans are supposed to be the strongest,
will undertake either to cross the Meuse in order to attack
the enemy towards the Belgian frontier, or to throw the
Germans back across the river if these should succeed in
traversing it. Our Third Army is stationed on the heights
which dominate on one side the right bank of the Meuse and
on the other the clayey plain of the Woëvre. This Army will
support the Fourth either in the movement towards the
north or in counter-attacking, on the right, German troops
which might venture to issue, in a westerly direction, from
their entrenched camp at Metz. For a moment the Generalissimo is not greatly concerned with what the Germans might
attempt to do in the north, except that he is taking the
necessary steps for one of our cavalry corps to cover the
concentration and the moving up into line of the British
army. He is arranging also that the fourth group of the
reserve divisions will be responsible in the environs of
Vervins to close any outlet either northwards or eastwards.
But the General Staff does not seem to think that the Germans
will try to attack Lanrezac's Fifth Army and stranglehold
our left wing.

9th August.—What Berthelot has telegraphed to us, and
on his return now tells us, impels the Government to beg
King Albert's acceptance of the French Military Medal ; I
assure His Majesty—in a letter which General Duparge is com-
missioned to carry—that this is the highest military award

and is borne alike by general officers and private soldiers who especially distinguish themselves on the field of battle. Our Consul-General at Antwerp telegraphs that from quite trustworthy information he hears the Germans are putting Belgian prisoners with their own troops in order that they may endure the fire of their compatriots. On the other hand, our Minister at Brussels reports that the Germans whom the Belgians have taken prisoner are very demoralised and all say that they were told by their officers they would be received in Belgium with open arms. We should be very foolish to let ourselves be dazzled by pleasant stories and in any way to undervalue the enemy's military strength, which Joffre fully recognises. In a letter to me of to-day's date he writes :

" I am advised that the mobilisation of the English forces who are to be landed here will only take place to-day, which puts back to the 26th of August the date on which these troops can move forward. Now, if we are not to lose the advantages of taking the initiative, we must not postpone until then our own advance against the German army, and I have decided not to await the arrival of the English troops before taking action. The British support will none the less be of the greatest possible importance in the development of operations so long as the arrival of the troops is not too belated. Perhaps the British General Staff could hurry up things a little. I think it will be a good thing to let their Government know what grave inconvenience will be caused by a long delay in the arrival of the English. As regards the Belgians, I am indeed glad to have noted the splendid energy they have shown in defending Liége. Our cavalry, thanks to General Sordet's activities, have been able to give them, if not very substantial help, anyhow a good deal of moral support. I should like the Belgian Government to be told this and to be assured that this service will not be the only one. We shall ask them in exchange to continue the action which they have so admirably set afoot on the north of the left wing of our army."

Viviani, Doumergue and Messimy, to whom I circulate the letter—and who, by the way, think that the letter ought to have been addressed to the War Minister and not to myself—are going to make representations to the British General Staff ; Doumergue will telegraph at once to London. Agreeably with the wishes of my colleagues, I write to King Albert, quoting the latter part of Joffre's letter.

" CHER ET GRAND AMI—Your Majesty has already replied to the hope which General Joffre expresses by letting me know your purpose to prosecute the war until every inch of Belgian territory is freed from invasion. With a very just appreciation of military requirements, Your Majesty has expressed the opinion that the French army should await its final concentration before taking the offensive. But the day is at hand when I hope we may be able to move forward. Your Majesty I think will agree with me that it will be well for the two armies then to co-ordinate action. In order to ensure liaison between the British Expeditionary Force and our armies it has been decided that English officers shall be attached to the French General Staff with reciprocity. The Government of the Republic earnestly wish that Your Majesty will consent to adopt the same arrangement during the campaign in Belgium. I shall be very happy to place at Your Majesty's disposal three officers who would come under your orders and to whom you could give the necessary information. General Joffre would for his part very gladly greet two or three Belgian officers to be attached to his Staff. The co-ordination of whatever programme is to be carried out would thus be ensured, while entire liberty would be left to the two High Commands. I beg Your Majesty to believe that this step I take is only a fresh proof of our profound wish to see the Belgian armies march to victory alongside our own. Croyez, cher et grand ami, à mes sentiments dévoués."

But already it is not only Belgium who is invaded, but France also on the Est. The Prefect of Meurthe and Moselle telegraphs he is without news of Briey, all communications being interrupted with this *sous - préfecture,* the postal office having been evacuated on the 4th . . .

" on the 5th [he adds] the German infantry crossed the frontier at Homécourt only less than 5 kilometres from Briey, and the next day the Germans moved towards Conflans, where I expect they are now; it would seem that the enemy may be in occupation of Briey."

The Government think rightly that the Prefect should at any cost have given us better and quicker information and that he had better be relieved. A German occupation of the basin of Briey spells little less than disaster, as it means their having in hand the rich metal and mining resources, whose value must be incalculable for whichever of the belligerents enjoys them. According to an order of the Commander-in-Chief, the ten kilometres given up before the declaration of war have been retaken. How can these have been lost—and more besides—without our being even warned of it? Then the Prefect of the Meuse telegraphs that he can no longer communicate with Bouvigny, Mangiennes, Billy and Spincourt ; that the gendarmerie of Longuyon has been pushed back to Marville, and that the French infantry has been in contact with the German cavalry this side of the frontier on the Spincourt-Montmédy line.

General Headquarters rounds off this gloomy news. Germans are at Othain, near Spincourt, which is in flames, and German cavalry yesterday evening got contact with a battalion of chasseurs holding an advanced post who had to fall back on Marville. So my poor dear Meuse is once more the prey of foreign armies. . . .

In Alsace we have reached Ste. Marie aux Mines, but farther south our troops have tried in vain to debouch from Mulhouse and have come up against the forest of La Hardt, which has been strongly fortified.

Although we continue to hear that Austro-Hungarian forces are being railed to France, Count Berchtold has categorically repeated to Doumergue that his Government has sent no troops towards our frontiers. Doumergue thinks this reply rather equivocal and instructs Dumaine to ask Count Berchtold if any Austro-Hungarian division has been sent westward outside Austrian territory.

At St. Petersburg there is always a plethora of proposals and projects. Sazonoff wants to give the Marquis de San Giuliano a solemn promise of military co-operation. Paul Cambon shakes his head at the idea, and Doumergue thinks that it would be quite sufficient if our Ambassador were to speak to the Italian Foreign Minister privately on the subject. Doumergue has good reason to be cautious ; he knows, from a " sure and secret source ", of a clever " combinazione " which has been devised at Rome. The notion is to ask England to intervene on the Italian coasts between the two groups of Great Powers so that neither shall get really the

better of the other. Doumergue has informed Paul Cambon
of this rather too ingenious idea.

Clemenceau himself, anxious as he is to see Italy come in,
fears that a little conspiracy has been woven to counteract
his efforts. He has been here to confide to me with revived
cordiality his hopes, and he seems afraid lest M. Tittoni, who
has just returned to the Embassy, may not wilfully make a
hash of the whole thing. But later in the day there comes a
Note from him :

" The Machiavellian plan has failed, or rather has not been
put in execution ; for I have been sent for. I was told that M.
Tittoni has completely come round to our way of thinking, and I
had a very pleasant interview with him for an hour and a half.
He wanted to be authorised to let his Government know of this
interview as well as the report of the former one at the Élysée. I
could not make any difficulties, and have reason to think that
M. Tittoni on arrival had found a despatch which caused him thus
suddenly to tack. I think you are very near getting what you
want."

I am much struck by the almost affectionate tone of the
Note which reflects Clemenceau's joyous patriotism. I only
wish his prognostications were well founded, but Doumergue's
" sure and secret source " murmurs that we must not pin our
faith to these conversations. The fact that we are still not at
war with Austria makes the Italian Government uneasy, and
San Giuliano once more expresses his surprise.

But the attitude of some of the other nations is very
wobbly. If we are to believe the assurances given by M.
Radoslavoff to M. Savinsky, Bulgaria has decided not to stir
up any trouble in Macedonia and not to engage in arms
against the Empire of the Czars. At Nisch, M. Pachitch has
repeated to M. Boppé that he is expecting King Ferdinand to
revenge himself against Serbia and Roumania.

The conduct of Turkey is even more suspicious. The
Grand Vizier has, it is true, assured the Russian representative
that the Porte will not allow the *Goeben* and the *Breslau* to
pass the Narrows, but meanwhile the two cruisers are roam-
ing like corsairs over the Ægean Sea, and it looks now as if
they had agreed with the Turks to help them make the diver-

sion which Germany wants on the hinterland of Russia. The Porte has given the command of the First Army to Liman von Sanders, who has now blossomed into Liman Pasha, and has acquired an extraordinary influence over Enver Pasha and, through him, over the Ministerial Council, where he is often called in. At Angora and Smyrna the command of the 4th and 5th Corps have been bestowed on German colonels ; Germans are all over the place in Turkey and acting as if they were masters in their own house. Russia's apprehension as the result of the Liman von Sanders' mission has only been too amply justified ; everything since that moment has been carefully prepared, and things are unfolding themselves precisely as the two Central Empires had foreseen and wished.

We are anyhow happier regarding the north of Europe, for from Stockholm comes authentic news that Sweden and Norway agreed yesterday as to maintaining complete neutrality with regard to all belligerent Powers. At Cettinge, King Nicholas makes protestations of loyalty to M. Vernet, while Austrian men-of-war have begun to bombard Antivari. The King has given orders to equip the Lovçen batteries and to fire on the Forts of Cattaro.

After a discussion between the Emperor and Prince Fushimi, the Japanese Government has decided to fulfil unreservedly the duties of an ally, and has said so to the British Ambassador. From Algiers, Tunis, Morocco, there come stories of the admirable spirit of the colonists and the natives, both equally eager to fight under the French flag. Notably General Lyautey telegraphs that the Sultan is giving proof of impeccable loyalty, the resident general adding that although he is quite ready to remain at his post, if such is the wish of the Government, this would be rather a cruel duty to impose on a soldier who also hails from Lorraine. He considers that Morocco should be a reservoir from which one can keep on drawing to swell the national forces.

Already the English are occupying the Togo, and the Governor of Dahomey has been told to join hands with Great Britain in taking over this German colony.

But a telephone message from Belfort drives from mind any far-off success. Thann has been retaken by the Germans,

where a French company has been surprised, and fighting is
going on in Mulhouse ; as a slight set-off General Headquarters says that we have made good, though with considerable losses, on several necks of the Vosges and that we
hold the crests. This side our frontier Blamont and Cirey are
held by the enemy, and altogether we have lost more than
we have gained. At Liége the fort of Barchon fell yesterday,
and the neighbouring forts are being attacked to-day, two of
them being very seriously pressed.

It is surely time for Russia to get to work to relieve the
pressure on Belgium and ourselves, and Joffre has begged
the Grand Duke Nicholas to move forward as quickly as he
possibly can. Paléologue forwards to our Commander-in-
Chief the Grand Duke's moderately reassuring pronounce-
ments. The plan of operation comprises (1) the army of
Vilna will attack Königsberg, (2) the army of Warsaw will
be placed immediately on the left bank of the Vistula on the
flank of the Vilna army, (3) the general offensive will probably
take place on Friday, the 15th August.[1]

M. Paul Deschanel, President of the Chamber of Deputies,
who comes to see me every day, and who, on his first visit,
embraced me effusively and enthusiastically, is to-day a
little depressed. M. Jean Dupuy, the Senator, tells me that
Clemenceau said to him : " The President must not think
that I am going to be friends with him ; it is a truce, not
peace, between us ". But what does it matter if only the
truce between Clemenceau and myself lasts until peace has
been signed with Germany.

[1] As the 15th falls on a Saturday in the Gregorian calendar, we wonder
if this is a mistake, or if it is meant as 28th August, Russian style. M.
Paléologue is asked and tells us that the Grand Duke meant Friday, the
14th, our style.

CHAPTER II

10*th August*.—Dumaine telegraphs, in clear, Count Berchtold's brief answer to Doumergue's renewed question.

" We are not sending troops towards the French frontier."

But what the Foreign Office and the War Office alike hear tends to throw a shadow of doubt on these official denials. Our Ambassador at Berne, our secret service, the Prefect of Doubs, agree that the Innsbruck and Agram Corps are directed on France, and that Austrian troops are in echelon not far from Basle and Schaffhouse. Doumergue therefore replies to Dumaine :

" If the Austrian troops are not being actually moved towards the French frontier they are anyhow in the neighbouring region, where we can only regard them as supporting the German troops opposed to us. Please call Count Berchtold's attention to this and beg him to assure us that no Austro-Hungarian units have been sent west outside Austrian territory."

To this Dumaine replies :

" Count Berchtold declares absolutely that no Austro-Hungarian units have been sent west outside Austrian territory."

Where does the truth lie ? And how can we decide between the repeated statements of our agents and the denials of Ballplatz ? Anyhow, Austria is at war with France's Ally while the Austrian fleet is cruising in the Adriatic and blockading the Montenegrin coast. No wonder Russia

28

begins to think our position a little equivocal, and Sazonoff
is insistent to know if our Mediterranean fleet is going to
remain inactive in face of the Austrian ships. Bompard also
urges us to emerge from our attitude of waiting on events.
If the *Goeben* and the *Breslau* find their way to the Sea of
Marmora, and even if, by some subterfuge, Turkey for the
moment disarms them, these ships will none the less constitute a potential naval force as, if the occasion presented
itself, nothing could be easier than to arm them anew.
Bompard therefore urges the expediency of France and
England crippling at once the Austrian fleet in the Adriatic.

Doumergue begs Szecsen to call and tells him very quietly
that we can scarcely take comfort from Count Berchtold's
declaration, as we have very precise information respecting
the movement of Austrian troops near our frontiers, and that
anyhow Austria is backing Germany in the field against
our Allies and thus enabling her to send forces in greater
strength against us. " Public opinion ", he added, " is beginning to get inflamed, and if things remain as they are I do
not quite know how I shall be able to guarantee the safety
of Your Excellency." Count Szecsen contradicts nothing
and acknowledges nothing, but only asks rather confusedly,
" What ought I to do ? " " I have no advice to offer you, my
dear Ambassador, but, as things stand, I shall be obliged
to recall M. Dumaine." " Then," was the reply, " will you
kindly prepare me my passports ? " Our Foreign Minister
promises to do everything possible to render Count Szecsen's
journey comfortable, and the Ambassador, with difficulty
restraining his emotion, bids him good-bye. A summary of
the conversation is sent in clear by both men to Vienna, and
nothing could have exceeded the courtesy of the two. In
parting with the representative of Austria I cannot help
rendering him the same justice as to Baron Schoen. During
1912 I received them both almost daily at the Quai d'Orsay ;
I have carried out every sort of negotiation with them in the
interest of general peace, and I have never been able to do
otherwise than congratulate myself on my relations, whether
official or personal, with them. What should I have thought
had I been told that some day I should have to treat as

enemies two men with whom I had always been on most correct, and indeed most happy, terms ?

But it is on Belgium that our gaze is most anxiously fixed. From King Albert comes a letter of warmest thanks for the Military Medal bestowed on him, but to our amazement we hear that the Belgian Minister at The Hague, at the request of the Foreign Minister, primed by the German representative, has just forwarded a Note to his Government from the Wilhelmstrasse, which runs :

" The Fortress of Liége has been taken by assault after a most courageous defence ; the German Government regrets very deeply that, as a consequence of the hostile attitude of the Belgian Government towards Germany, a struggle with much bloodshed has taken place. Germany does not come to Belgium in any enemy spirit ; it is due to the force of events that, on account of the military steps taken in France, she has been obliged to make her way into Belgium and to occupy Liége as a *point d'appui* for her further military operations. Now that the Belgian army has, by a heroic resistance to superior forces, maintained the honour of her arms, the German Government is prepared to make any agreement with Belgium which will fit in with arrangements between Belgium and France. Germany once more solemnly says that she has no intention of appropriating Belgian territory, far from it. Germany is always ready to evacuate Belgium as soon as the conditions of war allow."

So then, although the German General Staff had deliberately meditated the violation of Belgium, although the text of the ultimatum had been sent to Brussels before the declaration of war, although our Plan No. 17 provided for our having to defend ourselves on the Est, and although to-day we are in no position to reply effectively to Belgium's appeal for help, the Imperial Chancery persists in asserting that if neutrality has been violated it is the fault of France and even Belgium herself ; a piece of cynical hypocrisy of which our neighbours and friends will not be the dupes. The Belgian reply was as terse as it was dignified.

" The proposal of the German Government is a replica of what was set out in the ultimatum of the 2nd August. If she is to be faithful to her international duties, Belgium can only repeat her reply to that ultimatum, the more so because since the 3rd of August her neutrality has been violated, a terrible war has been waged on her territory, while the guarantors of her neutrality have promptly and loyally responded to her appeal."

The chivalrous spirit of the Belgian people has never exhibited itself more clearly ; everywhere everybody has hastened to endorse the resolution of the King and the Government, and 40,000 volunteers have come forward to serve.

From Italy no news. Doumergue has seen Tittoni, who remains as silent and impenetrable as a sealed grave, while the Minister points out to him, in very guarded language, the advantages which would surely accrue from combined action. There is no further trace of the eager satisfaction with which the astute Ambassador greeted Clemenceau's suggestion. The Marquis Imperiali has been to see Sir Edward Grey, but has contented himself with some rather banal laments as to the miseries of war, and has timidly remarked how desirable it would be to secure a suspension of hostilities. The Secretary of State drily replied, the only way of putting an end to the war was to persuade Germany to call a halt herself. Meanwhile England is astir. General Wilson, who has acted very cleverly as liaison between our General Staffs, and who seems to have a wonderful grasp of our military dispositions, is devoting himself with splendid energy to the transport of the Expeditionary Force. An advance party of thirty officers and eighty men in field kit have arrived at Rouen and are being received with as much rapture as if they had come to take part in a service of expiation for Joan of Arc. Our two Governments are also busy concocting plans—either joint or parallel—for occupying German colonies, England seeming disposed to accept our military co-operation in the Cameroons and Togo. Doumergue thinks also of offering to employ Madagascan troops in East Africa, but it may well be that in this part of the world the Colonial Office will wish to keep a perfectly free hand and act independently so as to run no risk of having to share with anyone any territory from which the Germans have been expelled.

Sir Edward Grey does not think the moment has come to do what Sazonoff proposes at Constantinople. It seems,

however, more and more probable that the Turks from now
onwards intend to open the Dardanelles to the *Goeben* and
the *Breslau* ; if necessary there will be a " got up " sale as a
pretext for allowing the two ships all liberty in the Marmora.
Bompard is forward to denounce this little bit of trickery
which the German officers are suggesting to the Porte, and
for the last eight days our Ambassador has moved heaven
and earth to try and keep Turkey quiet and neutral.   The
Ottomans, who have no grudge against France, are nervous
as to any big Russian success, which they think might mean
the loss of Constantinople or even a general break-up of
their Empire.   Bompard is very anxious to reassure them
on this point, and Paléologue is instructed to ask that the
Russian Government should administer a soothing draught
to Turkey.   The day does not finish without further news
of German incursions, and the Prefect of the Meuse telegraphs that the terrified inhabitants of Affleville, whose
Commune is on fire, have fled across the Woëvre to Etain,
where they have been kindly received and looked after.
Worse still, we have had to yield Mulhouse to the 14th and
15th German Corps and to fall back on the Remmingen-
Altkirch line.   Perhaps we ought to have advanced a little
more warily into this district; we should not have buoyed
the people with false hopes and then exposed them to the
reprisals of their masters of the day before yesterday.

11th August.—Count Szecsen has departed, congratulating himself on the attentions which have been shown him
alike by the French authorities and by the Paris folk ; but
between Austrians and ourselves the situation has not been
much altered, for if our diplomatic relations have been
broken, we are not at war.   This sketchy regime is favourable to Austria, who has her hands free for striking at
Russia, and whose fleet can career about the Adriatic.   It
would be well for us to have our own hands free also.   However little wish Italy may have to come to any terms with
Austria, we are running the risk of something of the sort
happening, and anyhow if we do not regard as enemies the
enemies of our friends, we look a little as if we were betray-
ing our alliances.   Doumergue again asks the British Govern-

ment to come to some arrangement with us as to what should be done, and proposes that our fleets should concert to relieve the Antivari blockade. But with absolute correctitude England does not wish to start any hostilities against Austria without the preliminary ritual of a declaration of war. Is the presence of Austrian troops near our frontiers a sufficient motive for such a declaration ? Our information, however trustworthy, is contested by Count Berchtold ; it might be better to say outright to Austria, " You are the original cause of the war. Germany only declared herself as against Russia and then against us to support what was a murderous act towards Serbia when Serbia had accepted your ultimatum. You in your turn had declared war against Russia, who, like us, was merely guarding herself against the aggression which Germany pretended was of a purely preventive character. You have therefore taken action against France which is unjustified by any provocation." Can the Ministers make this simple statement of fact without reference to Parliament, which is still in session ? The constitutional question arises and the matter is adjourned.

No further incident regarding Liége, where a large number of forts still hold out ; the besieging troops, which seem to belong to six army corps, have begun their entrenching in a most methodical way. Near Tirlemont, advanced parties of the First Belgian Division have been in touch with various German units, and the Germans have blown up the Liége-Louvain railway in two places. We have sent one of our best squadrons of aeroplanes to Brussels, and the officer pilots have been hailed with joy. The inactivity of the enemy on the Belgian front suggests that his armies are being reconstituted for the impending attack, but in my Elysian prison I get very scanty information as to what is happening at headquarters, and the War Minister assures me that he knows no more than I do. Messimy and I are arranging for our " liaison " with Joffre to function a little more rapidly and regularly; we do not of course wish to interfere in the slightest degree with the conduct of operations nor fetter the full liberty of the High Command, but it is

impossible for the Chief of the State and for the Government
to do their duty to the country unless they are closely
informed. Neither the Constitution nor the Law have
laid down precisely the relations between the public offices
in time of war ; still less have they defined the relations
between the Executive Government and the High Command.
It must therefore be experimentally, gradually and with
mutual goodwill that we shall co-ordinate the different
organisations, all equally necessary for our national life
and for paving the way to victory.

General Joffre lets us know that the Germans have taken
hostages in Alsace and in the French villages which they
have seized in Lorraine, and have shot a good many civilians.
The Wolff Agency, however, in a communiqué, puts the boot
on the other leg :

" The reports as to the fighting round Liége show that the
inhabitants have fired from ambuscades on the German troops
and have maltreated doctors who were attending the wounded.
News from Metz is to the effect that at the French frontier private
individuals have fired on German patrols.   These facts go to
prove that in France as in Belgium a campaign of *francs-tireurs* is
being organised against the German troops.   Our adversaries can
therefore only blame themselves if war be prosecuted with the
utmost rigour."

This Note is obviously drafted as a prelude to final
threats.   I do not see inoffensive Belgian peasants attacking
battalions of infantry, and certainly in the Est there is not
a single man capable of serving who is not mobilised ; the
francs-tireurs of whom the Wolff Agency so glibly speaks
must therefore be recruited from the old men, women and
children.

But can it be seriously thought that in our quiet villages
the few people whose age and sex keeps them at home have
taken sporting guns in their hands with which to pepper
enemy soldiers ?

Our Minister at Stockholm sends us fresh examples of
the false news plentifully put out in German propaganda.
In the Reichstag the Chancellor has explicitly recognised
that the invasion of Luxembourg and Belgium constituted

a violation of the right of nations, but he added, amid thunders of applause, that necessity knows no laws, and this particular necessity is of course that haughty and perfidious France has threatened to occupy Belgium. In a proclamation of the 6th—the third since the declaration of war—the Kaiser affirms that it is a question to-day of life and death for his Empire, and that to ensure victory Germany will sacrifice her last man and her last horse. The taking of Liége is alluded to in the Press as a feat of arms without precedent in history, and there crops up constantly the *leit-motif*, "the inhabitants of towns on the French frontier having fired on German soldiers, the latter will for the future give no quarter".

Another visit from Clemenceau, to whom M. de Freycinet has imparted his anxieties; he begs me to write to the old man, although as a matter of fact I saw him only yesterday. De Freycinet, Clemenceau reminds me, is eighty-six years old, was Minister of Defence in 1870, and for him it is much the same war now as then. In his reply to my note the veteran statesman says: "I would like to see the Russians with the fourteen army corps mobilised on the 26th July and their cavalry cross the Austrian frontier and advance into the country. It is the only means—and perhaps it is already too late—of preventing Austria from sending several army corps to our frontier, which would render our numerical inferiority far too pronounced. The Germans can already set twenty-three corps against our twenty, and an accession of Austrian corps would too far outbalance us. This is why, without in any way incriminating the Russians, I think it is indispensable that they should get busy immediately." I assure my old colleague that we have several times represented the same thing, and that, as well as to Russia, we have addressed ourselves to Serbia, to whom we had made pecuniary advances so as to be sure that our advice was being heeded. "For the moment," I can tell him, "one, or at the most two, Austrian corps have come north of Constance or in the direction of Fribourg to replace the Bavarians who had been sent to Austria. These Austrian troops may have been made up of the Innsbruck

corps with some Croats, but Count Berchtold has categorically contradicted the report, and anyhow there are no
Austrians at this moment on our, or the Belgian, frontier,
which does not at all mean that there will be none to-
morrow." M. de Freycinet is of course quite right. If
Russia, as we still believe, has mobilised more quickly
towards Galicia than towards Germany, she ought to be
able now to take the offensive against Austria without even
awaiting the date communicated by the Grand Duke
Nicholas. Doumergue will ask at St. Petersburg whether it
would not be possible to make an immediate move. We do
not know to-day the orders and counter-orders which, at
the end of July, led up to the partial and general mobilisation, and it is only much later that we shall learn what
really happened. But anyone can see that the delays in
mobilisation and concentration have prevented our Russian
Ally from getting down to work as quickly as one could wish.

Even now it is diplomatic strategy which is occupying
Russia. Her Ambassador does not despair of attracting
Turkey to the Triple Entente, and the daily conversations
of M. de Giers with the Grand Vizier are taking a more
favourable turn. The Russian Envoy thinks that it might
be possible to draw Turkey into a positive alliance if she
were promised—in the event of final victory—territorial
gains other than at the expense of Serbs, Greeks and Bulgarians. If there is really anything in the suggested
entente the French Government must in no way pooh-
pooh it. But does the idea emanate from the Grand Vizier
or M. de Giers ? Is it accepted by Enver Pasha ? What
will the Balkan people say ?

Sazonoff, always a little bewildering with his multiplicity of ideas, is now parleying with Bucharest and Rome.
But our Minister in Roumania rather fears that Russia
may be a little too importunate with these *pourparlers* and
that the *amour-propre* of King Carol may revolt, as the
Hohenzollern-born Roumanian is much put to it even to
preserve neutrality. Italy has given no mandate to her
Ambassador to negotiate with Sazonoff, and anything the
former says is of a purely personal character. With this

reservation the Marquis Carlotti has been at no pains to conceal that, besides Trentino, Trieste and Vallona, his country will require the Dalmatian littoral, and he has whispered in Sazonoff's ear that Germany and Austria are striving tooth and nail to bring Italy round to their side with the immediate promises of Nice, Savoy, Corsica and Tunis. Sazonoff will not take nay for an answer, and while Italy is making her choice between her suitors, he addresses his ingenuity to the game of cards being played in the Balkans.

The mobilisation decree for the Greek army was signed yesterday and will be published as soon as there appears the Bulgarian order for mobilisation, which has been announced for to-day or to-morrow. The return of the Queen of Greece is awaited with some uneasiness at Athens, as it is thought the Kaiser's sister may be enlisted on behalf of the Kaiser, whose representations have been so far without result. M. Venizelos has told our Minister that if Bulgaria should attack Serbia, Greece would at once declare war on Bulgaria.

M. Léon Bourgeois comes to see me and is terribly upset about the loss of Mulhouse. " We had no right ", he said, " to give the Alsatians hopes which were doomed to disappointment. We ought never to have entered Mulhouse unless we were sure of being able to stay there ; now we are exposing the people who have trusted us to cruel reprisals." I cannot contradict my good friend, and can only sit and suffer without knowing either the cause or the details of this miserable set-back.

The War Minister brings me in the evening an officer just arrived from headquarters, whose news is that we have to-day retaken Mangiennes, and that the Germans have summoned Longwy to surrender : in Alsace we have been obliged to give way to weight of numbers, although we still hold Altkirch. The officer cheerfully adds that the covering troops are intact, that the *moral* of the men is excellent, that our cavalry has made itself severely felt and can always account for the German cavalry, that our infantry is very full of " go ", and the General Staff full of confidence ; and that one could almost think we were engaged in a *Kriegspiel*.

This professional optimism is rather trying and I ask the officer to explain about Mulhouse, which he admits is a defeat. We were deceived by the faulty information of our aviators, who thought the country just there was free of Germans, whereas the Forest of La Hardt was crammed with them. After having advanced without any difficulty on to the plain below Mulhouse we were forced to beat a retreat ; we evacuated Cernay and apparently retired from Thann in the valley of the Thur to, and beyond, St. Amarin. We only hold a bit of the valley of the Doller, Altkirch and a corner of Sundgau, while the Germans are as far as at Masevaux. Those poor people who so joyously greeted the coming of our soldiers, what can they be thinking now ? The military repulse is of course nothing like irreparable, but how to repair the moral defeat ? The check to our 7th Corps has not in the least disturbed Joffre's equanimity, and he is bending himself to a general offensive in a few days. I pass the hours feverishly waiting for news, without leaving the Élysée for a moment, and dealing with a constant stream of Ministers, Senators, Deputies and military officers who are passing through.

12th August.—Colonel Aldebert brings me a letter from the King of the Belgians from Louvain, in which he thanks me most cordially for my letter of two days earlier and for all that I said about the Belgian troops, and assures me that we can count on the support of the Belgian army to the very utmost of their power on the left of the Allied armies.

At the Ministerial Council—when the officers have been nominated for King Albert's staff—there arises again the question of our relations with Austria. England is willing to recall her Ambassador from Vienna on condition that this step should be followed by a declaration of war ; Paul Cambon urges that we should do likewise. A good deal of discussion ensues, some of the Ministers being very anxious that in our declaration we should allude to the sinister movements of Austrian troops, but eventually the formula was adopted and communicated to Sir Francis Bertie.

" After having declared war on Serbia and thus taken the initiative in European hostilities, the Austro-Hungarian Government have placed themselves—without any provocation from the

Government of the Republic—in a state of war with France. (1) After Germany had successively declared war on Russia and France the Austro-Hungarian Government entered into the conflict by declaring war on Russia which was fighting alongside France. (2) According to numerous and trustworthy reports Austria has sent troops on to German soil in circumstances which constitute a direct threat with regard to France. In face of all these facts the French Government find themselves obliged to inform Austria they will take every step which will enable them to reply to these acts and threats."

Doumergue telegraphs to London, and as Dumaine has been recalled from Vienna and Count Szecsen has left Paris, we ask the British Government to forward our Note to Count Berchtold, together with their own declaration of war.

Before leaving his Embassy, Dumaine drafted a despatch to hand in on his return, in which he recites his last conversation with Count Berchtold and Count Hoyos. The former, with all his airs and graces, does not seem astonished that France did not accept the assurances given to her as to the movements of Austrian troops. He is by no means offended to see his denials contested anew. Even at this tragic moment he has said nothing to Dumaine, which discloses that he realises his responsibilities. Count Hoyos spoke much more freely. " Believe me," he said, " we could not do otherwise. In Serbia, in Russia, in all the Slav countries and in others which support them, there is a settled conviction that Austro-Hungary is breaking up and her complete disintegration is only a matter of three or four years. Better to precipitate the catastrophe than to accept the intolerable conditions of being regarded as condemned. We have been forced into proving that we are still capable of vigorous effort. God knows, however, that we earnestly desired to save Europe and ourselves from the crisis into which we are flung." In other words, the Monarchy of the Hapsburgs, believing herself doomed by the brittleness of her own interior constitution, has precipitated events and plays for neck or nothing.

Foreseeing that hostilities were imminent between Austria and ourselves, San Giuliano has given instructions in advance to Tittoni and Imperiali. He has told them that even so

Italy will continue to consider herself under no obligation to the Triple Alliance and will not take sides either against France or England for the specific reason that in attacking Serbia Austria has assumed the part of the aggressor. There in a nut-shell lies a balanced judgement as to the responsibility for the war. San Giuliano has put on record also that for the moment there are three opinions in Italy : first, for the maintenance of neutrality ; second, very feeble, for co-operation with the Empires of the Centre ; and third, which is much stronger, for action against Austria. But this last the subtle Italian Minister asserts will be much weakened by the immobility of the French and British squadrons in the Mediterranean. Thus San Giuliano, who is as clever as he is opportune, lets us know that " Italy remains neutral but may march alongside of you and against her northern neighbour, who was her Ally of yesterday and her perpetual enemy, if you and England decide to reduce to impotence the Austrian fleet ".

Sir Edward Grey will hand our Note to Count Mensdorff and tell him that this compels Great Britain to consider herself as at war with Austria ; the Foreign Minister has already consulted the First Lord of the Admiralty as to the most favourable moment for naval action. Before night Count Mensdorff receives his passports, and the British Fleet is ordered to weigh anchor, head for the Austrian ships and fire on them. Admiral de Lapeyrère is also told to move forward in the Adriatic.

As chance happens, Tittoni comes to thank me for my letter, which has appeared in the Press, recommending that we should help the Italians now living in France who are without resources. The Ambassador's eyes sparkle when I tell him of what we are doing in conjunction with England, and he repeats that his country considers itself as wholly detached from the Triple Alliance, the chief culprit in the matter of disturbing peace. " I have no right," I say after thanking him, " even as an individual, to offer you advice, but I know what would be my way of thinking if I were an Italian. England, France and Russia have not wanted war, but as war has been imposed upon them, they are all equally resolved

to fight to a finish.   This may mean the end of the artificial
Dual Monarchy.   Italy has her national aspirations and her
hour is striking.   I beg you to believe that if ever our fleet
should, in fighting Austria, find herself obliged to bombard
towns like Trieste or Pola we would only do so from sheer
necessity, and we should be deeply grieved to cause the
slightest damage to the Italians in those places." Tittoni
simply says he will convey what I have said to his Government, who will be much gratified.   I say no word to the
Ambassador as to Sazonoff's notions, which seem highly prob-
lematical and which M. Barrère considers very inopportune.

The *Goeben* and the *Breslau* are an infinite nuisance, and
yesterday they entered the Sea of Marmora, just when Enver
Pasha was pretending to lend a willing ear to M. de Giers's
proposals of alliance.   The two cruisers are said to have been
sold to Turkey, and Sir Edward Grey has told the Ambassador
to ask that they should be disarmed, and if this is not done in
twenty-four hours that they should be sent away altogether.
The Grand Vizier has very lamely explained to Bompard that
the whole thing is a consequence of England having seized
two Turkish ships as a security for an unpaid debt, and
that the Turkish Government, thus deprived of war-ships, is
obliged to purchase from Germany in case of trouble in the
Dardanelles.   The ships arrived after the bargain had been
concluded, but none the less they entered the Narrows under
the German flag and the trick has been scored.   Bompard at
once asked for an explanation, and the Grand Vizier promised
that the crews should be sent back to Germany.   He quite
seriously added that this deal did not in any way modify
the Ottoman Government's offer of neutrality.   Paléologue
telegraphs also that the Porte has nothing to fear from
Russia, the Czar and his Ministers having no idea of doing
anything to injure the integrity of the Ottoman Empire.
Whatever assurances Russia may give, Turkey does not seem
to be any happier ; she is held in leash by Germany.   At the
same time Austria is redoubling her pressure on Bulgaria and
has made solid offers at Sofia, promising Macedonia—it is so
easy to promise what is not your own—Salonika and part of
old Serbia.   She has also notified Montenegro of a blockade

of her littoral and of the Albanian coasts, and King Nicholas may well be uneasy as to supplies for Cettinge, and he urgently asks for a French squadron to come and save his hill people from famine.

There is no country in which German propaganda does not exploit and exaggerate our reverses. Unhappily there is a good deal of truth in some of the reports, and an official Note at Berlin can speak of a grave check to our troops near Lunéville ; thus it is through a German communiqué that we hear of a set-back as to which our headquarters have not breathed a word. I complain again to Messimy of this military reticence, which he himself thinks is quite wrong. One can understand absolute secrecy as to future operations, but there is no reason why we should not hear of untoward incidents which have actually happened. It is one thing not to depress the *moral* of the country; it is another to keep the Government uninformed of bad news when, if we were told what had happened, we might be of some use.

The news from Russia is scarcely more comforting. Without waiting for the Grand Duke's offensive the Austrians seem to have crossed the frontier in the valley of the Haute Vistule, and the Germans are so threatening Warsaw that the Russian authorities are preparing to leave after breaking the bridges behind them. But ill-tidings seem only to make the fires of French patriotism burn more fiercely, and from people in every phase of life and in every corner of the country I get letters offering help in whatever way help may be most useful. Prince Louis Napoleon, who sometime commanded a division in the Russian army, begs to serve in any capacity, but I am obliged to give him the same answer as to the Orleans princes and Prince Roland.

13*th August.*—Doumergue brings me very early in the morning such news as has come in the night from St. Petersburg and Brussels. The Grand Duke Nicholas takes over, this evening, command of all the forces and has on his Staff the French, English and Serbian Military Attachés.

The Germans have thrown up entrenchments in Liége this side of the line of the forts, and to the north of the town the retreat of the German cavalry is complete. M.

Klobukowski goes so far as to say it would look as if the proposed attack over Central Belgium has been postponed or given up, and it is thought that the Germans only want to open a way to the south of the Ourche towards the Haute Meuse and France. In another telegram our Minister adds:

" M. de Brocqueville told me yesterday that M. Vandervelde is at the moment of invaluable help, not only to his own Government but to the Allied Powers, because he does everything possible to stimulate his co-religionists in Holland to inform those who are in Germany and to restrain those who are in Russia. As to this last a little manifesto has been prepared to show that the German military party in letting war loose has classed itself as the enemy of humanity, and that its definite defeat will be an asset to social progress and will open the path to the union of peoples and to disarmament."

Just when we are receiving these messages the German Staff is publishing a long list of savage deeds traitorously committed by Belgian civilians, women as well as men, against soldiers off guard. But German militarism, however audacious in the art of calumny, is even more so when it comes to intrigues. At the other end of Europe there is evidence of what stratagems the Germans will employ to achieve their aims. Our Military Attaché telegraphs from Therapia that Liman von Sanders has been appointed to command the First Army due to concentrate toward Adrianople-Demolika so as to operate if necessary against Greece, and that all the German officers are staying on in Turkey and are being given commands. Bompard confirms this, and adds that he is pretty sure that the two cruisers are carrying the German flag. During their stay in the Dardanelles the crews behaved as if everything belonged to them and, in the Chanak Roads, made requisition for material from trading boats, French, British and Greek, and removed the wireless apparatus from the *Saghalien* under threat of sinking her. All this takes place in neutral waters. The Grand Vizier has quite courteously acknowledged our protest, but is powerless to do anything, as the War Minister shows a fine contempt for even his most formal injunctions. The Turks are now so saturated with the belief that Germany will win the war that the representatives of the Triple Entente are powerless even to protect their own compatriots. At the same moment, in order to administer a further narcotic, the Minister for Foreign Affairs telegraphs in clear to the Turkish Ambassador in Paris :

" In order to leave no doubt as to the pacific attitude which the Imperial Government has decided to observe in the conflict now going on, I repeat again that Turkey is resolved to maintain strict neutrality."

But if Turkish neutrality is more than flexible, Dutch neutrality is very solid ; Sir Edward Grey has received a categorical undertaking that the Netherlands will take no part in the war, a decision gladly heard at Brussels, where in the absence, so far, of any official communication there has been some anxiety on this score. Germany, however, loses no opportunity to try and enrol the neutral countries under her flag, and hopes to dazzle them by a recital of her conquests. She represents our armies as in full flight, and announces that revolution has broken out in Paris and that I have been assassinated. This devilry is especially addressed to Roumania, and under the influence of King Carol the Cabinet at Bucharest decides to reject Sazonoff's proposals and say that for the moment all they can do is to maintain the balance of power in the Balkans. Bulgaria promises "in the existing circumstances" to remain neutral ; while Venizelos has declared that if Turkey and Bulgaria attack Serbia, Greece will take up arms against the two aggressors. He wants to know if in such case she will be considered as an ally of the Triple Entente, a question which Doumergue hopes to answer in the affirmative.

Clemenceau sends his brother to tell me that Tittoni is now completely won over to the idea of an active alliance. I only hope this conversion is true, but we have good reason to fear that if so the eminent diplomatist has not imparted his conversion to his Government. The British Ambassador in Rome has seen the Prime Minister, and told him that Great Britain would welcome Italian co-operation just as much as France and Russia, but M. Salandra thinks it would be premature for the Allies to represent the matter officially at Rome.

The Russian offensive, which was to have begun this evening, and which was to have contributed so largely to relieving our front, is unhappily postponed until to-morrow evening or Saturday morning. Moreover, Sir Francis Bertie has called at the Quai d'Orsay to-day to warn us that, according to information received at their War Office, Russia will keep in hand a large part of her forces for eventual action against Turkey. Sir George Buchanan has been instructed to remind Sazonoff that it is of vital importance for Russia to back us up against Germany, as there is every sign that the German armies will in a very short while launch a very powerful attack against us.

Our reverse at Mulhouse is not only a serious moral defeat but a very awkward tactical failure. One of our brigades pushed forward without taking proper precautions as to scouting and has been forced to retire. General Pau, the splendid soldier who was wounded in 1870, has been sent to Belfort and is making immediate dispositions. The 7th Corps was to evacuate Alsace to-day, recross the frontier and concentrate on the parade ground protected by the memory of Denfert-Rochereau and the majesty of the Lion of Bartholdi. Thank God, the African troops are reinforcing our rather tired divisions. The 19th Corps have already sent to France two contingents, altogether 23,000 men.

The Prefect of Meurthe and Moselle has been relieved of his duties and replaced by M. Mirman, formerly deputy for the Marne, who telegraphs that the population of Pont-à-Mousson has had a very bad experience in the bombardment (of which I learnt first from the newspapers) : five civilians have been killed and many wounded. All round Briey is occupied by Bavarian infantry and squadrons of chasseurs, dragoons and hussars, and wherever the Germans are they have made a clean sweep of all articles of food and have forwarded to Metz by waggon and lorry everything they can gather from the harvest : the Mayor and the curé are locked up in a fortress on a groundless charge of spying.

There is a very slender slice of comfort in the news that General Cordonnier's brigade has severely punished the 21st Regiment of German Dragoons and has taken many prisoners.

14th August.—Our Council this morning is closely engaged with internal affairs which press for attention, but matters of international importance of course take up the larger part of our time.

Japan has wasted no time and has declared war on Germany without waiting for an agreement either with us or with our Ally Great Britain. Germany hopes that this spontaneous action may dispose the United States against the Triple Entente, and in Berlin a rather theatrical display in honour of America is being arranged.

M. Jules Guesde, one of the leading Socialists, asks for an interview and expresses the opinion that we should officially notify Germany that we are fighting not her but the Empire, and that when the war is over we should give an option to Alsace and Lorraine and not claim any victory. I tell him that I have been careful to make quite clear the distinction he recommends and I have spoken of legitimate reparations. " You agree with me ", I say, " that these reparations are due to us and are an essential condition for the future balance of Europe. But it might be imprudent to say we are going to give an option to Alsace. The Germans, it appears, are now putting the Alsatians in their front ranks, so that we may be obliged to fire on them ; a rash word on our part might only aggravate the risk which these unfortunate men are now running. For forty-four years Alsace has been invaded and every effort has been made to detach the new generations from France; who knows whether on the morrow of the war a false plebiscite may not be taken. Personally, I hope we shall recover our lost provinces, and I do not think we can lay down our arms without doing so. But beyond this I do not think we ought to annex an inch of European territory, but that we should show the world what is meant by a great democracy which only fights for her independence and her rights."

My distinguished compatriot, M. Maurice Barrès, is going to the Front to serve as war correspondent for some big newspapers, and comes to ask me for facilities to enable him to go to the most exposed points at the Front. I the more readily promise to do what I can for him, because his patriotism and his great talent have conspired to give us articles such as those which, in the *Écho de Paris*, dwell so admirably on the work of the Secours Nationale, the Croix Rouge and the Légion Alsatienne. I know perhaps better than anybody the quick sympathy which he sometimes conceals under a rather cold and disdainful manner; but to-day he is his own real self and sees Ehrmann harnessed to the service of France, and Colette Baudoche married to a Parisian.

M. Sabini also turns up at the Élysée and tells me that Tittoni is definitely in favour of Italy breaking off immediately with Austria. He shows me a report which he is sending to Rome, and in which he declares himself authorised to pronounce that in the event of concerted action Italy will derive from France the immediate funds necessary, and that, independently of territorial advantages, she will obtain a commercial treaty. I remind my friend that constitutionally I have no sort of right to guarantee anything of the sort, that the Government could not promise a commercial treaty without the consent of Parliament, and that he had better advise Tittoni to go and see the Foreign Minister, who would certainly do nothing behind the Ambassador's back. So, M. Salandra says we must do nothing in a hurry, M. Tittoni sits tight, and M. Sabini continues to busy himself without our really knowing whether he is or is not the authorised spokesman of his Chief. I cannot help finding this sort of *combinazione* rather trying.

Sir Francis Bertie brings his rosy presence into my room and leads me back into less tortuous paths. He tells me in confidence that Sir John French, who has been appointed Commander-in-Chief of the British Army in the Field, will be in Paris to-morrow, but this is a scrap of news already to hand both through the Havas Agency and from Paul Cambon's telegram; the Government think it well that everybody should know of the British General's arrival, so that he should get a warm welcome.

Sir Edward Grey is less and less favourable to the hurried and rather ragged proposals which Sazonoff is piling up for the Balkans, and is contemplating a plan for federating in joint neutrality Roumania, Bulgaria and Greece. Grey wants Venizelos to take the initiative in this matter at Bucharest and Sofia, and we are the more willing to fall in with the idea because a telegram from Bucharest makes it clear how very indisposed Roumania is to be tutored by Sazonoff. M. Bratiano has told the Russian Minister who was pressing him unduly : " If your Government insist on having a reply to-day Yes or No, our reply will be No. Anyhow, please wait until the Roumanian Minister has arrived at Petersburg." Paul Cambon, who is extremely well informed as to things in the Near East, again tells us that in his opinion the diplomacy of the Triple Entente at Constantinople can have no influence on Turkey, and that military events will alone affect the attitude of a Power which is accustomed to pay respect chiefly to force of arms. Turkey will dawdle and dilly-dally so long as she has any doubt of German victory, and will only throw in her lot against us when she is sure of our being worsted.

The Berlin propaganda is raging everywhere, and Jules Cambon who has just arrived at Christiania telegraphs : " I am thunderstruck by the amount of false news which is spread here and at Copenhagen by the German Legation, and our agents seem to have the greatest difficulty in contradicting the falsehoods."

To-day General Dubail and General Castelnau, at the head of the First and Second Armies, are marching on Delme and Sarrebourg ; we have reached the Donon, where we have established a regular stronghold, and General Headquarters look for great things from these operations in Lorraine. But in Belgium the Lonçin Fort has been very heavily shelled, and Joffre understands that the German forces between Luxembourg and Liége comprise at least eight infantry corps and four cavalry divisions. Evidently the enemy is going to move in great strength across Belgium, and General Lanrezac has drawn Joffre's attention to the necessity of protecting our left wing.

15th August.—The Feast of the Assumption ; a day of anxiety. The Germans are "practising their strokes". The last forts of Liége are holding out, but Lonçin has fallen, and General Leman is wounded and a prisoner. The German cavalry has crossed the Meuse ; shells have fallen on Dinant ; there has been much fighting round Jarny and Conflans ; Longuyon is strongly held by the Germans.

As to Russia, Paléologue says that England is wrong in supposing that the Czar would keep back any troops for action against Turkey, and that Russia understands perfectly well that she must deliver an immediate and powerful stroke against Germany. She is setting four armies, composed of fifteen fine corps, against the Kaiser's forces, whilst three armies, comprising twelve corps, will deal with Austria. Germany has apparently concentrated against Russia five regular and eleven reserve army corps ; the fighting, both in the East and the West, bids fair to be something fearful.

There is to hand a new offer of alliance ; Portugal would like to come in with us, but the Council of National Defence, although very grateful, is a little nervous as to whether this might not disfavour Spain. The overtures from Lisbon are therefore warmly but cautiously acknowledged, and nothing must be done in a hurry, especially without England knowing all about it.

The Czar has addressed a manifesto to the Polish populations in Russia, Germany and Austria, in which he solemnly declares he intends to re-establish their national unity. According to what Sazonoff has told Paléologue, Poland reconstituted will acquire an entire local autonomy, with perfect freedom as to the Catholic religion and national language ; she will be governed by a Viceroy of the Czar. The proclamation signed by the Grand Duke Nicholas runs :

" The hour has struck when the dream of your father and of your ancestors is to be realised. A century and a half ago Poland's body was torn to shreds, but her soul lives on. She has lived in hopes that the day will come for a new birth of her people and for reconciliation with mighty Russia. May the Polish people find

their unity under the sceptre of the Czar ! Under this sceptre
Poland will be born anew, perfectly free as to her faith, her
language and her internal administration. . . ."

Here again Russia has done something without telling us.
Nothing could be better than her wish to set forward a re-
vival of a reconstituted and a sovereign Poland. But to
offer to the Poles of Silesia, of Posen and Galicia, complete
liberty as to religion, language and administration, under the
Imperial authority of the Romanoffs, is scarcely the right
way to their hearts ; anyhow, it is to tell Germany of veiled
annexations as to which no agreement has been concluded
between Russia and ourselves, which may traverse the whole
idea of a defensive war and may risk the restitutions which
France has the right and the desire to claim. I cannot help
wondering whether Russia is not making another blunder in
discarding, as outside the province of practical politics, Sir
Edward Grey's idea of a neutral federation of Greece, Bulgaria and Roumania. The British Secretary of State's idea
—and it is a very clever one—is to render Bulgaria immobile.
Sazonoff, however, will not listen to this English proposal and
continues to run from pillar to post without settling anywhere. But to do him justice, the Russian Minister of Finance,
M. Bark, has a very practical notion. He insists that we
should give the French holders of Russian bonds facilities to
collect their coupons. He tells Paléologue that it is more
than ever necessary for Russia to prove that her credit is
sound, and he asks that a special fund should be constituted
at the Bank of France. Russia wants the Bank of France to
make prospective advances which are sure to become effective
and will very likely grow. But how to refuse ? How can
we leave unpaid during a war which is just beginning the
coupons which represent here the savings of so many
peasants and of the lower middle class ?

Sir John French comes to see me a little before three
o'clock, accompanied by Sir Francis Bertie. Although his
arrival was quite unofficial, he received a great ovation at the
Gare du Nord. To-morrow he will go to Vitry-le-François to
confer with Joffre, and thence proceed to Le Cateau to join the
army which is now arriving and of which he is to take com-

mand. He is a small man, quiet in manner, with nothing
particularly military in his appearance, except that he looks
you straight in the face ; his cheeks and chin are closely
shaved, his moustache is grey and rather drooping. Sir
John, it would seem, has made proof of military skill and
courage in Egypt and South Africa, but one would take him
rather for a plodding engineer than a dashing soldier. Slow
and methodical, he does not seem to have much " go " in
him. Although he has been accustomed to spend his holidays
in Normandy, and although, as I have heard, he has a son-
in-law who is a French officer, he speaks our tongue with
great difficulty, and Sir Francis Bertie has to act as interpreter. Sir John explains to us in English that his troops
can hardly take their place in the front line before the 25th
of August. The disembarkation of the cavalry, he says, has
taken a long time and has been very difficult ; it will need
ten more days to get everything ready. Ten days ! So
the English will take no part in the opening battles. How
French opinions have been misled ! We thought them ready
to the last button to fight, and now they will not be at the
rendezvous.

Late in the afternoon we learn that thirty storks have
been seen over Belfort coming from the valley of the Rhine
and flying prematurely towards the south. They are flying
from the cannonade. When will they be able to come back
without hearing the roar of the guns and find a footing in
Alsace on French soil ?

CHAPTER III

Sunday, 16*th August.*—Always this fever of suspense. I know nothing of the military operations except the scraps I glean daily from the liaison officers. Our troops have re-taken Blamont and Cirey and have re-entered Thann, but any exhilaration derived from these little successes is dashed by the thought of the blood which France is shedding. And from the Prefect of Meurthe and Moselle comes an ugly story of the excesses of the German troops, who are behaving as if they had received orders to terrorise France, as if a ruler, drunk with pride, thinks to excuse savagery under the pretence of shortening the war. During the eight days the Germans were at Blamont, for no rhyme or reason they killed three people, of whom one was a young girl and another was an old man of eighty-six ; while at Breux a patrol of Uhlans came in contact with our Customs House officers and wounded two of them, as well as a child of twelve years old. Scouting parties have slipped into the village of Nonsard, whose inhabitants are all my faithful friends ; the Germans have pushed even further on in the Commercy arrondissement for which I was so long the member, and ten men have been taken prisoner near Montsec. All these names bring to my mind familiar figures, and the war has scarcely begun before I see the enemy in the heart of the country where I was born and only a few kilometres from the country home of my childhood. In the Vosges we still hold Ste. Marie aux Mines after a sharp tussle, and we have made some progress in

Schirmeck, that picturesque valley through which only the other day my wife and I were motoring. At Dinant in Belgium we have met with success against a Guards division and the enemy's 1st Cavalry Division, and it is good to hear that at St. Blaise on the 14th the 1st Battalion of Chasseurs secured a German flag. But to me it seems a bad omen that Germany is already on the outskirts of St. Mihiel, and I feel it the more acutely as, knowing every inch of the country of the Meuse, I can see with my mind's eye the bitter struggle which is staining it with blood.

While the fortune of war seems to fluctuate, German propaganda is raging abroad, and from Christiania we have some choice specimens of the stories the Germans are flinging about.

" Brutality of the Belgians at Antwerp against deported Germans ; the 1500 French prisoners who arrived at Berlin were in ragged uniforms and were a pitiful sight."

A communiqué published in the *Gazette de l'Allemagne du Nord* has been distributed over Norway.

" Despite the right of nations, a people's war is being organised in France. We shall fire without pity on civilians who take up arms or destroy means of communication. It is France, and not Germany, who will be responsible for all the blood which will flow. . . . Belgium has wanted war ; civilians and even children are attacking us. If the war takes on a ferocious character Belgium must bear the responsibility."

At Stockholm there is announced : " Revolution in Poland confirmed ; a Hohenzollern who is a Catholic is a candidate for the throne ". From Copenhagen M. Bapst telegraphs :

" They are saying in Berlin that the German Government has, through a neutral Power, told the French and the Belgian Governments that if the fighting becomes savage, the fault will be Belgium's, whose civil population has shown methods of barbarism towards the German troops which are an insult to civilisation."

Poor Belgium ! she is now charged with being the guilty party. Germany, who, like ourselves, was a guarantee of her neutrality, has cold-bloodedly invaded the land she had sworn to protect, and now has the audacity to try and incriminate in the eyes of the world the peace-loving country which, without the slightest provocation, she is over-running. Belgium, however, taken unawares as she is by the aggression of her truculent neighbour, scarcely knows how she is going to find the money for the unexpected expenses which an act of treachery has imposed on her, and she rather confusedly turns to the other guarantors of her independence. The Governments in London and Paris must find the means to advance the funds she requires, but in order to lend to a friend in need they must borrow for themselves. Belgium is pluckily arming to defend herself. I have had much talk to-day with M. Vandervelde, the Belgian statesman, at the Élysée, who in presence of the danger which threatens his country seems to have put aside altogether any party questions. He speaks of his King with the greatest respect, and is evidently on the friendliest terms with his colleagues in the Cabinet. If he is a little cold in manner, he evidently combines mental alertness with a very resolute character, while he enjoys a very convenient deafness which does not prevent his hearing all he wants to know and enables him to dismiss whatever he considers negligible. He is very insistent as to the detachments of the French cavalry being sent on to the left bank of the Meuse so as to back up the Belgian army, and above all, to hearten the population. The same request has been made to us from Belgian Headquarters, and we put in a word with Joffre, who is telling General Sordet to cross the Sambre with his cavalry, and to move on in Belgium towards the Est.

Up to now the Departments of the Nord and Pas de Calais have not been included in the zone of the armies, and even after the invasion of Belgium our General Staff could scarcely believe that the war would be carried so far northwest. Our plan of campaign attributed to the enemy France's own notions of chivalry. But the constantly growing strength of the Germans on the edge of Belgium, the weight of men that has already penetrated to neutral territory, the arrival of the British Expeditionary Force, the very alarming prospect of much larger developments than we had envisaged, the necessity which is now recognised of stretching our line along the Belgian frontier as far as the coast—all these and other considerations determine General Joffre to ask that the Nord and the Pas de Calais shall be included in the zone of fighting.

The constant pressure on our front compels Joffre to stir up anew his Russian colleague; not that the Grand Duke Nicholas personally requires any stirring up, but because, as he said himself to me in 1912, in a huge Empire, when an order is given, no one is ever sure whether it is delivered. Our Russian friends took the offensive on the 14th August; the three armies of the North-West, comprising twelve corps, have attacked the Germans, two on the north of the Vistula and the third south of the river, while three army corps are marching on Posen and Breslau. On the south-west, three armies, consisting of about twelve army corps, are to take account of Austria. The Czar, the Grand Duke and General Yanouschkevitch vie with one another in saying they will open the way as rapidly as possible to Berlin; that operations against the Austrians will be considered as of secondary importance, and that before all things it is necessary to secure the destruction of the German army. Paléologue says also that England need not have any qualms as to Russia keeping back a single man for eventual operations against Turkey, and our Ambassador assures us that the manifesto to the Poles has been well accepted by Russian opinion; the Press in St. Petersburg and Moscow indulge in glowing periods as to the reconciliation of the great Slav family. But I would like to know what Warsaw has to say on the subject, and I still fear that the sceptre of the Czar will scarcely suggest itself to Polish eyes as an emblem of freedom. Anyhow, the Russian proclamation has stirred up German bile, and the diocesan authorities of Posen have been ordered to publish a paper recording the persecutions endured by the Catholic Poles under the Russian rule, and inciting their flocks to fight faithfully under the German flag. There are other Russian initiatives, and especially those of M. Sazonoff, which add to our anxieties. M. Bratiano, unduly pressed by the Russian Minister at

Bucharest, has said again that he cannot promise anything
to anybody, and if he is required to give an immediate
answer to Russia, that answer will be in the negative.   M.
Sazonoff tries to console himself for this rebuff by recommending *pourparlers* with Turkey.   He wants us to say to
the Porte : " If you will remain neutral, England, France
and Russia will not only guarantee you your territory, but,
in the event of victory, will rid you of the very oppressive
custody which Germany has kept over you in many ways,
and especially with regard to the Bagdad railway ".   Sir
Edward Grey, who is very much on the alert, has told
Sir Francis Bertie to convey to Doumergue an analogous
proposal.   Without entertaining any great illusions as to
the value of the step proposed, the Cabinet here agrees to
this, but there has hardly been time to send the official
reply before Isvolsky tells Doumergue of a further notion.
Sazonoff now wants to ask Turkey, as a preliminary, to
demobilise, but we think this would be to go too far and
might risk everything.   M. Bompard does not conceal from
us that as a matter of fact Turkey is leaning more and
more towards Germany ; and if the first big battle issues
in a German victory, it will be very difficult to keep the
Ottoman Government neutral any longer.

On the other hand, the British Foreign Office is more
favourably impressed by what is going on in Greece.   For
some days it would seem King Constantine has been under
a hail of letters and telegrams from his Imperial and im-
perious brother-in-law.   Queen Olga has come to the rescue
on more than one occasion, but Venizelos, who is closely
watching these manœuvres, has been very uneasy.   Now,
however, the Kaiser has overstepped the line.   The German
Minister—no doubt under precise orders from Berlin—has
told the King that he must make up his mind one way or
the other and say whether he is for or against Wilhelm,
and his tone was such that King Constantine took offence
and broke off the audience which he had granted.

As to Italy, Doumergue has indeed been well inspired
not to hurry things.   There is no doubt but that the Italian
General Staff is apparently preparing military measures

sooner or later against Austria. But we know that to-day the Marquis Imperiali has been told to go slow ; that Italy has no immediate intention of shedding her neutrality, and before any new decision can be made, cut-and-dried military and political agreements would have to be come to with the Powers of the Triple Entente, and that these would be secretly negotiated in London and nowhere else. Italy has no misgivings about Doumergue, but for a long time she has not been sure about Isvolsky, the Russian representative in Paris ; she prefers the caution and discretion of the British, and Imperiali is even deputed to beg Sir Edward Grey to do what he can to prevent the French and Russian Ambassadors at Rome from alluding to the point in any conversation with San Giuliano. What Italy does not add, and what perhaps accounts for the preparations being made in the direction of Trentino, is that she proposes, meanwhile, to parley with Austria, Germany being intermediary. Italy is determined to weigh minutely the respective advantages which may accrue to her, either from neutrality or from war with her old allies ; once more the Consulta is showing herself the cleverest and the most subtle of all the European Chanceries.

In the evening, there is still no news at the War Office as to whether we have taken the offensive on the Belgian frontier as announced ; all that we know is that our position is made good in Haute Alsace, that in the region of Schirmeck we have taken a thousand more prisoners with field and heavy guns, and that beyond Cirey, which we have again captured, the Bavarian corps has had to retire.

Just before midnight there is to hand a telegram, sent from Malta, from Admiral de Lapeyrère :

" I have surprised this morning off Antivari the cruiser and torpedo boat which were making the blockade. The cruiser has been sunk ; the torpedo boat seems to have escaped."

17th August.—Paléologue telegraphs :

" In the course of an interview this morning I urged Sazonoff to say whether in the event of victory Russia would formulate any political or territorial claims against Turkey."

Our Ambassador reminded the Minister that the territorial integrity and political independence of Turkey were one of the chief factors in French diplomacy. Sazonoff replied :

"Even in the event of victory we shall respect the independence and integrity of Turkey if she remains neutral in this war. The utmost we should ask is that a new régime should be drawn up for the Narrows, a régime which shall apply equally to all the States on the coast of the Black Sea, Russia, Bulgaria and Roumania."

Sazonoff on this occasion is quite explicit and fairly satisfactory. It suffices to show that never before the war —although certain slanderers have said otherwise since— did France betray, for the sake of Russia, her old policy in the Near East, and that thus neither in 1912 nor in 1914 was there anything promised to the Czar, his Government, or Isvolsky, even in the matter of the Narrows. Sazonoff cannot quote any engagement made by us, and for good reason. But from Therapia we gather that Russia has not yet given up the idea of claiming Turkey's demobilisation, an idea which Bompard thinks a very unfortunate one ; Doumergue is urging Sazonoff not to pursue a course from which Germany would certainly suck advantage in Constantinople. How difficult it is to drive the Triple Entente in triple harness.

M. Quinonès de Leon, just arrived from Madrid, brings me the warmest messages from the King of Spain, who wishes him to say that, when the moment comes, he will be too happy to play the part of mediator, but that meanwhile he will not make any proposal which might embarrass us, and will await some request from ourselves. I beg kind M. Quinonès, who enjoys his Sovereign's entire confidence, to thank the King most sincerely and to say that our Allies and ourselves intend to carry on the war which has been imposed upon us until victory is within our grasp. It is now too soon or too late to call a cease fire.

The charming Greek Minister M. Romanos also pays me a visit and tells me that a fortnight ago King Constantine let the Kaiser know that if Bulgaria were to set herself

against Serbia, Greece, in virtue of her treaty, would have
to support the latter by force of arms. Although the Kaiser
knew perfectly well that Greece was bound by explicit terms,
he would not admit that she would think it necessary to
hold to them, and was much irritated by the communication.
The two brothers-in-law are *en froid*, and Romanos was
evidently very pleased to tell me so. He thinks, moreover,
that it would be very difficult for the King to go against
public opinion in Greece. The day does not finish without
Sazonoff being delivered of another scheme. In order to
immobilise Turkey, he wants to promise her the island of
Lemnos ; neither Grey nor Cambon nor Doumergue could
or would agree to this, and Paléologue must try and curb a
little the zeal of the Minister. Our Ambassador replies that
Sazonoff is wholly loyal to the spirit of the Alliance, and
this is perfectly true, as it is that the Minister is quite straightforward with the representatives of France and England.
But perhaps things would be a little easier if the Russian
Minister would not let loose on us every day all the resources
of his active and fertile brain.

At the Council of National Defence, Messimy gives some
explanation of Joffre's dispositions. On the Belgian frontier
we remain, standing to arms, and based on the Chiers, watching the movements of the German army. When we resume
the offensive in this sector we shall put in all our weight so as
to try and thrust the enemy back across Belgium towards
the North Sea. With regard to our left wing, in order to
keep touch with the English, General Lanrezac's Fifth Army,
which has just been reinforced, is moving to the Sambre.
From left to right there will be écheloned the Fourth Army,
now under the command of General de Langle de Cary ; the
Third Army, commanded by General Ruffey and which is
concentrated near Verdun ; the Second Army, under General
de Castelnau, which is operating in the neighbourhood of
Nancy, notably with the 20th Corps in charge of General
Foch ; while the First Army, under General Dubail, will be on
the right in the Vosges and Haute Alsace. We shall speed
up at once our offensive in the Est, and Headquarters are
preparing to invest Metz, whose outworks it is thought are

only manned by one army corps. It is hoped also to push our troops into Alsace, beyond the Vosges, between Sarrebourg and Strasbourg, and to turn at Saverne the force which is opposing us in Lorraine. We hold the Donon and the valley of the Bruche as far as Schirmeck, and our cavalry has pushed on to Lützelhausen, but we are still far from the objectives which Messimy has in view. Meanwhile the Prefect of Meurthe and Moselle reports some odious cruelties perpetrated by the oncoming German armies. At Badonvillers eleven persons, of whom one was the Mayor's wife, have been shot, seventy-eight houses set on fire, and fifteen people taken away as hostages ; at Bréménil five inhabitants have been killed, of whom one was an old man of seventy-four ; at Blamont there have been three civilian victims, including a young girl.

While we are marking time on the banks of the Chiers, Germany is driving forward her compact and powerfully armed armies towards Belgium. The last forts of Liége have fallen ; the way is open ; nothing can any more ward off the storm. The Belgian seat of Government has been moved to Antwerp, where are the Queen and her children ; the King remains with the army. Our Minister at Brussels telegraphs :

" Commission of Enquiry as to the maintenance of the Rules of War notifies acts of cruelty and savagery committed deliberately and under official authority in Belgium on wounded soldiers as well as on an ambulance carrying the Red Cross flag, and on old men, women and children." [1]

18th August.—From hour to hour hope alternates with anxiety. This morning while the Council of National Defence was sitting, Messimy receives a very reassuring telegram from Joffre as to operations in Alsace and Lorraine ; our cavalry is at Marsal and at Château-Salins. This, of course, fills us with joy, but for the last fortnight our joys have been

---

[1] Telegram, 17 août, No. 217. Cf. *Documents pour servir à l'histoire de l'invasion allemande dans les provinces de Namur et de Luxembourg*, publiés par le chanoine Jean Schmitz, secrétaire de l'évêché de Namur et Dom Robert Nieuwland, de l'abbaye de Maredsous. Van Oest et Cie, éditeurs, Bruxelles.

fleeting.   Messimy explains briefly to us the position of the
other armies.   The First Army occupied yesterday, in the
Lorraine which has been annexed, Hattigny, Fraquelfing,
Gondrexange, Heming, Hertzing ; while General Maud'huy
is on the threshold of Sarrebourg.   In the afternocn we learn
that the town was taken by our 8th Corps at 1 P.M., but already
there is news of the enemy gathering in the neighbouring
forests.   In Haute Alsace, General Pau, who has been given
charge of the 7th Corps and of four reserve divisions, is
installed at Thann, Cernay and Dannemarie, and yesterday
he made some further progress and will try and re-take
Mulhouse.

All this information is given us by the Commander-in-
Chief under the seal of absolute secrecy.   The classification
of the armies, their positions, and the names of the Generals
who command them are veiled from the public, and in this
respect the official communiqués are methodically discreet.
So far, then, the defenders of France are anonymous, and
General Headquarters seem to think that publicity might
flatter ambitions in some breasts and excite jealousies in
others.   But it is possible to think this obligatory silence
may rob certain military virtues of a wholesome stimulant
and rightful reward ; I am all for fame being regarded as a
luxury, but it is a luxury of which men fighting for their
country should not always be deprived.

In Belgium and in Luxembourg the Germans seem to
have twelve army corps available, of whom seven are grouped
south of Liége, while the other five are massed somewhere
round Arlon ; they are advancing with three armies in the
direction of Namur and Givet.   In order to keep touch with
the Belgian army we have pushed some cavalry as far as
Fleurus, where they will recall souvenirs of Marshals Luxembourg and Jourdan, but on our frontier and on the Chiers
we are stationary.

Sixty-five thousand English soldiers are already round
Le Cateau, but will not move until the first hundred thousand
men have not only landed but are in position, which
will no doubt bring us—as Sir John French told me—to the
25th of August.   Although the enveloping movement set afoot

by the enemy seems to increase both in volume and in threat, General Headquarters cannot, of course, know whether the Germans will not interrupt their march, wheel to the right and face our front so as to fall suddenly on the centre of our armies.   In his Orders of to-day, Joffre thinks it wise not to exclude this hypothesis, and should it materialise, our Fifth Army will cross the Meuse from west to east to fall on the German right flank ; if, on the other hand, the Germans continue to march westward, this same Fifth Army, in conjunction with the Belgians and the British, will block the road for the oncoming German wing, while our armies of the centre, the Fourth and Third, will devote their attentions to the enemy centre.   Before either of these battles can occur there is brought under my eyes a very stirring symbol of victory. Yesterday two officers brought to the Élysée a regimental colour as large as an ordinary flag, taken from the 4th Battalion of the 132nd German regiment by our 10th battalion of chasseurs à pied.   It is a gorgeous bit of stuff, with a design embroidered on it, "Pro Gloria et Patria", and in each of the four corners the Kaiser's crown.   Curiously enough, this trophy was handed to us by Colonel Serret, our former Military Attaché in Berlin, who a little while ago prophesied to me so clearly the course which Imperial militarism would run.   This morning a company of the Republican Guard conveyed the colour to the Invalides, and the non-commissioned officer detailed to carry it, bore it, not aloft, but across his shoulder like a dead thing.   General Niox, the Governor of the Invalides, has lodged the trophy in a good place in the old Hôtel de Mansart.

As the concentration of the troops has now been effected, I tell Messimy that I want to go as soon as possible with him to the front in order to give some official words of encouragement.   Messimy is all for this, but on referring the matter to General Headquarters we are told that my visit would be premature ; until further orders, the head of a Republican State is obliged to look rather like a *roi fainéant*.   But it is for the soldiers to say what is right and wrong, and I can only hold my tongue and bow in silence to a military decision.   M. Clemenceau, however, does not

hold *his* tongue ; he comes to me to complain that the
communiqués from Headquarters conceal our reverses and
make far too much fuss about our successes. He declares
that a regiment of Marseilles reservists have been made
prisoners, and that as a result of a rash attack a battalion
of chasseurs has been decimated ; he emphasises the many
and serious blunders which, he says, have been committed
in the first march on Mulhouse. " I fear ", he adds, " that
if some day or another we sustain a real defeat, which is
always quite possible, there may be a sinister reaction in
public opinion, as false hopes have been inspired, and these
may be suddenly shattered." I share Clemenceau's opinion,
but I am constitutionally deprived of any means of interfering personally, and up till now Headquarters and the War
Office have given me but little more information than what
is bestowed on the Press and the public. It is no use for me
to claim anything else, for I am only met with silence and with
a knowledge of my own forced inactivity.

M. Ernest Lavisse tells me that Isvolsky, who is as rest-
less in war as he is in peace, has summoned several Poles
resident in Paris, including Madame Curie, to the Russian
Embassy in order to give them a bit of his mind. These
Poles have asked Isvolsky if the manifesto of the Grand Duke
Nicholas, granting to their native country an autonomous
regime, expresses, as has been affirmed, nor only what is in
the mind of the Generalissimo, but what is the will of the
Emperor. The good people have been surprised, and are not a
little uneasy, to receive from the Ambassador an evasive and
ambiguous answer. They want France to ratify, by some
public declaration, the Grand Duke's promise. The moment
will doubtless come when some such guarantee can be given,
but it is too early to discount the future and to make engagements the fate of which must hang on what will be the extent
of victory. To-day, it is true, the telegrams are optimistic,
and we know that the Second Army occupy, beyond the
Seille, all the lake region up to the west of Fenestrange.
From Nish, M. Boppé tells us that there has been sharp
fighting between the Serbians and the Austrians at Loznitza
and Chavatz ; three enemy regiments have been smashed

up, fourteen guns have been taken, and the Austrians are in full flight with the Serbians at their heels. From Moscow Paléologue telegraphs that the ceremony at the Kremlin this morning was marvellous to witness. " The enthusiasm of the crowd ", so says our Ambassador, " is proof of how popular the war is in Russia." One can only hope that this enthusiasm and this popularity may last as long as is necessary to serve the interests of the Alliance, but while the sun seems to be shining in our eyes here and there, some pretty dark shadows are growing. The German army is making rapid progress in Belgium and has taken Tirlemont, and the Belgians, who have lost heavily, have been obliged to retire ; it is evidently in the north that the menace is growing greater.

News from Turkey is a little brighter, and the Grand Vizier, satisfied by the assurances of the Triple Entente, seems to have made up his mind to remain neutral ; he has promised that the *Goeben* and the *Breslau* shall not emerge either on to the Black Sea or the Ægean Sea, but there is always the question as to whether the Grand Vizier is master in his own house.

Venizelos is burning to enter the lists with us, but as his intervention might have just the effect of landing Turkey in the opposite camp, Sir Edward Grey and Doumergue beg him to remain quiet for the moment. Talaat Bey has arrived at Sofia, whence he will repair to Bucharest to discuss the eternal question of the islands with Roumania and with the emissaries of the Greek Government ; he evidently wants to assure himself *en route* as to Bulgaria's favourable disposition in case Turkey should finally draw the sword. Each succeeding day makes the Balkanic imbroglio more complicated.

19th August.—This morning, in Council, we hear from Messimy that General Headquarters have at last taken a corps both from Dubail and Castelnau and railed them to the north, and part of the English army will be ready to take the field any time after to-morrow evening. There is no question but that it will be west of the Meuse where— unless we take the initiative—we shall have to meet the chief shock of the enemy. For some days the Cabinet has been busy as to the steps to be taken to reorganise the economic conditions which mobilisation has upset. From to-morrow the ordinary service of trains will be resumed except in the Est, where everything must yield to the movement of troops. Viviani has long conferences with the Finance Minister, the Governor of the Bank of France and the directors of other great establishments as to determining the moratorium and amending conditions for discounting bills. The banks have at last agreed to pay their depositors immediately an additional instalment of 10 per cent, apart from the 5 per cent provided for by the moratorium.

They will, moreover, continue to pay customers, on production of satisfactory evidence, any further sums which they undertake to employ in the purchase of raw material. Then for its part, the State will lend money to the Municipal Unemployment Bureau, and the Prefect of the Seine will arrange for a certain number of the public works yards to be reopened as soon as possible.

The war is beginning to devour the country's substance, and the Government must needs have recourse to palliatives and expedients or a crisis might occur which must anyhow be held off until the enemy has been expelled from our territory and France is safe.

German propaganda is incessantly active, and from General von Stein's headquarters is issued, through the Wolff Agency, " The True Story of Liége ". This " story " has it that the first German attack took place with non-mobilised troops in order to frustrate an occupation by the French which was imminent : whether this is a hallucination or a fib one does not know, but a falsehood does not become true by being repeated.

In London the Marquis Imperiali, full of enterprise, has tried to extract promises from Sir Edward Grey, who merely answered : " When Italy has made up her mind to come in with the Triple Entente, we shall be more than ready to go into the matter of what she wants ". But San Giuliano has telegraphed to the Ambassador :

" We must not let any hopes be entertained of co-operation until we have assurances of definite advantages to be derived.'

Such is the vicious circle in which we shall turn until Italy can balance minutely what the Central Powers will offer against what she will get by taking the field. On the Russian front there has been brisk fighting not far from Eyd Kunen, and the 1st German Infantry Division has gone back, having lost heavily ; in a radius of 100 kilometres round Warsaw there is not a single German horseman, and the Russian armies of the north are carrying out their offensive all along the line. On the Serbian front there is much fighting with varying result, and we are rather hazy here as to the general happenings. Round Sarrebourg there has begun a pitched battle, of which, however, as yet, we know nothing.

20th August.—This day last year I had a birthday telegram from King George ; to-day there comes a gracious message of more general interest ;

" I am anxious to convey to you, on the occasion of your birthday, my sincere good wishes and my heartiest congratulations. I am entirely convinced that success will favour the arms of our two nations in the great struggle which we are making against a common enemy, and that, in concert with our other Allies, we shall prosecute the war to a satisfactory end."

My reply, as approved by the Ministers, runs :

" I thank Your Majesty for your cordial good wishes, and I beg you to accept anew the assurances of my friendship. I fully share Your Majesty's confidence as to the issue of the war which has been imposed on us, and which we shall prosecute, with the help of England and our other Allies, until success has assured the definite triumph of a Righteous Cause and of Civilisation."

My birthday brings me a few, but very fitful, moments of pleasure. Towards noon we learn that yesterday evening, after bitter fighting, which ended with an attack at the point of the bayonet, French troops re-entered Mulhouse. The enemy put up their strongest resistance at the gates of the great Alsatian city and in the gardens and villas of Dornach, but our soldiers, having carried everything before them, spent the night in the town they had retaken, and where their unlooked-for return was rapturously acclaimed.

Messimy tells us also that the Germans have evacuated
Longuyon and Briey, and that in Lorraine they are giving
way to Generals Dubail and Castelnau, but just when the
War Minister is imparting to us this pleasant news, the
news itself is no longer true. Our 93rd Division has had to
retire on the Donon, and the 14th Corps has lost Schirmeck,
while the Germans are making an attack on the Second
Army, which has thrown two army corps back south of
Bisping and Dieuze and caused the whole force to retire.
The First Army, which yesterday and to-day did so well at
Sarrebourg and Walscheid, and which itself could go forward,
now has its left wing uncovered and must comply with
general orders for retreat.

Things in Belgium are no less alarming. Klobukowski
went yesterday to Malines, where he found Colonel Aldebert
and our Military Attaché very much upset. Orders had come
from headquarters for a retirement on Antwerp, leaving
open the road to Brussels and cutting contact between the
Belgian army and our own. M. de Brocqueville told our
Minister that the situation had become really critical. The
day before yesterday a Belgian force of 50,000 men had,
between Tirlemont and Westerlo, felt the weight of four
German army corps, and the Belgian General Staff were
pretty sure that their troops are threatened with an enveloping movement, which is intended to drive wedges
between them and to invest Antwerp ; it has been decided
to withdraw the troops within the fortifications of that
town. Colonel Aldebert, in his anxiety at seeing the left
of the French and British armies suddenly exposed, has
taken upon himself to write to the Belgian Chief of the Staff
pointing out the danger of losing touch. M. Klobukowski
thinks the terms of the letter rather sharp, and Doumergue
and Viviani have sent a copy of it to Messimy, who has
referred it to Joffre. All four agree that Colonel Aldebert's
emotion is a little excessive. The Belgian army cannot, they
think, hold out indefinitely in open country against weight
of numbers, and there is nothing amiss in the retirement
on Antwerp. General Sordet, who is operating in Belgium,
will not be really taken by surprise, as he only has under his

orders some cavalry and an infantry brigade in motor cars. From a purely military point of view the German entry into Brussels has no great importance. The delay imposed on them by the resistance which Liége put up has allowed us to complete our concentration, to bring north our Algerian troops, and to have some of our Moroccan troops hard by, while the respite has enabled the English to take up their position. Messimy assures us that there are now 100,000 British near Le Cateau, that their cavalry can be on the move from to-day and their infantry within forty-eight hours. In a word, the Government bows to the inevitable, and only regrets that Colonel Aldebert should have seemed to reproach Belgian troops for failing us. M. Klobukowski has been received by King Albert, who spoke most admirably to him. The King was in undress uniform with our Military Medal as his only decoration.

" I know I am not worthy of it," he said, " but I have the greatest esteem for those who conferred it on me. I am very grateful to the French Government for casting no doubt, in the present stress, on the sincerity and the stability of my attitude. I am very anxious there should be no sort of misunderstanding, so I am going to speak to you, as one friend to another, and I beg you to remember and repeat what I am going to say. The move which has just taken place and the rendezvous of our army at Antwerp is a result of the pressure exercised by forces largely superior in numbers to ourselves and threatening to envelop us. The retirement was only ordered after consulting the Generals commanding the three divisions engaged, of whom one is General Bertrand, who delivered so powerful a stroke at Liége. If we had continued to hold our ground, we should have run the risk of being cut off from Antwerp, and then what would have happened ? Our army would have been cut to pieces, Antwerp would have been invested and we should have been unable to do anything effective in the way of defending our country. As a result of the steps we have taken, that danger has been warded off ; our army has not been broken up as the enemy intended it should be ; at the given moment we shall be able to resume the offensive, and I am determined that we shall do so. The defence of Antwerp is in the hands of the Military Governor, General Dufour, who is as keen as he is energetic ; the presence of the Chief of the Staff is no longer so requisite, and I have therefore, this morning, decided to send him to Sir John French and to General Joffre, so as to arrange the details for some concerted action as to which we are agreed and in which we shall take our part in the future as loyally as in the past! At Liége we have checked the exuberance of the Germans, and our forts have managed to hang up three army corps, and while the enemy was engaged on the left bank of the Meuse, we have disputed ground with him foot by foot at Hasselt, Dietz and Tirlemont. And this has been going on for fifteen days, fifteen days with an army whose units are by no means of equal value, whose cadres are incomplete, and where for one seasoned soldier who can hold out because he has fifteen years of service behind him, seven are liable to give way, not from any lack of courage, but because they are not fully trained for the field. At Liége we have lost 20,000 men, and our casualties—especially in the fighting of the 18th of August—are heavy. The same men are marching and fighting who have been marching and fighting since the outbreak of hostilities, and it is only after desperate struggles that the order to retire has been given ; thus we have not been crushed, according to German plan. The first phase of our task is over, and the second is about to begin with the concentration at our stronghold, it being all the more necessary to rally our forces there because the defence of the place is not yet complete. Antwerp is a first-rate *point d'appui*, and it is not a question of shutting ourselves up in a fortified camp, but simply, as I would say again to you, of taking breath before resuming the offensive. The order for retreat has, it is alleged, broken off touch between us and the left wing of the French army, but the only contact which we really had was that kept up between our advanced posts. Even if we had made an effort to maintain or to render closer this contact, our army, echeloned over more than eighty kilometres, had not sufficient depth or cohesion to stand up against a powerful German thrust. It might then have been a case of something like a helter-skelter flight, and this must be borne in mind by those who are conducting the operations. Thus the Note drafted by that distinguished officer, Colonel Aldebert, surprised as much as it pained me, as it expresses a doubt which nothing either in the past or the present can warrant. I should have been neither surprised nor offended if it had been a question of criticising our tactics, but between criticism and blame there is a long stretch. Belgium has proved that she knows how to fulfil her engagements, and France must not have any doubt on that score."

The Government think that after this incident it would be better for Colonel Aldebert not to remain in Belgium, and he will be given a military command. The Belgian

Minister here, Baron Guillaume, whose unhappiness is quite pitiful, comes to talk to me about the unexpected retreat on Antwerp ; he is especially disturbed by the imminent German entry into Brussels, and he wants to know what I think about it. I can only tell him that we are unhappily sure that this will happen, and that we feel very sorry indeed for the population of the town, who will no doubt be subjected to infinite annoyances, but I add that the occupation, however painful, is not a military disaster. The Belgians have played an admirable part in holding up the Germans for a fortnight, and it is only natural that their army should be reorganised under the walls of Antwerp, while the English and ourselves make ready for the great battle which will take place on the frontiers.

M. Dreyfus, Senator for the Seine et Oise, brings an Alsatian, one M. Blumenthal, to see me ; this very intelligent little Jew was Mayor of Colmar until the 31st of July, when the Germans replaced him, as he was suspected of having too much sympathy with France. He made his escape through Switzerland, and the purport of his visit is to advise me to organise as quickly as possible, even while war is going on, civil administration in Alsace and Lorraine, modelled on the German system. The people who have been imported will disappear ; the Alsatians who have latterly fondled the Germans should be quietly removed, but he assures me that the great majority of the population will be infinitely glad to see the provinces restored wholly to France.

Jules Cambon, who has just arrived in Paris, gives me a vivid description of his tedious and odious journey, and has also some scraps of information which he picked up in Copenhagen, Christiania and London. The King of Denmark said to him : " Do not tell anybody, except the President of the Republic, that I have received you. Here we are under observation to an unbelievable extent. Our innermost wishes are all for France and England, but we dare not express them, as we have so much to fear from the anger of the Empire." Princess Marie, wife of Prince George of Greece and daughter of Prince Roland Bonaparte, called on Cambon several times, and in reply to his sugges-

tion that he should call upon her instead, she reminded him :
" You could not come to me without people knowing it, and
no one must suppose that you meet my husband ; all the
Royal Family of Denmark is spied upon." Cambon says
that, in spite of this general sense of fear, Danish opinion is
much in our favour, while at Christiania King Haakon said
to him : " We are with you at heart, but are obliged to
remain neutral, the more so because we have just signed an
agreement with Sweden in order to make sure that she
remains neutral herself. As a sailor, I am rather perturbed
as to the difficulties in store for the British Fleet, which has
no naval base, and if they were to try and secure one on our
coasts, we should be obliged to say No, for to consent would
be to emerge from our neutrality. . . . Anyhow, I hope that
in spite of everything you will be victorious, for if you were
to be beaten we should very soon find ourselves under the
heel of Germany." Mr. Asquith and Sir Edward Grey, in
conversation with Cambon, admitted that the absence of a
naval base was a great handicap to England, and the same
indeed might be said of ourselves in view of our operations
in the Adriatic. The British Ministers seemed to indicate
that after successes had been scored on land, they might
try to get Denmark's consent for our requirements by
promising her the restitution of Schleswig and of the Danish
part of Holstein. England is also determined to give an
international and neutral character to the Kiel Canal, and
King George has declared very forcibly indeed that his
country will continue to fight until the Hohenzollerns are
overthrown.

In thanking Cambon for his information, I beg him not
to be sparing, in these difficult days, of his advice to the
Government and myself, and, as a matter of fact, there is
to hand for him a mission of special interest. A telegram
from Rome announces the death of Pope Pius X., who has
been in poor health for the last year, and who has succumbed to an attack of catarrh on the lungs. We are no
longer represented at the Vatican, but the Government is
telling M. Camille Barrère, our Ambassador at the Quirinal,
to conform precisely, in the matter of offering condolences,

with the British Ambassador. Viviani and Doumergue also agree with me that before the Conclave we ought to come to some understanding with the French cardinals, and that it would be a good thing to ask Cambon to confer officially on this point with Cardinal Amette, the Archbishop of Paris, who is a liberal-minded prelate and an admirable patriot. M. Barrère thinks that Cardinal Ferrata, sometime Nuncio in Paris, may have a very fair chance of being elected, and it would be well for the French cardinals to vote for him. I knew Cardinal Ferrata well, for when I was Minister for Public Instruction I was also Minister for Culture, and professors, bishops and artists used to meet in my room ; Cardinal Ferrata knows France well, and esteems her highly, but there must be no idea of his being our candidate or he would be foredoomed to failure.

21st August.—Once more I gather from the newspapers a sad bit of news, the details of which one has great difficulty in obtaining from General Headquarters. At Morhange our troops of the Second Army came up against positions strongly organised and bristling with barbed wire, and the 20th Corps, which is under Foch, was forced to retire, the 15th and 16th Corps, having engaged with largely superior forces, being obliged to do likewise. General Castelnau has had to move his army back on the Grand Couronné of Nancy, which has only just been put in a state of defence, and General Dubail has been unable to emerge from Sarrebourg and must move back towards the Meurthe. In view of these reverses Joffre, who is as calm as ever, has decided to hurry up the offensive of our Fourth and Fifth Armies against the enemy's centre, and he ordered an attack for yesterday evening at half-past eight.

M. Tardieu, the well-known Deputy of the Seine et Oise, who, as a reserve officer, is attached to the Headquarters Staff, seems to have been authorised to let the Press Bureau of the Ministry know about our set-back ; as a matter of fact he did so, but as the news only reached Paris after the usual bulletin had been brought to me, it was not thought wise to send the unhappy corollary. This respect for the Presidential slumbers seems to me excessive, and I insist once more that information from headquarters shall reach me more rapidly and more readily. As Maurice Barrès said to me the other day, it is a war fought in shadow, and not much light is vouchsafed either to the public or to the Government.

Clemenceau comes to my room with the M. Blumenthal of yesterday and two other Alsatians, the Abbé Wetterlé, Deputy for Ribeauvillé, and M. Laugel, Deputy for Molsheim, both equally loyal to France. They all three think that it would be well to consult them before organising an administrative regime for Alsace, whether for the period of the war or for the transition period which will follow the making of peace. They tell me, to my surprise, of a Commission which has just been detailed to study Alsatian questions, and they ask to be made members of it. I have never heard a word of this Commission, which seems to be functioning in the premises of the Conseil d'État, with several members of the Haute Compagnie sitting daily in uniform and distributing amongst one another administrative posts in Alsace. It would be an amazing farce if the conditions were not so tragic. Nobody knows exactly how, or by whom, this Commission has been instituted, and I have no idea whether it is a self-sprung phenomenon or a creation of General Headquarters.

In the afternoon the Prefect of the Nord telephones that the population of Lille is very uneasy, and rumour has it that the Germans are marching in force on Mons and on Charleroi. One of the cavalry divisions is moving to Lille, but Messimy reminds us that Lille is now an open town, and that General d'Amade, who is there, has only at his disposal depôt, reserve and territorial troops, who are nothing like fully trained. The War Minister fears that a sudden attack might well succeed, and he again deplores the slowness of the English, as according to our military agreements it was for them to cover our left wing, while they have not as yet performed any manœuvre.

Cardinal Amette writes to beg me to be represented next Wednesday at the Mass which will be celebrated at Nôtre Dame in memory of the late Pope, and he adds in graceful

phrase that if I would like to see him before he leaves for
Rome, he will keep any appointment I may like to make. I
tell Viviani and Doumergue that, in spite of the Separation
Laws, I ought to be represented at the religious service, and
this as due to diplomatic etiquette as well as to all that is
meant by the Union Sacrée. They both agree with me, and
also that I should receive the Cardinal if he would like to
see me, but they think it would be better for Jules Cambon
to tell His Eminence what is in our mind. Cambon will
therefore see the Cardinal to-morrow and tell him that the
Government relies on a patriotic agreement between all the
French cardinals. The Government knows that they will
vote for the candidate who is alike the most worthy and the
most favourably disposed towards France, but they must
use great tact and prudence, and, in relation with the other
countries, they must not seem to be merely obeying a
national *mot d'ordre*. To avoid this danger it might be
better for the Archbishop not to come to the Elysée until
after his return from Rome ; this point, however, I leave
entirely to his discretion.

The situation in Belgium grows darker. Von Klück
has led his army into Brussels and levied a war tax of two
hundred million francs on the town. A cavalry force with
artillery is marching on Courtrai and communications have
been cut between Antwerp and Ghent.

From Serbia alone come telegrams which are more satisfactory. The Austrians seem to be in full flight on the
Losniza-Lesnitza line, and Colonel Fournier informs M.
Boppé that the Austro-Hungarian troops which had crossed
the Drina are retiring in disorder, hotly pursued by the
Serbians, whose guns are firing on the military bridges over
the Drina. " The Serbian victory is complete, and many
trophies remain in the hands of the victors."

Bargaining continues at Constantinople under the name
of negotiations. Djavid Bey has told M. Bompard that the
opponents of France, who have the ear of the Ottoman
Cabinet, are dangling wonderful German promises and are
reproaching Djavid Bey, Djemal Pasha and the Grand
Vizier for turning them down without offering anything on

behalf of the Powers of the Triple Entente. Djavid Bey would like to counter this by being authorised to make some definite promise such, for example, as the suppression of the Capitulations. Bompard reminded him that when he was in Paris he could have learnt for himself that we were quite disposed to go a long way in this direction, and Djavid ended by saying that some striking success of our arms in Belgium would be the best thing to set a term to the tergiversations of the Turkish Cabinet. There Bompard was at one with him, and Turkey, like others, is evidently more than ready to fly to the help of the conquerors.

Sazonoff, who has heard of the same sort of parleying, has told Paléologue he would be willing to guarantee for fifteen, twenty or even fifty years (why not more, I wonder ?) the integrity of the Ottoman Empire : that he would gladly consider some judiciary regime under which the Capitulations might be gradually abolished ; and that he would also regard benevolently any proposals which the Turkish Government might submit with a view to recovering their economic independence. Let us hope that these Russian assurances will tie Turkey down to neutrality, but the fighting in Serbia, from which we derive new disappointments, will send up the stock of the Central Empires in Constantinople as elsewhere. They were in too great a hurry at Nish and Kraguievatz to sing about victory, as the enemy has brought up much larger forces than the Serbians thought possible, and the struggle has been resumed under far less favourable conditions.

22nd August.—I wrote yesterday to the War Minister to ask for further details about the defeat in Lorraine, and I have expressed the fear that this would be exploited by the Germans in neutral countries before we ourselves were informed. This is just what has happened, and we hear from our representatives in Turkey, Rome and the Netherlands that according to the communiqués of the German General Staff, eight French army corps are " in full flight " between Metz and the Vosges, leaving 10,000 prisoners and fifty guns in the hands of the pursuers. One quite understands that headquarters do not give all the information they might to the civil power for fear of something like panic behind the lines, but it is none the less intolerable that we should be left in ignorance as to the result of battles on which hangs the fate of France. I beg Messimy to tell Joffre that I must have regular and full information, and he promises to do what he can to obtain this for me as well as for himself. This morning's bulletin is again almost silent as regards Lorraine, but the liaison officer tells me that Joffre is going to send us further details, and at noon an artillery officer brings me a telephone message from the Generalissimo:

" Our forces attempted to debouch from the Seille on the 20th August ; they came up against fortified positions and were subjected to a violent attack of the enemy. The troops which debouched between Mitersheim and Marsal were never able to secure the heights on the right bank ; *per contra* the 20th Corps which debouched by Château-Salins was able to move forward towards Morhange and it advanced perhaps a little too quickly, and before the troops detailed to cover the left flank could get up. It was this corps which, taken in front and flank, suffered the most ; they have lost heavily and have been obliged to abandon twenty-one guns. The Second Army has retired towards Nancy for rest and reconstruction. The enemy seems to have lost heavily also. The fighting, with its very heavy casualties, has necessitated the retirement of our units who were operating towards Sarrebourg and in the valley of the Bruche, and in order not to have their heads exposed they have retired on the line of La Verouze and of the Col de Saales. The situation in Alsace is still good, and we are on the threshold of Colmar, while in the north we are moving forward. The enemy is trying to invest and attack Namur and has shown himself on the Sambre."

We have evidently suffered a serious set-back in Lorraine, where we have lost all the ground which our armies of the Est had so painfully acquired. The artillery officer, who has arrived from the Est, tells me that the German version is untrue ; there has been neither rout nor flight. The 15th Corps had to give ground before superior numbers, but it remained entirely in hand, and the number of prisoners lost was not serious. The German losses are heavy, while own own casualites, including the missing, come to about 5000 men. The 15th, 16th and 20th Corps are being reconstituted, and are by now ready to take the field again : the German heavy artillery has done immense damage, their fire being remarkably accurate. This time, anyhow, there is no juggling with words, and the truth has been faced.

At four o'clock in the afternoon comes a telephone message from Lunéville :

" Shells are falling on the town and our position is becoming untenable ; the telegraph officials are quitting and destroying their apparatus."

Half an hour later a curious and even more serious message comes from Nancy :

" Under orders, the personnel is leaving Nancy for Paris."

What does this mean, and who has given the orders ? Is Castelnau's army in flight ?   And anyhow, why have the officials abandoned their posts without being asked or even authorised to do so by the Government ?   Nothing is known at the War Office, and from there and from the Élysée we telephone again and again without getting any reply.   It is like the silence of the grave.   For more than half an hour Nancy gives no sign of life, when an inspector, who has remained behind with a very reduced staff, explains to me personally that he had been ordered to evacuate the telegraph office and destroy the apparatus, that he had remained behind to ensure the telephone service till the last moment, that the guns can be heard, but that Nancy is not occupied ; he does not know if the town is really threatened, but anyhow, our troops are still on the Grand Couronné.

Colonel Pénélon, who is now attached to headquarters, arrives at the War Office from Vitry, and is passed on to the Élysée ; he says that the Germans have turned the position of Morhange into a regular entrenched camp with concrete and wire fortifications.   On the 19th of August Castelnau's army had been ordered to advance, and the 15th Corps entered the pretty little town of Dieuze to be acclaimed by the compatriots of Edmond About and the

famous mathematician Hermitte. The 6th and 23rd battalions of chasseurs secured Vergaville, and the 29th Division
was hurrying on to Biedesdorf, when they met with a terrific
bombardment which compelled the 15th Corps to retire on
Dieuze. The 16th Corps had already been pushed back the
evening before, and was scarcely on its feet again, and our
offensive on this side broke down without our being able to
extricate ourselves from the lake region. Most of the 20th
Corps, on the other hand, had gone forward very methodically
towards Morhange. The next day the First Army, under
General Dubail, tried, but failed, to move on Gosselmingen
and Fenestrange ; nor was the Second Army any happier. The
16th Corps, attacked by the enemy in strength round Dieuze,
was obliged to make a further retrograde movement, while
the 15th Corps, no less violently assaulted from the height
of the wooded slopes, was obliged to fall back even farther
than the day before. On the left, however, the 20th Corps
had made a splendid dash on Morhange and on Marthil-
Baronweiler, but had been stopped by a storm of artillery
and obliged to retire on Château-Salins. The gallant 26th
regiment, in which I had served my *volontariat*, had captured seventeen munition waggons and a quantity of horses
and baggage besides taking a number of prisoners, but for
them also it was retreat and defeat. General Castelnau,
foreseeing that heavy pressure might be brought on him by
the enemy, thought well to order a general retirement, and
taking up his quarters at Arracourt, had made all arrangements for the troops which had so cruelly suffered. He had
ordered the 16th Corps to fall back on Lunéville, the 15th
on Dombasle, the 20th on St. Nicolas and Laneuveville,
while the reserve divisions were to establish themselves in
the fortified positions of the Grand Couronné. We were
thus obliged to give up the strip of Lorraine which, for a
moment, was in our hands, while the enemy, making his way
on to our territory, was engaged in devastating the country
and burning Nomény, and at the same moment the First
Army was descending the slopes of Donon and must lose
the splendid observation post which they had been so justly
proud to secure.

Colonel Pénélon's short but extremely melancholy story leaves one under no illusions as to happenings in the Est, and one wonders whether there is anything much better to hope for on the frontier of the Nord.   Joffre has instructed the Colonel to tell me that there is complete agreement between the French, British and Belgian Staffs, and that co-operation is sure to be all it should be in the forthcoming fighting in Belgium, as to the issue of which the General-issimo is wholly confident.   On this point Colonel Pénélon does not seem to me to be quite so comfortable ; he seems to fear that General Lanrezac, whose force is stationed between the Sambre and the Meuse, may not be able to prevent the Germans crossing the latter stream between Namur and Dinant ;   he will have to deal with the enemy in force and with fresh troops.

The Special Commissary of Givet notifies us that Uhlans and German Hussars are in the neighbourhood, that two army corps have invested Namur, that the Germans have crossed the Sambre and already attacked the line of front held by our 10th Corps and 5th Division.

I hear by telegram that the son of Georges Clemenceau has been wounded in the leg by a revolver bullet, but that he managed to kill the officer who attacked him.   I have sent a word alike of sympathy and congratulation to the father.

It is impossible to know who gave the evacuation order to the Nancy telegraphists ;   neither the Prefect nor the military authorities can throw any light on the affair   Is it a matter of espionage or of a hoax ?   The employés who have arrived in Paris will return to Nancy and resume their strangely interrupted duties.

CHAPTER IV

Sunday, 23rd August.—We are much happier as to Nancy, and
the beautiful city, in which the Kaiser hoped to march round
the statue of Stanislas, is no longer threatened with a foreign
occupation. But Lunéville, less happy than her great neighbour, has fallen into the hands of the enemy, and fighting is
going on there in the faubourgs. I remember the happy far-off
days I spent there as a young deputy and a second lieutenant
of chasseurs. Now the shells are falling in those beautiful
old avenues and blood is flowing in the streets through which
I used to march at the head of a section; my former comrades
are fighting for their country while I am shut up in the Élysée
remote from the ravaged places in which the fate of France
is being decided.

The idea of grouping the armies of the Vosges, Alsace and
Lorraine under General Pau has been abandoned, but yesterday the General secured in beautiful Alsace the slope of the
valley which runs from the Fecht to near Colmar, although
unhappily at the same time the First Army lost the line of the
Vezouse. Prince Rupert of Bavaria crossed our frontier of
the Est, and we had to hurry back over the Meurthe, blowing
up the bridges behind us, while the enemy's guns were posted
on the heights round Lunéville. . . . And with that battle
over, the 21st German Corps has made a pompous entrance
into the town, where the inhabitants are in a state of consternation. Farther north and near Nancy the enemy is
making, but without success, two violent attacks on the
Rembêtant. General Castelnau has just lost a son on the

field of battle, but his grief does nothing to disturb his devotion to duty, and his Second Army seems to be sufficiently pulled together to resume fighting with every hope of success. The First Army has been instructed to concert with the Second to prevent the Germans slipping —as they will no doubt try to do—through the gap in front of them beyond Mortagne near the little town of Charmes, where, not far from the birthplace of Claude le Lorrain, Maurice Barrés loves to listen to the running waters of the Moselle.

My post-bag brings me to-day a quantity of letters from good folk who criticise with some warmth the military operations, who distribute blame among the Generalissimo and his army commanders, who find a good deal of fault with myself, who give much advice and tell me what ought to be done. Now that the pulse of France is beating very fast, my correspondence is of a rather heated character. Every non-mobilised Frenchman has his own ideas of strategy, dreams of victory and, when the slightest reverse occurs, wakes up and is all agog to put things right. In the mass of letters which I have to wade through, there are as many curiosities and contradictions as in the daily communications from the Eiffel Tower. Day by day the Tower gives out to everybody, and especially to Germany, wireless messages specially designed to mask the movements of our troops. The Tower picks up also conversations which take place outside France and intended for the International Press; this stream of invisible waves distributes through the world parcels of false news cunningly made up to mislead so-called Intelligence. Thus, for instance, there are successes in the Near East which make up for the lamentable effect produced in neutral countries by our defeat in Lorraine; the Russian army has seized Goldap and Lyck; Germans have been put to flight in the region of Gumbinnen; in Serbia fighting has begun again round Tzer and has resulted in the destruction of several Austrian regiments.

In council this morning we have to deal anxiously with matters submitted to us. Our big offensive has begun on the Belgian frontier, and we eagerly await definite news which

somehow does not reach us.   There are immediate questions
to hand.   The delayed Japanese ultimatum to Germany ex-
pires to-day, and our Minister at Pekin has been questioned by
his Japanese colleague, and our Consul at Hongkong by the
English Admiral, as to what part we are likely to play against
Germany in the Far East, especially with regard to operations
against Tsing Tao.   This is a matter on which we shall have
to agree with England.

Montenegro seems to have an idea of attacking Albania
and occupying Scutari, and is dying to do just the very things
which worried us in 1912 and 1913 ; Doumergue has to telegraph to Cettinge to discountenance an adventure which
would have bad effects in Italy and Turkey.   Our 1886 rifles
seem to be running short if there is a question of arming the
territorial reserve ; the War Minister feels that if we give
these men the 1874 pattern they may think they are armed
with an inferior weapon, and he suggests that we should purchase from the enormous surplus stock in Japan.   Japan will
probably prefer England, who is her Ally, to be the buyer, and
Doumergue is to ask the British Government to undertake
the negotiation.   We hear that some of the Belgian Ministers
have complained that Belgium was not helped these last days
by France as she ought to have been, and one must admit
that there is some apparent reason for the reproach.   A press
communiqué has been sent out emphasising our resolve to
defend Belgian territory as our own, and, in agreement with
England, we are opening the money credit which Belgium
wants and sending her some extra munitions.   It is none the
less regrettable that, with this sudden invasion of Belgium,
our concentration arrangements should have detained us so
long this side of our frontier of the Nord.

M. de Panafieu informs us that the representations of
Talaat Bey at Sofia have fizzled out and that his proposal of
a definite alliance between Turkey and Bulgaria has been
cold-shouldered.   There is no doubt but that the Bulgarian
Government, and above all King Ferdinand, mistrust
Russia altogether and their sympathies lie with Austria ;
but for the moment they prefer to keep themselves to themselves and not make any engagement.   M. Venizelos, speak-

ing on behalf of King Constantine himself, has told the
British and Russian Ministers that Greece is very willing to
hold her naval and military resources at the disposal of the
Triple Entente, and Sir Edward Grey suggests that we shall
say that, if Turkey falls in with Germany and Austria, England would be only too happy to consider Greece as an ally.
Also, if Bulgaria were to attack Serbia, and if Greece, agreeably with the stipulations of her Treaty, were to intervene,
England would be more than willing to support her.

Jules Cambon has seen Mgr. Amette, who is leaving to-
morrow for Rome. The Archbishop of Paris will do everything he can to get the French cardinals to be of one mind
and mouth as to their candidate — probably Monseigneur
Ferrata. The Archbishop thinks that Cardinal Mercier, the
Spanish cardinals and the Archbishop of Westminster will
agree with their French brethren, and our Ambassadors in
London and Madrid have been urged to do their utmost to
promote this minor *entente*.

The day passes without any information as to our offensives, and the communiqué in the evening does nothing to
enlighten us, but with the night comes Colonel Pénélon, on
whose face, which is usually wreathed with smiles, I can
read that things have gone amiss. " Is it defeat ? " I
bluntly ask him. " Yes ", is the straightforward answer.
It would seem that Joffre, noting the enemy's turning
movement, had moved the Fifth Army up towards the
Sambre and had slipped the Fourth Army, previously held
in reserve, up to the frontier. He had further borrowed
from the First and Second Armies of the Est those corps which
had been detailed to strengthen our actions in the Nord.
The Fourth Army, thus composed of first-rate troops under
General de Langle de Cary, was stationed in the regions of
Montmédy, Stenay, Buzancy, Mouzon, Bouillon, Bièvre,
with General Ruffey's Third Army on its right. There had
also been constituted on the 19th of August an army of
Lorraine under General Maunoury, which was to mask Metz,
while two corps of the Third, Fourth and Fifth Armies were
to take the offensive towards Arlon, and the Sixth Army,
under General Sarrail, was to watch events round Fresnes.

The next day the final instructions were given as to the
attack which the troops had been so eagerly awaiting ; the
rôle of the Fourth Army was to march straight north and
fall on the flank of the German army, who were making
their way westwards across Belgian Luxembourg, the Third
Army being ordered to cover the movement of the Fourth.
As far as one could gather, three German armies, under the
Crown Prince, Duke Albert of Wurtemberg and General
von Hausen, who is the Saxon War Minister, are confronting
our forces, with apparently Verdun, Arlon and Givet as
their objectives ; in other words, we are up against fourteen
army corps, of which several are stiffened by reserve corps.
On the 21st, our Fourth Army tried to debouch beyond the
Semoy and get contact with the enemy.   Our infantry
dashed forward with admirable pluck, but without either
proper precautions or any real artillery preparations and
with quite insufficient touch being kept between the units.
The result was that they were decimated by a force of German
cyclists armed with machine guns.   The 12th Corps managed
to reach Florenville, but the Colonial Corps, after a long
night march in torrents of rain, lost all contact with its
neighbours.   The 2nd Corps, also drenched to the skin,
strayed into the middle of the German forces, while the
Third Army advanced to the environs of Virton, where the
enemy was found.   A thick fog enveloped the whole Forest
of Ardennes and impeded all our movements.   The happenings of the 22nd, according to my informant, appear to have
been even more disastrous.   The Fourth Army was told to
move northwards with its left wing in front and to attack
as soon as opportunity should present itself ; the Third
Army was to conform to the movements of the Fourth and
deal with any attack which might come from Arlon and
Fontoy.   But the 11th Corps, which was directed on Paliseul,
could not hold the ground it had taken, and the 17th Corps
could not emerge from the Forest of Luchy in which it was
fighting, and had to fall back behind the Semoy ; the 11th
Corps had seized, at the cost of heavy casualties, St. Médard
and Névraumont ; the Colonial Corps had thrown itself
valiantly against Neufchâteau, where they found the enemy

hidden among the corn or in trenches full of machine guns, and after a very sharp fight had been forced to yield to over-whelming numbers. The 3rd Colonial Division had occupied certain points successfully, but only after a terrible struggle, in which, among others, there had fallen Generals Raffenel and Rondony, and a young lieutenant who was Ernest Renan's grandson. The 2nd Corps, on the right of the Colonial Corps, had made progress as far as Virton, when it was checked either by the carefully concealed infantry or by the admirably directed fire of the 105 and 150 guns. The net result yesterday evening, so Colonel Pénélon assured me, was that the Fourth Army had not retired very appreciably and had inflicted very severe losses on the Germans, but had suffered itself severely and its attack had broken down.

The Third Army, which was to direct the attack on Virton and disengage Longwy, had, in the fog, hurled itself against troops strongly entrenched and had been broken up by machine guns. The 5th Corps had crossed the fron-tier and penetrated to Gorcy, but had found everywhere heavy artillery and barbed wire ; it was unable to rescue Longwy and was stationed on the right bank of the Chiers. The 6th Corps, heading northwards, had met the Metz Corps in great strength opposite Crusnes and on the Chiers, and in the evening was in position about Arrancy, with the hope of resuming the offensive to-day. At nightfall, there-fore, yesterday, nothing had been gained, but nothing actu-ally lost. During the night Generals de Langle de Cary and Ruffey gave orders to attack at dawn, and the Fourth Army tried to start again in the direction of Beauraing-Laroche, but was suddenly opposed by an entire German army, so far unidentified,[1] and was obliged to fall back fighting. The 9th Corps has retired on the Semoy, the 11th on Bouillon, the 17th on Amblimont, the 12th on the north bank of the Chiers, the Colonial Corps on St. Welfroy and the 2nd Corps on Villers-la-Leue. It is on this line, Colonel Pénélon says, the Germans will be made to halt. But our offensive has failed and the battle of the Ardennes has been lost.

Colonel Pénélon does not disguise that faults have been

___

[1] It proved to be General Hausen's.

committed.   There have been individual and collective
mistakes, divisions badly delivered, deployments rashly
made, hurried retreats, wastage of men and altogether lack
of military efficiency among the troops and their leaders,
both as regards the movements of the infantry and the
employment of the artillery.   General Headquarters may
perhaps be charged with some imprudences.   As our concentration—on account of the violation of the Belgian
neutrality—was too much disposed to the east and too weak
towards the north, it seemed dangerous to launch an offensive on woody and very difficult ground where communication roads are few and where flank attacks [1] were to be
feared.   But our General Staff has been imbued with the
idea—derived from the school of military thought more
inclined to enthusiasm than caution—that boldness is sure
to be crowned with success, and however right this doctrine
of offensive, it has too often happened that on the battle-
field we have neglected what are elementary methods of
safety.   Have not several of the pupils from St. Cyr gone
into the fight in full dress, with white plumed casoar, and
fallen at the head of their sections ?

Colonel Pénélon's story of the Fifth Army was no better ;
General Lanrezac had occupied the Charleroi region and had
found himself opposite Von Klück and Von Bülow, who
were marching rapidly towards the west with the evident
intention of crossing our front and overwhelming the little
British army.   To ward off this danger Joffre had created
a new army—to be posted on the British left—and placed
it under General d'Amade, who had made a name for himself
in Morocco.   Lanrezac had for days been longing to take
the offensive, but he had to wait till the English got up
in their places.   This General had been a member of the
War Council since last April, and Joffre speaks of him as a
thoroughly scientific soldier and a future Generalissimo.
Lanrezac wanted to move earlier on Maubeuge, but General
Headquarters, preoccupied by what was taking place on
our frontiers of the Est, could not at first detail enough men

---

[1] *Le Haut Commandement français et la bataille des Ardennes*, by General
Palat, etc.

in the Nord to prolong our front, and, being obliged also
to wait for the concentration of the English troops, orders
could not be given soon enough to start Lanrezac's operations. As soon as news came of the occupation of Brussels,
and of the amazing march of the German armies, everything
was done that could be done to speed up his attack. Unhappily the British army was not ready. Sir John French
had scrupulously refrained from promising that his divisions
would be in line before 25th August; it was hoped he might
be ready on the 20th or 21st, but it was only on the 22nd
Sir John was able to give orders to attack as to-day. Now
the bombardment of Namur began the day before yesterday
morning at ten o'clock, and Lanrezac knew that another
German army was coming up from the south of Namur to
pounce on Dinant and Givet. Two of our Corps, the 10th
and the 3rd, were "in the air", and he thought it risky to let
his army remain inactive and ordered it to debouch yesterday
afternoon across the Sambre. But already Namur, under
intense bombardment, was unable to give our people any
sort of help, and could not even immobilise the besiegers.
After some bloody fighting the 3rd and the 10th Corps were
obliged to retire, while the Fifth Army had to make its way
back for more than ten kilometres from Charleroi to the
south of the Sambre.

This morning Lanrezac was no less determined to move
forward again as arranged, but the enemy has entered Namur
—in spite of the reinforcements which General Franchet
d'Esperey had sent up—and has burnt and sacked the
gallant little town of Dinant; the sudden influx of these
troops has decided the fate of the battle and our Fifth Army,
with its flank threatened by constantly increasing forces,
is completely paralysed.

The British army has come up in line near Mons and has
already shown of what admirable stuff it is made; discipline,
coolness, courage and moral, no less than physical, strength
are evident; but their right has been uncovered by the
retreat of our Fifth Army, and the Germans, flushed with
success, have flung themselves on Mons, which Sir John has
been obliged to evacuate. Moreover, the check to us has

decided Sir John to retire on Maubeuge, and one does not yet know whether Lanrezac will order his army to make a fresh stand or whether, with both his wings threatened, he will not be obliged to fall back.   Joffre thinks that he will be able to hold his ground, but Colonel Pénélon says that whatever happens, we must give up all hope of pushing the Germans back towards the North Sea, and that if either to-morrow or the day after our new endeavours are un-successful, we must make up our minds both to retreat and to be invaded.   So much for the illusions which we had nourished during the last fortnight ; our very safety must depend on our powers of resistance.   But will the highly strung French people be able to put up with this ?   Will they understand what it means and be willing to play a waiting game ?   True, the national spirit has never been more sound, but may not discouragement come with the flux of time, with suffering and mourning, and all the horrors of war ?   We are a brave, generous and impulsive nation ; does it lie within us to show ourselves tenacious, long-suffering and doggedly determined ?   My own duty is quite clear ; at whatever cost, to keep smiling, conceal my anxiety and vigilantly watch over the moral of the country.   This is the least anyone can do who is not able to shed his blood for France.

24th August.—From information, a little vague as usual, which reaches us from headquarters, fortune did not favour us yesterday in the Est any more than in the north, and anyhow, the Germans are noisily celebrating their victory in Lorraine ; in every town flags are flying, fanfares are being sounded, and the streets are blazing with illuminations. But, nevertheless, our First Army is in close touch with the Second, and has changed front from north-east to north and north-west : the First Army halted in its retreat yesterday to join hands with the Second, which is now ready to spring on the flank of the enemy if they advance into the open angle.   Throughout the morning alarming news keeps com-ing in from the Belgian frontier, and we hear that the enemy is within six kilometres of Jermont and that Tournai has been occupied by a detachment of 3000 men : 20,000 Germans have passed St. Genois, moving on Menin, and

Belgian refugees are crowding into France from Philippeville and Charleroi; enemy patrols, scouting in front of
large forces, are on French soil near Aniévrechain and
Blanc-Misseron.

These scraps of news dribble in while the Defence Committee is sitting, and with the growing danger, Messimy gets
gloomier and gloomier and foresees a great defeat. Viviani,
who is so easily upset by little things, is quite proof against
big happenings and remains perfectly calm and cool. He
complains, however, of M. Briand, who, he says, is accusing
Ministers of inefficiency both in the Press and in the corridors
of the Chambre, and who is trying to force the Prime Minister's
hand, so as to be admitted into the Cabinet. Viviani, however, thinks that Parliament would not at the moment
agree to the return to power of the man, however eminent,
who only a few months ago was supposed to side against the
Left, and to whom Havre tried lately to give so unpleasant
a reception.

But far be it from us to recall the Périgueux speech; it
seems more and more necessary to broaden the Government,
and Briand surely is one of the first-class " brains " of which
we should avail ourselves. After a little hesitation Viviani
agrees that I should ask Briand to come to the Élysée and
talk things over with him.

Towards noon the news is confirmed that the Department
of the Nord is being invaded at several points, and that
Lille is threatened. There are 10,000 Territorials in the
town, but—according to Messimy—General d'Amade thinks
that if we try to hold the town whose " déclassement " was
proposed in Parliament, the troops will be wiped out and the
town mercilessly bombarded; the General thinks it would be
better to withdraw the troops and not to expose, without
any valid military reason, the inhabitants to disaster.[1]
Rumours of defeat are also reaching us from England and
from the Prefecture of the Nord, even before General Head-

---

[1] The War Minister had in 1911, agreeably with the advice of the War
Committee, proposed that Lille should be made an open town, but a vote
had not yet been taken on it in Parliament. M. Clemenceau revived the
proposal in 1919 and it became effective before the end of the year.

quarters send us exact information, but in the afternoon a telegram from Joffre blows into thin air our last illusions. Our great offensive has broken down everywhere, and we have been driven back beyond the Belgian frontier and on our own territory ; we are evacuating Alsace as far as south of Mulhouse, which we have so cruelly lost a second time, and the army of General Pau, which was successful yesterday, has shed much of its strength and has been repulsed in the north. General Headquarters say again that in the battles of Ardennes and Charleroi our troops kept altogether insufficient touch with one another, that the junior leading was poor and that the liaison between the arms was defective. Whatever the cause, the result is certain ; so far we are beaten, and we have to begin all over again and on our own invaded ground. Towards eight o'clock in the evening Colonel Magnin is sent to us by Joffre to assure us that in spite of everything the Generalissimo remains quite confident. For the moment he has given up the idea of taking the offensive, but asks us not to lose faith. A solid defence is going to be organised both so as to gain time and to allow the Russians to push forward. The communiqué this evening winds up with phrases, half contradictory and half sybilline :

" Under orders from General Joffre our troops and British troops have taken up position on the line of support which they would not have left had not the splendid effort of the Belgians allowed us to enter Belgium. These troops are intact ; our cavalry has not suffered at all and our artillery has given evidence of its superiority ; our officers and men are in admirable condition, both physical and moral. Under general orders the fighting will for some days present a different aspect. The French army will for a while stand on the defensive ; at a moment to be chosen by the Commander-in-Chief a vigorous offensive will be resumed. Our losses are heavy and it would be premature to give exact numbers. It would be no less so in the case of the German army, which has so suffered as to be obliged to call a halt to their counter-attack and assume new positions. As to the situation in Lorraine we counter-attacked four times yesterday from the positions which we hold north of Nancy, and we inflicted very serious losses on the Germans. Generally speaking, we have preserved full freedom to use our railways, and the sea is everywhere open to us for supplies. Our operations have enabled Russia to take action and to penetrate to the heart of eastern Prussia. One must of course regret that the plan of offensive, owing to faulty execution, did not succeed; had it done so the war would have been shortened; but our defensive situation is intact in face of an already weakened enemy. Every Frenchman will deplore the momentary abandonment of portions of territory annexed which we had occupied, and also certain parts of French territory will suffer from events which will occur there. This is an inevitable but only a temporary trial. Thus, some units of the German cavalry have reached the region of Roubaix-Tourcoing which is only defended by Territorials."

Here we have a triple avowal of defeat, invasion and the loss of Alsace. What effect will Joffre's emotional proclamation have on our provinces just liberated? Where are the high hopes raised by the great advance of our armies? The Commander-in-Chief has in mind to resume the advance when the moment seems to him opportune. But when is he going to put a term to our retreat and halt our troops? Anyhow, the war will go on for a long while, and it is no more a question of so many days of high courage and enthusiasm. Victory will only be attained with stubborn efforts, and the plain duty of the Government and myself is not only to tell the country the truth, but to try and prepare the people for the terrible trials which await them.

In giving the order to fall back, Joffre wrote to the War Minister:

"The fears which I entertained earlier as to the aptitude of our troops for taking the offensive in open country were confirmed by yesterday's occurrences, which definitely put a spoke in our big attack in Belgium."

And again:

"One must accept the evidence of things themselves: our Army Corps, in spite of their numerical superiority, have not shown in open country the qualifications for attacking which partial successes at the beginning caused us to look for. . . . We are therefore condemned to take up a defensive line based on our fortresses and on local defences while yielding as little ground as possible. Our object must be to hold out as long as we can while wearing down the enemy and then at the given moment resume the offensive."

I do not know if these remarks are not too severe on our soldiers : courage is not everything, and the Germans have just shown that on well-organised terrain, and with proper resources in material, it is always possible to resist any attack which may be made in open country.   As a beginning the Generalissimo has ordered the army to retire on a line from Arras to the north of Verdun, through Valenciennes, Maubeuge and Stenay.

The Ministers are for the most part in a state of consternation.   " My good friend," I say to Viviani, " there is something wrong as to the relations between the military Command and the Civil Government.   You have complained, and not unreasonably, that the Generalissimo wrote to me direct and not through the War Minister. When I mentioned this to the liaison officers, I understood the reply to be that General Headquarters considered themselves, in time of war, as wholly independent of the Government, and only regarded as superior the nominal and irresponsible authority of the President of the Republic.   We agree, you and I, that such a theory, if it were to materialise, would run clean contrary to the spirit of our Republican institution, and I am quite sure that the irreproachable loyalty of Joffre would never allow such to be sustained. But there is considerable risk in these circumstances of uncertainty.   The laws of 1882 and 1905 have entrusted to the War Minister—that is to a member of the Government jointly responsible with his colleagues—the administration of the army.   It is for him to furnish the High Command with everything that is necessary to take the field, and the responsibility to Parliament lies with the Government as a whole in the matter of determining general, political, financial, economic and diplomatic conditions under which war must be prosecuted.   Thus, General Headquarters must not shut themselves up in an ivory palace and strip themselves of all control.   Of course it would be as dangerous as it would be ridiculous for the Government to interfere in the conduct of military operations, but they ought to be better informed than they have been up to now.   The regularised control of the Government is the only way of

preventing Parliament from substituting itself and abusing
its own rights of intervention—a state of things which would
be highly dangerous with the inevitable multiplicity of
proposals." I added that my personal opinion is that the
Cabinet ought to be enlarged and thereby fortified, and I
suggest in reply to Viviani's loyal scruples, that it might be
possible to eliminate no present member and merely to add
Ministers without portfolio. The name of Clemenceau of
course occurs, and Viviani asks me to get in touch with
Millerand, Delcassé and Briand, who seem to him the three
representative Moderates whom Parliament would be willing
to see in office. Viviani leaves me and returns after a short
while saying that he has found Clemenceau in a state of
violent exasperation. " No, no," he expostulated, " don't
reckon on me ; in a fortnight you will be torn to ribbons.
I am not going to have anything to do with it. Besides,
you are victims of Jesuitical generals. Castelnau is to
blame for the defeats in Lorraine. The thing has got to be
put a stop to." After this paroxysm of passion Clemenceau
burst into floods of tears, and flung himself into Viviani's
arms, but still declined to give us any support. I beg
Viviani to try again. " No thank you," was the answer,
" I have had enough of him. Besides, he will not accept
anything except the Premiership, which of course I would
willingly give up if you would like me to do so." This
suggestion I decline and remind Viviani that the day may
come, if the war go on long enough for Clemenceau's ad-
hesion to us. For the moment his leadership, however
energetic, would be fraught with danger, as he would certainly slash about the army commands. " Stay where you
are," I tell Viviani, " and call in men whose authority is
indisputable, and who are not all members of the same
political party." Unfortunately, as Viviani feared, the
least shuffling of ministerial cards revives what almost
always happens with Parliament, and in the half-empty
couloirs of the Chambre buzzing whispers and back-chat
abound. Viviani brings Marcel Sembat to see me, and the
Socialist orator says very straightforwardly that in the
existing circumstances I can always count on his support,

but he thinks it too soon to enlarge our Cabinet and put
down our last card. Millerand, Delcassé and Briand are
conditionally willing to come in. Millerand would like a
" general post " in the Cabinet, and would like to see
André Lefèvre as Finance Minister and himself or Delcassé
at the Foreign Office. I mildly suggest that Gaston Doumergue is doing extremely well at the Quai d'Orsay ; Briand
is by no means convinced ; he sits astride on the chair, his
elbows on the back, with eyes flashing, lips closed, and
mind evidently made up. Delcassé, less taciturn, criticises
with some bitterness the present supineness of our diplomacy,
knowing nothing of what has been done since he left the
Embassy at St. Petersburg ; Briand, cleverer and more
subtle, thinks we ought to try Clemenceau and Sembat
again. The discussion drags and we part at 1 A.M. without
having come to any decision.

25th August. — Another protracted talk with Briand,
Millerand and Delcassé, when we seem further than ever
from agreement between them. They think the Ministry
is doomed to an early death, and they want to establish a
stronger one, but do not say under whom it should be.
Viviani proposes to split the War Office in two and give
Millerand the charge of the administrative side. To this
suggestion Millerand vouchsafes no answer. Viviani offers
Briand the Portfolio of Public Instruction, but the latter,
who held the post with signal success in peace, does not care
to resume it in war. Delcassé does not say a word, but only
nods his head to show that he agrees with his colleagues.
The Socialist party, after a consultation with Sembat,
registers its decision : " We will support the Cabinet whatever happens ; but, in the actual circumstances, we do
not think we ought to refuse even more active co-operation. We only ask that two Portfolios should be reserved
for our party in the Government, and that these shall be
given to Jules Guesde and Sembat." This communication
weakens very appreciably Briand's resistance, but Delcassé
only opposes us the more strongly, while Millerand sits
motionless as a statue and impenetrable as a sphinx.

Eventually I discover that what they all three object to

is the presence of Messimy at the War Office. They know that he has not given much attention to military operations and that he knows nothing of the meaning of our defeats. They fully admit his intelligence and his patriotism; they think that he is overwrought and " nervy ", and they blame him for the communiqués—for which he is anyhow indirectly responsible—which these last days have been foolishly optimistic and have systematically harped on the alleged weakness of the enemy and have kept from the country the realities of the war. Here they are not far wrong, and what they say agrees pretty closely with what I have said to Viviani. But in some respects the fault lies rather with our General Headquarters than with the War Office. After a prolonged interview the three inseparables go away together, promising me a reply the next day.

Clemenceau, according to the agent of the " Publicité Lenoir," is willing to form a new Cabinet himself and to take in Millerand, Briand and Delcassé. When I told my three visitors this story Briand only smiled, Delcassé remained coyly silent, and Millerand drily remarked : " As far as I am concerned, there must be two to play that game ". There is no doubt whatever that in public Clemenceau has gained ground in many points. He pleases a good many people by his unbounded energy, his perfect coolness in the presence of danger, and even by the very roughness of his manner. But one never knows whether, if he were head of the Government, he would not try and substitute for military authority his own overwhelming and too often capricious influence. He does not like Joffre, and has often found fault with him ; might he not try and replace him by some General who would be a mere figurehead ? All these questions obsess me, and I ask myself with something like dismay what in the event of such a crisis my duty as President would be.

The day drags on even more mournfully than the others. Last night Joffre ordered our armies of the north to fall back, and fearing that Paris would be uncovered, Messimy, with my knowledge, sent Colonel Magnin to headquarters

at five o'clock this morning with this order to the General
Commanding the Army of the Nord-Est :

" If victory does not crown the success of our arms, and if our
armies are obliged to retire, an army of at least three regular
corps should be moved to the fortified camp of Paris to ensure
the safety of the town.   This order is to be acknowledged."

Everywhere, except in the Est, the situation grows worse,
and in Belgium the enemy continues his forward march.
The English army has retired on the Valenciennes-Maubeuge
line, and a German cavalry corps has been pushed forward to
Orchies ; but to the east, although the first Bavarian corps,
the 21st and 15th Corps have advanced on the Mortagne and
Meurthe lines up to the Vosges, General Dubail—having
just retired his right wing on the neck of the Chipotte—has
solidly dug himself in and is preparing a counter-attack.
The Second Army has received a simple order from Castelnau.
" Forward and strike home ".   Our 16th, 15th and 20th
Corps have vigorously pushed the Germans back at several
places, but my poor Lorraine is in worse and worse plight ;
Crevic and Gerbéviller have been burnt by the Germans.

A Zeppelin has flown over Antwerp and dropped eight
bombs, killing seven people and wounding others.   Klobukowski telegraphs that the objective was the King's palace,
the Grand Hotel where the Ministers are and the powder
magazine.   At 10 P.M. Joffre, who is quite unruffled, issues
a general instruction, in which he sketches the plan of the
future fighting as he sees it :

" The offensive manœuvre not having been carried out,
further operations will be such as to reconstitute on our left wing,
by linking up the Fourth and Fifth Armies, the English army and
some new forces taken from the Est, a mass of sufficient strength
to resume the offensive while the other armies will check, for the
necessary period, the efforts of the Germans.   In their retirement
the Third, Fourth, and Fifth Armies will each keep touch with the
army next to them, and the movement will be covered by rear-
guards left in favourable folds of the ground ; every natural
obstacle must be used to hold up or anyhow delay by sharp short
attacks, to which the artillery will chiefly contribute, the advance
of the enemy."

While he has made up his mind that nothing can prevent the invasion of the country, Joffre in a General Order points out one or two lessons to be derived from our abortive offensive. General Headquarters perceive, rather belatedly, that they neglected, in the Ardennes and at Charleroi, the requisite co-ordination between infantry and artillery, that there was not sufficient artillery preparation for the infantry attacks, that these attacks were delivered from too distant a point and without sufficient cover, that too many units were thrown in, and in too close order, that, in a word, the mistake was made of thinking that courage and dash would be all-sufficient. These painful reflections do not, however, discourage the Generalissimo ; according to the Orders of the 25th his offensive will not be long delayed. The 7th Corps and four reserve divisions will be brought by rail up to the Somme, and a large force will be concentrated, based on Amiens, to attack the right flank of the German Armies.

26th August.—While alike on the frontiers of the Est and the Nord French blood is being poured out, I am condemned to sit in my gloomy study in the Élysée and try and reconstitute a Ministry. Viviani is assailed by all sorts of ambitious candidates for office who—so he says—are as little suited for it as they are determined to secure it. Millerand declines co-operation with Messimy at the War Office and will only accept the Portfolio if he is himself in direct communication with the army in the field. Millerand's untiring energy and sangfroid are qualities just now indispensable, and the only thing to be done is to ask Messimy to resign his post. Augagneur, who is always prone to forcible arguments and never minces his words, undertakes the necessary interview and says to the Minister : " Believe me, you are tired out. I am a doctor and I know what I am talking about. I tell you straight if you go on like this you will end by being a neurasthenic. Rid yourself, while there is time, of a load which is too heavy for you, or anyhow agree to share it with someone else." Messimy has indeed good cause to be tired out ; his work is more than strenuous, and his responsibility is more than heavy, although, rightly or wrongly, everything to do

with actual operations in the field is outside his knowledge.
For many days also he has been desperately anxious with
regard to the delays in preparing the fortified camp here, and
for this he is disposed to blame the Military Governor, General
Michel, with whom to-day he has exchanged winged words.
Viviani had to intervene, and it was finally decided that
Michel should be put in charge of a sector and that General
Galliéni, who is as great an administrator as he is a soldier,
should, although he has already reached the age limit, be
appointed Military Governor of Paris.   In addition to the
troops already detailed for the defence of the town, the
fortified system will be manned, as Messimy has already desired, with a mobile army of defence.   For this three Regular
Corps will be placed at Galliéni's disposal besides the Territorial troops which are now in, and near, Paris.   Galliéni's
title will be Governor Commanding the Armies of Paris.   All
these arrangements having been made, with the idea of the
eventual defence of the capital itself, Messimy, much relieved,
gracefully resigns his place to Millerand and tells us that he
is going to the Front.

Briand, while still holding himself at Viviani's disposal,
continues to urge a regular reshuffling of the Cabinet.   He
hints, rather than says, that he would like again to be, as in
1912, Minister of Justice and Vice-President of the Council.
Viviani sees no objection to this, and M. Bienvenu Martin,
who is modesty—as well as disinterestedness—itself, will, if
he is asked, give up his seat in the Place Vendôme and his
Keepership of the Seals.   Delcassé who is more exacting
than Briand, has found his tongue and says that the Portfolio
of Foreign Affairs must be entrusted to him.   " My name ",
he reminds us, " has a meaning which no one can mistake.   It
is my policy which is being vindicated to-day.   I was a good
deal blamed for having tried to encircle Germany, and it was
I who signed the *ententes* with England and Italy and the first
entente with Spain.   It was I again who prepared the ground
for the Russian alliance.   Everybody expects to see me at
the Quai d'Orsay."   It is perfectly true that Delcassé did—
in the teeth of innumerable difficulties—pave the way for the
alliances which just now constitute our strength, and no one

can contradict him when he reminds us of his signal services. But for the moment he might leave it to others to write his record, and not insist on ejecting Gaston Doumergue, who has likewise done his duty admirably and who is really dealing with Foreign Affairs with perfect competence and tact. There would be nothing derogatory in Delcassé accepting some other post and in working with us for the common good. But he does not see things in this light and merely repeats : " My place, as everyone will say, is at the Quai d'Orsay ".

What is poor Viviani to do ? It seems very unfair to turn Doumergue out, but when he tells him of Delcassé's peremptory demand, he is met with the answer: "That's quite enough, my dear fellow. I know exactly what Delcassé wants, and I will gladly give way. People may say that I have not been up to my work, but that doesn't matter. Situated as we are to-day, I am ready to serve just where I am wanted." Nothing could be more dignified than this answer, and I congratulate Doumergue on his unselfishness and cannot resist embracing him. By the end of the afternoon everything is settled except that I would have liked the Right to be represented in the Cabinet ; I had suggested the names of Albert de Mun and Denys Cochin. But Viviani and Malvy do not think the Parliament will go quite so far, and it is settled that Bienvenu Martin will take the Ministry of Public Works, while Doumergue has consented to go to the Colonial Office. Some Ministers have of course been left out to avoid constituting the Aulic Council, of which Delcassé was afraid, and one or two of these are rather sore about it. They do not complain openly, but later they will be sure to air their grievances in the *couloirs* of Parliament and will bear a grudge against Viviani and myself, no less bitter because they wrap it up. Their recriminations will not be always and altogether harmless, and will do something to create absurd stories which will make their appearance in the troublesome hours ahead. The Cabinet is, therefore, thus composed : Viviani remains President of the Council without a Portfolio ; Delcassé resumes, as he was determined to do, his seat at the Quai d'Orsay ; Malvy, to the satisfaction of all his colleagues, keeps the Ministry of the Interior ; Ribot, in whom everybody recognises one of the greatest of our Parliamentarians, replaces Noulens at the Ministry of Finance ; Millerand goes back to the War Office, where he did such good service in 1912 ; Augagneur remains in charge of the Navy, and Sembat, the Socialist, takes over Public Works ; Jules Guesde, another Socialist, is brought into the Cabinet without a Portfolio ; Bienvenu Martin exchanges the Law for Labour ; Fernand David will be Minister for Agriculture ; and Doumergue will look after the Colonies.   Viviani introduces the new Cabinet to me, the only absentee being Jules Guesde, who is rather annoyed at Ribot being included, as he professes to like neither his opinions nor his character.

The news from the Front is no better.   Our First and Second Armies have pushed the enemy back, and the gap at Charmes has been filled in, but the Fourth Army, heavily attacked at Sedan and Blagny, has retired its right over the Meuse ; the Germans have invaded the arrondissement of Avesnes, and are moving on to the Cambrai-Le Cateau line. Meanwhile, the Belgian Army, which yesterday scored a considerable success round Malines and pushed on to Vilevorde, is now very nervous about our retreat and tells us that if we get out of touch they will have, instead of advancing, to look to their own safety.

Sir John French, who on the 25th moved back to the Cambrai-Le Cateau line, has ordered a further retirement this morning, and as he thinks he cannot take up his position behind the Somme, he has ordered his forces to go back to the Oise.   Thus Joffre's fight will be no longer from Amiens to Verdun, but much farther south.   While these retirements are going on, our towns and villages, occupied one after the other by the enemy, are the victims of ruthless pillage.

Our failures, of course, do us disservice in the eyes of the neutral countries, and the most is made of them everywhere. Bompard telegraphs from Pera :

" The Turkish Government is to-day unable to send away the crews of the *Goeben* and *Breslau* as well as the German Mission. Nothing but some marked success on the part of our armies will give Turkey the power as well as the energy to break with the Germans, who are making their strength felt here more and more every day."

The Austro-Hungarians are moving on in the Sandjak, and the German and Austrian Consuls are trying to rouse the Egyptians against England and to whip them up against the French Colony. At Petersburg, however, Sazonoff has told Paléologue that Joffre's decision to give up for the moment any plan of offensive is approved by the Russian General Staff, who want us to nurse our strength and preserve freedom of manœuvre until the moment when the Russian army can deal a decisive blow. Our Military Attaché, who has been these last days at the Front, telegraphs that a Russian attack is being vigorously made at several points, and he seems to be full of confidence. Is it from this quarter that much-needed help is coming to us ?

27th August.—The new Cabinet is very well received by public opinion, and at our first meeting Millerand says he is going at once to headquarters to talk to Joffre. He is quite right to do so, and I only hope he will bring about closer and more regular correspondence between the Government and the High Command. The War Minister has also had a long interview with Galliéni, who is not comfortable about Paris, and says that within four or five days the German cavalry might make a raid as far as our walls. He is very anxious to speed up measures of defence, and would like the troops which Messimy detailed to be sent to him at once ; Sembat would like the public to be warned.

Clemenceau is on the war-path again ; after a few weeks of truce he and I are at loggerheads just as much as before the war, and now, as before, I really cannot accuse myself of having done anything to bring about the rupture. M. Dubost and M. Deschanel tell me that he brought the Deputy Mayors of Lille to see them, and they protested against our troops having given up the town. I can only say that Messimy assured me that the evacuation of Lille was not only proposed by General d'Amade on the score of his Territorials not being able to defend the town, but was also asked for by the Mayor himself, who, knowing that the inhabitants could not hold out, did not want to see them exposed to heavy gunfire. It was on this double request that Messimy decided to authorise the General to retire his troops, but the mistake was made of leaving motor cars and cereals in the place. Clemenceau saw in this incident the result of carelessness on the part of the Government, and according to his usual bent he blamed myself even more ; for the last eighteen months indeed he has fixed the blame on me for everything which he thinks blameworthy. M. Ribot, it would seem, had called yesterday on Clemenceau, with whom he is openly on fairly good terms and whom he found very acid as regards me. I know exactly whence this bit of ill-temper springs. I had committed the unpardonable fault of not listening to the suggestion which came through the Lenoir agency; I did not offer to Clemenceau the Presidency of the Council. I did not do this because it would have been an abuse of power and an act of injustice towards Viviani, while, despite Clemenceau's great intellectual worth, his patriotism and his courage, I am always rather nervous, perhaps a little too nervous, of his whims, his very versatility, and his fine contempt for everybody except himself. He always reminds me of the dictum of Aeschylus—so often forgotten by politicians—" Pride, born of Success, who devours his father ". It is certainly not from mere ambition that Clemenceau wants to be in office ; it is because he is convinced that he will save the country and that he alone can do so. If ever the real moment comes I shall call upon him without hesitation, but in a war like this one must put square pegs into square holes, and anyhow it is better not to put all one's eggs in the same basket. So as to be on the right side, however, I ask Clemenceau to come and see me, and try and give him Messimy's explanation both as to the evacuation of Lille and the "déclassement"[1] asked for by the War Council. He scarcely listened to me, and scolded me for the appointment of General Perçin, of whom he spoke as sharply as he did the other day about Castelnau ; he can indeed be very eclectic in his animosities. I told him that Perçin had been nominated six years ago, when I had nothing to do with public affairs, but I don't think he heard what I said. He reproached me for not having looked after, or

---

[1] This was revived by Clemenceau in February 1919 and legalised under his sign-manual that October.

anyhow for not having re-edited, the communiqués, as if any
Minister would have allowed any such meddling on my part,
or as if he in the same circumstances would have allowed it
himself.   He said pleasantly that I had composed a Cabinet
of nullities so as the more easily to dominate them, as if he
himself had not formerly recognised and pronounced Viviani's
worth, and as if I had played any other than my constitutional
part.   He accused me of having a shady Ministry to which
the Socialists would bring their political stock-in-trade, and
in which Briand, Delcassé and Millerand would bring about
disorder and failure.   To his mind I had sacrificed the
destinies of France to my own selfish good.   In a word, he
addressed me for several minutes with the spiteful and
incoherent violence of a man who had completely lost self-
control, and with the frenzy of a disappointed patriot who
thinks that he alone can secure victory for our flag.   If I
were a free agent I should have asked him to leave the
room, but in deference to my own function and his age I
kept myself in hand except that I could not resist interrupting him once and saying: "That's a lie".   His answer
was: "People who talk about lies are the people to whom
one can return the compliment".   He then continued his
diatribe.   I kept my eyes fixed on him, looking with amazement at this angry old man who was relieving his pent-up
feelings by vomiting over me all his grievances.   I let him
go on as he pleased without saying another word, and he
finally rose, shaking with rage, and flung a last word at me.
"Besides, what on earth are you thinking about at a moment
like this?   Do you want to be the idol of the *Figaro* and of
Alfred Capus?"   I did not understand till later the meaning
of this last sally; it appears that in passing through my
Secretary-General's room he had seen Alfred Capus there,
a great friend of his, but of whose presence I was entirely
unaware.   The veteran's paroxysms were not finished even
when he was leaving; he kept on repeating that with the
Socialists in power I should destroy France, and by way of
good-bye he called out: "I am very glad to get out of this".
Seeing him in this frame of mind I only answered: "You
are crazy".   He had told me, I am bound to say, that he

couldn't get any sleep and only kept himself going with bromide. The *Temps* this evening regrets that Clemenceau has no office. This was his fault only ; he did not want to be a Minister, he wanted to be the Ministry. The more I think of the matter the more I say to myself : " So long as victory is possible he is capable of upsetting everything ". A day will perhaps come when I shall add : " Now that everything seems to be lost he is capable of saving everything ".

For the moment let us forget this storm in a teacup and get back to work. Mournful news again to-day. The Belgian army has had to suspend its forward movement south of Malines, and to fall back on Antwerp under the attentions of two German divisions ; in France some of the enemy cavalry have reached Combes, ten kilometres from Péronne, while others are in St. Quentin ; Maubeuge is completely invested by the 9th and 7th German Corps. On the front of our Fourth Army the battle is in full force. We have counter-attacked, but have not been able to prevent the enemy getting across the Meuse in three places, while some of their columns have arrived at Consenvoye and Damvillers. It is only in the east that things are a little brighter. Our First and Second Armies continue to clear the gap at Charmes and are making good our frontier here. In the Near East there is a ray of hope ; the Austro-Hungarian troops who were in the Sandjak of Novi Bazar are retreating, while in the Colonies fortune is actually smiling on us ; the German troops at Togo having announced that they would only surrender with the honours of war, have surrendered at discretion ; this morning the Allied troops have entered Kamina. But these far-off happenings are poor compensation for our sets-back in France. Joffre, who is preparing a counter-blow, wants us, by some well-earned praise, to encourage Sir John French for the next offensive ; Sir John himself has sent to the British Government a very flattering account of the French army.[1] Agreeably with the wishes of our Generalissimo I hasten to telegraph to King George :

[1] Telegrams from Paul Cambon and from our Military Attaché.

" The General Officer Commanding-in-Chief the French Armies has told the Government of the splendid courage which Your Majesty's army has shown alongside our own soldiers against our common enemy. I beg Your Majesty to accept my profound thanks, and I shall be greatly obliged if Your Majesty would consent to convey to Marshal French and to all officers and soldiers under his command, my sincere and grateful congratulations."

Information to hand to-day from other parts of the world shows the diabolical cleverness of the continuous German propaganda. In the Socialist quarters of Norway, which are favourable to us, an edition of the *Vorwärts* states that Germany will leave France not only her existence but her dignity unimpaired, and that she will invite all the nations of Europe, including England, to build up universal peace and to create a federation against Russian tyranny. Through Swedish intermediaries she insinuates to the English that the British troops, victims of our incompetent commanders, will be destroyed all in vain ; the Belgians are told that we first pushed them into the war and then left them to their fate and that Antwerp is lost. At Munich there are posters up which announce an alleged violation of the Swiss frontier by French armies, and we are accused of using dum-dum bullets. At the same time we hear from Bucharest and Sofia of constant arrivals of German officers at Constantinople. There are already 150 of them there, and with the crews of the *Goeben* and the *Breslau*, together with the German Military Mission, they constitute a small highly organised force which completes the handiwork of the Hohenzollerns with regard to Turkey. The director of the Banque de Commerce at Stockholm has just returned from Berlin and given the British Minister in Sweden his political impressions. Germany is determined to bring all her weight against France, to break down quickly our resistance and to offer peace on these conditions: the pre-war integrity of our country ; prohibition to fortify for the future our frontier of the Est ; a moderate indemnity ; Colonial compensations and the creation of a neutral principality between France and Germany : Germany would then turn round on Russia.

Thus war has been declared upon us, we have been invaded, and we shall be asked to leave our frontier open for the future, to indemnify Germany who has already burnt several of our towns, to give her up part of our Colonies, and above all to betray our Allies in the middle of hostilities. It is more than likely that Germany will try to sow dissension between her adversaries, and in view of this danger I have over and over again pointed out to the Government that it will be well to submit as soon as possible to England and Russia the proposal of a pact under which we can mutually undertake not to make a separate peace. Paul Cambon and Paléologue have been informed of this ; Sir Arthur Nicolson has already given his approval, and we only await Sir Edward Grey's.

But Italy is making a little retrograde movement. San Giuliano has told our Ambassador that Germany and Austria have given them assurances which relieve any anxiety they had entertained as to the attitude of the Central Empires towards them, and it was thus unlikely that Italy would emerge from her neutrality. What is to be said ? What promises have Austria and Germany made, and at whose expense will they be carried out ? Here is a well-preserved secret of that temple of prudence which is called the Consultà.

The enemy is drawing near St. Quentin,[1] and it was on the 27th August 1557 that the town, defended by Coligny, was taken by the Spaniards. Will it, on the 27th August 1914, be captured by the Germans ?

28th August.—The King of England telegraphs :

" I thank you most sincerely for your amiable telegram. I have, with profound and grateful satisfaction, conveyed your praises to Field-Marshal Sir John French and the officers and men under his command, who will, I know, appreciate deeply the manner in which you recognise their splendid services. I have every hope that the gallant French troops, acting with our forces, will successfully repulse the enemy."

[1] I telegraphed to the Mayor, the Sous-Préfet and the Curator to try and save the wonderful collection of pastels, but it was too late, and the Germans carried them off to Maubeuge, where, however, they left them when they beat a hurried retreat in 1918.

Millerand has come from General Headquarters, where he finds Joffre and his immediate subordinates confident and resolute as ever. They have substituted for their original idea, which failed, a plan which, so far, is being duly carried out; a general retreat to a long line between the Somme and the Vosges which, if necessary, may be bent back towards the south; a stand to be made on this line at a point which is as yet not decided and will depend on circumstances; fighting to be kept up all along the front and, if possible, the offensive to be resumed. To prepare for this new great battle, which will doubtless decide the fate of the war, troops have been brought from the Est towards Amiens, and this is being quite smoothly done. General Headquarters repeats that at the beginning there was doubtless faulty work, and this not only on the part of the troops; some of the senior officers and even the corps commanders could not be held blameless. A good many officers have been relieved of their posts, perhaps some with undue haste, but it is essentially necessary that vigilant and inflexible authority should be recognised and exercised. Millerand even thinks that some of the penalties err on the side of leniency, and he wants them to be extended and increased. Joffre disagrees with Galliéni as to there being any danger of a cavalry raid on Paris, and does not think that our left wing is in any risk of being overrun. But if his new scheme comes to grief, the three corps detailed for Paris will be sent to our fortified camp, while the rest of the army will remain in the field. Millerand seems to be very satisfied with the explanations given him by Joffre, who, he says, is taking no chances. Unfortunately, Paris is far from being in a proper state of defence, and Galliéni, who always talks very straight, is very down on General Michel for what he considers protracted neglect.

Millerand gives the Ministers a very clear—and fairly cheerful—account of the situation, but in certain quarters of Paris something like depression has set in. M. Caillaux, mobilised in the Army Pay Department, has begun by having a bone to pick with his military seniors; when he was on leave in Paris he appears to have told people whom he met that he had very little hopes as to the result of the war. He asked apparently to be allowed to serve under General Sarrail and was told by Millerand to go back to his post at Amiens, but it is not very likely that a Minister and a former President of the Council—especially if that individual be named Caillaux—will submit, without being forced, to the requirements of military discipline. Clemenceau's outlook is even gloomier than Caillaux's, and he is as excited as ever. Primed by him, M. Jeanneney, a senator who usually keeps a very level head, comes to see my Secretary-General, to tell him that unless the Government convene Parliament at once they will incur a very heavy responsibility. Clemenceau also tries to stir up Presidents Dubost and Deschanel, and has some success with the former, while the latter is proof against him. As a matter of fact, Parliament is still in session and was only voluntarily prorogued. But what possible use would it be for the Chamber to reassemble on the eve of battle ? Deeds, not words, are what are required now.

The blunder committed at Lille has been partially repaired, and the Prefect du Nord has been able to organise and send to Dunkirk a convoy loaded with rifles and military equipment, but he can only communicate with Dunkirk and Hazebrouck, most of his other communes being now cut off. Late in the afternoon we hear that the Germans poured into St. Quentin about half-past five.

The reports from St. Petersburg continue to be fairly good ; in Eastern Prussia the Germans are said to be retreating on Königsberg and Allenstein, while in Eastern Galicia the Russians are striding out towards Lemberg ; but the rather nebulous successes on the Russian front do little to console us for the miseries and dangers with which we are surrounded here.

According to the German newspapers the Governor of Metz has put up a placard :

" In the battle round Noměny civilians took part in the fighting against our brave troops of the 4th Infantry : I have therefore ordered as a punishment that the village should be burnt to the ground. Noměny is thus by now destroyed."

Always the same excuses and always the same savagery. The German Headquarter Staff has issued a triumphant communiqué :

" German victory all along the line. Klück has driven the English back and turned the French left south-west of Maubeuge. The armies of Bülow and Hausen are fighting between the Sambre and the Meuse ; the army of the Duke of Wurtemberg has crossed the Semoy and the Meuse ; the army of the Prince Imperial is now facing Longwy ; the Prince Royal of Bavaria is moving forward in Lorraine ; and the Hoeringuen army is pursuing the French in the Vosges."

In America German bluff hardens daily, and the Ambassador Count Bernstorff is tireless in his efforts to lead astray public opinion. He emphasises the danger of Japanese predominance in the Pacific and largely exaggerates the success of the German army. But his rhapsodies seem to have been carried a little too far and have irritated American common sense ; the *World* publishes an article under the title " It is France who is telling the truth ".

Mr. Sharp is replacing our excellent friend Mr. Herrick at the Embassy here, and has been told not to present his credentials until the different questions apart from the war, to which Mr. Herrick has been attending, have been settled satisfactorily between the two countries. Our Ambassador, M. Jusserand, was received yesterday by the President of the United States, who spoke with considerable emotion about this terrible war, and, however guarded his words, Mr. Wilson expressed a good deal of sympathy for France. Jusserand was careful to point out that the Germans, who wanted to sell to America the ships stationed in American ports, had, according to the London Convention of 1909, no right to carry out this transfer of flags, and that the Government of Washington could not lend themselves to such a deal. Mr. Wilson, a very rigid lawyer, only answers that he will give the matter his serious attention. No one knows what will be the result of the Presidential reflections. Mr. Wilson knows very little about Europe, and Europe knows very little about him. France has many warm friends in America, but what is in the mind of the great doctrinaire in whose hand are for a moment the destinies of the United States ?

Late in the evening comes very bad news. General Lanrezac, seeing that the retirement of the English behind the Oise between Noyon and La Fère will uncover the left wing of the Fifth Army, has himself retreated farther. He has just received orders from Joffre to turn west and attack the flank of Von Klück's army, which is pursuing the English and which must be held up at any cost. Joffre attaches the utmost importance to the battle which is imminent. He has decided to break up the army of Alsace, as events, he says, have made this part a secondary theatre. It must have cost him a pang to describe Alsace as a " secondary theatre ". The chapter which opened so splendidly and caused our hearts to beat so high has been closed.

CHAPTER V

The battle of Guise—The Russians in Galicia and Eastern Prussia—Our retreat continues—At Joffre's request the War Minister insists on the Government leaving Paris—Authors and military service—Visit of Mr. Myron Herrick—A sad departure—Before the battles of the Ourcq and the Marne.

29th August. — Modest and quite selfless as ever, Léon Bourgeois comes to see me to thank the Government for having appointed him President of the Commission of Assistance and Supplies on which Millerand, Briand and Delcassé are to sit ; he is one of those rare souls who are only too happy to do whatever work is entrusted to them. But his duty is one which will become daily more important, as, besides the allowances granted to soldiers' families, there are to be considered the cases of workmen unemployed on account of age and health, women without resource or means of gaining their bread, and a host of other unfortunates, while the question of supplies for the civil population is by no means easy. For this sort of task Léon Bourgeois' lovable character is no less valuable than his experience as Minister of Health.

Per contra, M. Touron, Vice-President of the Senate, rushes into my room like a whirlwind. He is in such a state of excitement as to be scarcely recognisable, and he declares that the General Staff is either uninformed itself or is deceiving us, that our left wing has been turned and that the Germans are at La Fère. What he blurts out is very much what I feared myself and what I hinted to the liaison officers yesterday. But, for the moment, in spite of the enemy being at Péronne and St. Quentin, General Headquarters do not seem to be over-anxious, and Colonel Pénélon has just telephoned to the Élysée that Joffre thinks the situation has improved since yesterday. The short communiqué this morning announces that the forward movement of the Germans has slackened, but one quite understands that M. Touron, who is one of the industrial magnates of the Aisne, is by no means reassured. In the back of my mind I am scarcely more comfortable than he is, and the question is whether something of self-deception may lurk in the optimism at General Headquarters.

We learn successively that in Belgium the Germans have burnt the famous library of Louvain, that in France a brigade has reached the Somme at Brie, that a strong column has entered the forest of Nouvion, that a division of infantry has attacked our 9th Corps near Dommery, and that German troops have pushed forward on the left bank of the Meuse, while in Lorraine our First and Second Armies have resumed the offensive but are making very little progress, and that in Haute Alsace large bodies of troops seem to be converging on Belfort. However discreetly worded, the official bulletins are beginning to trouble public opinion, and in some of the Paris clubs which have remained open there are members who have little else to do and who bandy about discouraging stories ; a new evil for which a new name—defeatism—has to be found is beginning to show itself. My post-bag gets more and more swollen and bulges with criticisms, complaints, recriminations, as well as petitions from priests or women who urge me to dedicate France to the Sacred Heart. Many of these requests are touching in their sincerity, which is born of grief and of devout faith ; others seem to be unhappily inspired by political passion rather than by religious feeling, and our defects are represented as a well-merited punishment inflicted by the Almighty on the Republic. Is the Union Sacrée, therefore, in any way threatened ? Surely not. The disaffected letters, however numerous, are but a negligible quantity compared to the expressions of heart-whole confidence which abound.

Towards two o'clock Colonel Pénélon brings me better news. The four German army corps which were advancing in parallel columns on our left wing, and whose advance guards had already passed the Somme, seem to have exposed

themselves rashly. They have on their right our 7th
Corps, which has just detrained at Amiens and which, with
the reserve divisions, Sordet's cavalry divisions and four
battalions of chasseurs on foot, compose the new Sixth Army
under General Maunoury : the Germans will quickly feel the
attack of these combined forces. Against their left flank,
the four German corps have Lanrezac's entire army. Unfortunately this army is so tired that Lanrezac wants to
take it back without further fighting to the south of Laon
and there refit and reform it for further engagements.
Joffre, who will not at this moment hear of any delay,
considers this proposal as an exhibition of faint-heartedness,
and has given Lanrezac definite orders to take the offensive
in the region of Guise, and has further told him that if he
hesitates or disobeys he will be shot ; the Generalissimo has
gone himself to the Front and has great hopes of the forthcoming battle.

All day the most contradictory rumours reach my ears.
A deputy of the Aisne, one Magniaudé, comes to the Élysée in
travelling clothes, but with the Parliamentary badge in his
buttonhole and a tricolour scarf round his neck, as if he had
appointed himself, on his own authority, as Commissary for
the Armies of the Republic. He has arrived from Vervins
in a great state of excitement and has, he declares, seen our
troops in great disorder round Laon, while the Sous-Préfet
of Vervins has confided to him that our leaders are either
depressed or incompetent. At Laon itself he has not seen
a single French soldier, but at Compiègne he has been struck
with admiration for the splendid turn-out of the English.
Our men themselves are for the most part excellent and full
of go ; but the leaders ! " Commissaries ", Magniaudé says,
" are absolutely necessary to look after things and to raise
the moral of the troops." Then back comes M. Touron,
more out of hand than ever ; he again says to Viviani and
myself that we are being taken in and that our armies are
surrounded. In vain we try to calm him ; the poor fellow,
who is generally a very reasonable and thoughtful individual,
has lost all self-control. Late in the afternoon, while the
Ministerial Council is sitting, Touron returns and is received

by my Secretary-General. He has been talking on the telephone with M. Sébline, another Senator for the Aisne, who
has a property a little to the south of St. Quentin, now in the
hands of the enemy. The Germans are treating Sébline
quite politely, but they tell him again and again : " Paris
will pay for France ". Sébline has told Touron that from
the roof of his house he has had a good view of the battle,
and that at first our men, attacking towards St. Quentin,
gained some advantage, but as soon as the enemy brought
up reinforcements, borrowed from the advance guard on the
Somme, they were easily repulsed. A few hours later one
of the liaison officers brings me the daily bulletin which confirms M. Sébline's gloomy story. But, on the other hand, the
Prefect of the Aisne telephones from Laon that we have
secured a real success round Guise. Unluckily the left of
our Fifth Army has a little later on been obliged to retire
towards the Oise, and in spite of the partial advantage
gained near Guise, the manœuvre, planned by General
Headquarters, has once again failed. Our attack on the
four corps which formed the right wing of the enemy has
not succeeded, whereas a German assault on the right wing
and rear of Lanrezac's army has not been decisively dealt
with. Not only has the German advance not been checked,
but it looks very much as if we might be caught up and
pinned down in our retreat.

The Council is compelled to consider the likelihood of Paris
being invested, and Millerand says that in such case, and
agreeably with Joffre's wishes, he will propose the departure
from the capital of the Government, which has no right to
allow itself to be cut off and isolated from the people. This
idea seems to be a little premature, and I arrange that it shall
be reserved for future discussion, but Guesde and Sembat
ask that, if the exodus takes place, some members of the
Government shall remain behind to represent it, and the two
Socialists wish the inhabitants to be armed to defend the
town. Millerand promptly says that to arm the population
of Paris would be to expose them to horrible reprisals, as
the Germans have everywhere given alleged shooting by
civilians as an excuse for setting on fire the houses of inoffen-

sive citizens. It is decided that questions affecting the
defence of Paris are to be discussed to-morrow with Galliéni.

The telegrams which we receive during the day from other
parts of the world do nothing to console us. We are still in
a fog as to what Turkey means to do, but a quantity of
Pan-Islamic emissaries are leaving Constantinople for North
Africa. German soldiers and sailors keep on passing through
Bulgaria on their way to rejoin Liman von Sanders, and the
representatives of the Allied Powers in Sofia in vain protest
against this cynical violation of neutrality. Germany is
also busily manœuvring at Bucharest, so as to push King
Carol into taking a decision contrary to the general feeling
of his country, and our Minister, who is very anxious as to
this, wants Russia to offer Roumania a district in Bessarabia,
so that the whims of the Sovereign may be checked by the
force of public opinion. Trains crammed with German
officers and soldiers, who are easily recognisable despite
their mufti, have passed through Roumania *en route* for
Bulgaria and Constantinople, and the Government at
Bucharest has been obviously very much embarrassed by
our Minister's complaints on this score ; the Government
know perfectly well that a wrong thing is being done, but
on account of the King, they dare not close the frontier.
The Ambassadors of the Triple Entente are submitting to-day
to the Porte a proposal which has the double disadvantage
of being belated and rather nebulous :

" The three Powers declare to the Sublime Porte that they are
prepared to guarantee the integrity of Ottoman territory and to
examine in a friendly spirit the claims which Turkey may wish to
address them on economic and judiciary subjects. The Sublime
Porte will for its part undertake to observe an attitude of strict
neutrality with respect to the conflict which is at the moment
dividing Europe."

One cannot help fearing that, after Germany's loud
trumpeting over our defeats, this proposal has little chance
of being accepted.

The military news from Russia, however, continues to
be good ; in Eastern Prussia the Russians have occupied
Allenstein, and in Galicia there has been a regular battle on

a front of 300 kilometres from the Vistula to Lemberg.
Sir Edward Grey has told Paul Cambon that, like us, he
thinks the Allies should come to an understanding not to
conclude any separate peace ; it remains to establish this
convention, and I am asking Delcassé to push it on. Our
1904 Agreement does not make England our Ally ; she has
become so by reason of the war, and the actual alliance
must last the war out.

30th August.—In Lorraine our troops have gone ahead, and
we hold the line of the Mortagne, while our right continues
to advance. But we never get any kind of success without
a corresponding reverse, and in the Vosges we seem to be
moving back. The town of St. Dié is still occupied by the
Germans, and the Prefect telephones that the enemy want
to imprison the Mayor with his deputies and other persons,
because at St. Marie and at Saales our military authorities
thought well to take some women and children as hostages.
The Government accepts the exchange and promises restitution ; I cannot understand how French officers could have
had so stupid an idea as to molest inoffensive people, and I am
urging that exemplary penalties should be inflicted. North
of Rethel the Saxons have attacked our 9th Corps, and our
Fourth Army has had to retire still farther. Indeed, it
seems as if we are obliged to yield ground everywhere. A
regular pitched battle seems to have been fought round Guise
to disengage our left wing, and we have managed to resist
the pressure of the 11th Corps and the Imperial Guard, but
then farther west we have been less happy, and the Germans
have crept up in the direction of La Fère. M. Touron was
not altogether wrong in the information with which he so
emotionally supplied me yesterday, and part of the First
Germany Army has reached Chaulnes, Lihon and Rozières.
In commenting this morning on the recent military happenings, the liaison officer does not conceal from me that the
situation is becoming intensely serious. Viviani tells me
that he remained till very late at night at the War Office, and
that Millerand was telephoning to Joffre, who thinks that he
can no longer prevent the Germans from entering Paris,
especially if the Government stays there. The Commander-

in-Chief is strongly of opinion that we ought to move away so that we shall not ourselves be the means of drawing the enemy on the capital ; in a word, the battle of Guise has not given the results expected. Viviani dislikes the idea of leaving no less than myself, but he is much disturbed by what Joffre has said, and states that the Presidents of the Two Houses have asked to see him. What do they want ? And what could Parliament do if it were to sit now ?

Messimy, in the uniform of a commandant of infantry chasseurs, and overjoyed at joining his battalion, comes to wish me good-bye. He leaves with me a sort of little last will and testament which, among other recommendations, contains these two lines :

" 30*th August* 1914.—Above all do not allow yourselves to be shut up in Paris, and, when retiring, destroy all works of art even on the road."

By not being shut up in Paris, he means not to allow the garrison itself to be invested. It would be impossible to defend Paris as a fortified town, even with the three army corps which he asked for, and he thinks it would be much better for them to deliver one or more regular battles outside the walls rather than immobilise themselves within. I can only tell him that neither the Government nor myself would, in a purely military question, interfere with the military authorities. Messimy begs me—on his knees, he says—to let the War Minister know his opinion, and I enclose his note to Millerand, who can, if necessary, show it to Joffre and Galliéni.

The Commander-in-Chief is just now specially concerned with what Sir John French considers he has a right to do. Will the English consent to break off their retreat so as to fight again without taking the time to refit ? They seem to be retiring on Meaux, whence they wish to reach the Lower Seine in order to get nearer their naval bases ; they will skirt Paris by the south, so as to go and reorganise themselves somewhere round Rouen. Joffre is very unhappy about this and wants Sir John French to give up the idea.

Galliéni comes to my room before the Ministerial Council

and, in presence of Viviani and Millerand, explains his views with a clarity and force of expression which cannot but have a profound effect on us. Straight as a dart, with head erect, tall upright figure and piercing eyes, he cannot but impress himself on everyone with whom he comes in contact as an example of powerful manhood. Although he is only sixty-five years old, his constitution has been severely tried by long residence in the Colonies and especially by those nine years—crowded with important events—which he spent in Madagascar. He thinks that the defence of Paris is not sufficiently ensured, that the forts are not in proper condition, that the entrenched camp is not organised as it should be, and that we require eight or ten days to catch up the time lost by General Michel. But, he adds, even if all is done that has been left undone, Paris will not be able to stand up against an assault with the heavy guns which the Germans can bring into play. We ought, therefore, to constitute, with the four army corps or, at least, with the three indicated by Messimy, a mobile army under the command of the Military Governor which should form the extreme left wing and which, at the given moment, should fight just outside the town. We beg the General to give his views to the Ministers, and he does so with the same clearness and precision as to us. At Millerand's request he furnishes a written report, which is not very pleasant reading, and which is at once brought under the notice of Joffre, as the despatch of the troops which are wanted for Paris must depend on material conditions which only Joffre is able to appreciate.

In the afternoon another Council is held, and M. Dubost and M. Deschanel appear before it. The former is very sulky to-day and grinds his false teeth to show his resentment. He alleges that the Cabinet cannot legally transport itself anywhere outside the capital except with a Parliamentary vote, that the seat of public office was fixed by the law of 1879, and that therefore if we want to leave we must first summon Parliament and pass a Bill for the transfer. He says further there need be no further heated debate about military operations, and that the good feeling shown on the 4th of August will be quickly recovered and that the Govern-

ment will gather strength from another demonstration of
goodwill in Parliament. I do not think—and I say so—that
M. Dubost's thesis is juridically correct. It is anyhow no
question of transferring the permanent seat of Government ; it is merely that, should military requirements not
allow the Government to remain in Paris, a provisional place
of reunion shall be found ; thus it will be not a change of
domicile but of temporary residence. As a matter of fact,
Ministers have often met outside Paris—at Rambouillet,
at Fontainebleau, at Havre ; M. Dubois does not contest
the justice of my observations and only urges that the
Government should pass, as it has the right to do, a decree
to close the extraordinary Session and thus free him from
having either to convoke the Upper House or to evade
individual demands for Parliament to meet. Viviani, Ribot
and others remind him that such a decree, if it were passed
at once, would alarm public opinion, and that any convoca-
tion of the Chambers, however discreetly worded, would give
rise to various, and probably very unhappy, comments,
both here and at the Front. The idea might get abroad
that the Government is about to sue for peace, and such
an idea might do something to discourage the troops. The
two Presidents having left, the Council decides that they cannot take the responsibility for calling Parliament together.
Dubost on the telephone expresses his annoyance and says
that he will himself assemble the Senate unless the Government gets me to sign now and here the decree of closure.
It is finally decided that the decree shall only be gazetted if
the Government is obliged to leave Paris, and on the motion
of Guesde and Sembat it is laid down that, if the case should
arise, the decree will be due to the impossibility of conven-
ing anything like integrally the two Chambers, as so many
members are serving with the Colours. "It is quite evident",
Viviani says to me, " that it is Clemenceau who has pushed
Dubost into this." Possibly this may be so, but there are
occasions when Dubost does not require any pushing. While
this little civilian struggle is harmlessly proceeding, a motor
is whirring in the skies. A German aeroplane flying over
Paris throws three bombs on the Quai de Valmy and the

Rue des Vinaigriers, killing one man and wounding three others. The aviator has also thrown a silly proclamation, in which Parisians are notified that the best thing they can do is to flee the city as the Germans are at the gates of the city in the same way as in 1870. Although the incident is reported to the Press and becomes common knowledge, the people pay scarcely any attention to it. But the deputies and municipal authorities are beginning to be very anxious as to the fate of the town, and some ardent patriots want the inhabitants to be armed in view of street fighting. But what opportunities for devastating revenge we might thus furnish to the Germans !

. . . There is always the same little shaft of light in the Near East. General de Laguiche telegraphs that the last Russian successes have assured to our Allies the possession of Eastern Prussia :

" After masking the fortresses with some regular and reserve troops, the bulk of the armies has been railed rapidly west and is developing an offensive towards Berlin.   In Galicia the big battle begun a few days ago continues with excellent results in the east, but not yet decisive in the west."

Anyhow, the activities of the Russian armies will bring us a measure of relief on the Western Front, and Joffre is very grateful to the Grand Duke Nicholas for what he has done.

31st August.—My old friend Alphonse Deville, Municipal Councillor for Paris, is good enough to tell me that there are very odd stories about myself ; as I have had neither time nor opportunity to go out these last days, I am said to have been sequestrated by the Government. As a matter of fact I have arranged to visit the Hôpital Militaire des Recollets this afternoon, where it is my privilege to congratulate brave men on behalf of the nation and, all unworthily, to express to them the gratitude of the public. But the men need neither consoling nor encouraging ; they are all in fine fettle and longing to get back to the Front. The rapturous reception which I get going and coming, simply shows that I represent a France who is threatened, but undeterred and resolute. Will the Government make up its mind to quit Paris and to leave behind so many unhappy people who are entrusted to us ?

Thank God, Colonel Pénélon brings me from head-quarters news which allows me to hope that the question of our departure may not arise. Joffre has said that if only the English will agree to keep their rear-guard in contact with the enemy, Lanrezac—after the heavy fighting of yester-day in which the enemy, and especially the Imperial Guard, were severely punished—might again ' go for " the German flank while Maunoury's Sixth Army could contain their right wing and part of their front. And if, at the same time, success should wait on our offensive at Rethel, on the Meuse and in Lorraine, there might be real hope of sharply checking the German advance. Should this plan not meet with the ex-pected results, the 18th Corps would at once break off from Lanrezac and repair to Paris with the Sixth Army, and battle would be given in front of the town with these forces and those of the garrison. Thus Joffre does not think it neces-sary that the Government should pack up at once, and I am indescribably relieved, as the nearer the dreaded hour ap-proaches, the less one can resign oneself to quitting Paris. One Minister, anyhow, M. Ribot, thinks as I do, and thinks that anyhow we ought to wait for the battle which will take place under the walls of the town. I tell Viviani and I tell Pénélon—in order that the latter may repeat it to Joffre—how I hope on that day to be with the armies, and that person-ally I should not leave Paris unless defeat obliges us all to go. Léon Bourgeois, in turn, begs me to protest against any pre-cipitate departure, and, backed by Ribot and Sembat, I re-turn to the charge at the Ministerial Council. But Millerand energetically supports the views of the High Command with which he has identified himself, and says that, as Minister of War, he could not accept the responsibility of letting the Government be besieged. A party of Uhlans, he says, might well cross the Seine and blow up the railway behind Paris, and it would be preposterous to expose to this sort of risk all the central administrations and the organisations on which the existence of the country depend. Doumergue sees eye to

eye with the War Minister and delivers himself of a phrase :
" M. le Président, one's duty is sometimes to allow oneself to
be accused of cowardice ; it may require more courage to con-
front popular reproach than to run the risk of being killed ".
I know quite well that Doumergue is right, but, on the other
hand, I don't think that I am altogether wrong, and to leave
Paris, especially to leave it so hurriedly, might be to expose
the people to something like a feeling of despair and perhaps
the country to revolution.

Since Joffre has let me know that if the English would
agree to slow down their retreat and hold up the Germans
there would be a great chance of success, I beg Sir Francis
Bertie to come and see me, and he has promised to telephone
to Sir John. About ten o'clock in the evening Sir Francis
brings me a British officer with a message from the Field-
Marshal :

" In view of the heavy losses in men and material which the
British army has suffered in its retreat from Mons, and in view of
the fact that until yesterday the troops have been continuously
engaged with the enemy, my army needs at least eight days to
be refitted and reorganised and so to become again an effective
fighting unit. The utmost I can say is that I will not go further
back than a line drawn from east to west by Nanteuil so long as
the French army does not go south of its present position. After
this respite, I shall be ready to hold the British forces at the
disposal of the French Commander-in-Chief under whatever conditions he thinks best, provided only that my independence of
action shall be preserved and that my lines of communication
shall be assured. Up till now I have no information as to the
French army resuming the offensive."

Eight days ! Eight days ! Within eight days will not
the Germans be in Paris ? Sir John's orderly officer tells
me that the English have lost 6000 men with guns and
ammunition and that they are dead tired. The last part of
the Field-Marshal's note, however gracefully it is couched,
does not correct the negative meaning of the earlier words.

Contrary to the hopes entertained at General Headquarters the situation of our armies does not seem to get
any better. From Lille the Prefect telegraphs that there are
at Cambrai 50,000 German infantry and 10,000 cavalry, who

have come straight from Trèves without striking a blow; these troops have ordered food to be ready for them at four o'clock in the afternoon, and have threatened to shoot a third of the male population if the slightest violence is offered to them. A German lieutenant has told the Mayor that a General and two divisions will be in the town to-morrow and that the forts will be occupied; other German officers have warned the municipality of Douai that three of their divisions will cross the town this afternoon, while the Prefect of the Pas-de-Calais lets the Minister of the Interior know that a German army corps is advancing on Lens and that Arras is threatened with occupation. Farther east the enemy is still nearer Paris and their First Army continue to make head-way southward, in several columns, on the Montdidier—Senlis and Roye—Estrées St. Denis roads, while a cavalry corps has passed the Oise and reached Offémont; it would seem that the march on Paris is being accelerated and that the great battle of Paris cannot be far off.

Nor has the East Front anything to offer in the way of compensation. The Russian Government appears to be frightened by our retreat and to fear that we may be driven to make a separate peace. Operations continue in Galicia without anything decisive occurring, and in Eastern Prussia the Germans are putting in a counter-stroke with fresh troops. England has an idea—perhaps rather a hazy idea—of asking Russia to send us three army corps by Archangel; the troops would be transported on British vessels, and Delcassé has supported the notion. The Government in Russia says, however, that the difficulties and delays as to transport prevent their answering in the affirmative, but M. Sazonoff tire-lessly reels out rather crude proposals with the alternative objects of coaxing and threatening Bulgaria and Italy. The English join with us in trying to dissuade the Russian Minister from these windy enterprises, with which, however, now we say that we will have nothing whatever to do. Austria has just declared war on Belgium under the pretext that the latter has given her support to France and the British Empire. The appearance of this enemy neither sur-prises nor discourages our neighbour. Their gallant Queen has left Antwerp this morning for England to take her children there, but she will return in a few days. She saw M. Klobukowski before her departure and told him that she would never falter in her belief that final victory would lie with us.

"She spoke to me with much emotion", our Minister telegraphs, " of the acts of cruelty committed by the German armies on a quiet and inoffensive population, and in her own words ' Those who planned this war and are carrying it on are mad ; nothing but madness can explain such a horror '."

At the close of the day the amiable Roumanian Minister sends me a little word full of hope :

" M. le Président, I have just received from my wife a telegram dated yesterday from Bucharest in which she says ' The dispositions of which my letter speaks are developing ; the promise of money has been almost secured '. This was the arranged term for saying that the moment was approaching for us to take up the attitude which I so long for, you know what I mean. Votre tout dévoué LAHOVARY."

In the evening there is nothing to suggest that the German march on Paris has been arrested or slackened or that they have in any way altered their objective. According to headquarters, and especially according to the wireless between the German commands which we intercept, Bülow's Army, the Third and Fourth Armies are the only ones following up our men to the Haute Seine and the Aube. Klück's First Army is detailed to cover the right wing of the others towards Paris, to destroy the communications round the capital, to contain the troops in the fortified system and, if possible, to besiege them.

Our General Staff have been aware of this plan for some days and this is what has induced Joffre to insist on the Government leaving Paris. But this morning one of our cavalry officers, reconnoitring to the north-west of Compiègne, was surprised to learn that Von Klück's advance guard, instead of continuing to march straight on Paris, has suddenly turned off and is heading towards Meaux. We know nothing of this here ; still less do we know that this deflection is Von Klück's own idea. The independent retreat of the English had led him to hope that he would be able to turn the left wing of our army, attack it from the rear, put it to flight and then march back in triumph on Paris. Von Klück is, however, reckoning without Maunoury's army, without Joffre, without Galliéni and without Foch, but his obsession will anyhow delay any danger to Paris ; this also we do not know, as we have been told nothing of what the officer, Captain Lepic, has found out. General Headquarters may have wished to verify the news, but if the Government had known of the change of direction on which Von Klück had seemingly determined, I should doubtless have been able to arrange for our departure from Paris to be postponed, and once it had been postponed it would never have taken place ; I should thus have been spared one of the saddest events of my life.

1st September.—I hear that M. Doumer, sometime President of the Chamber, is complaining rather sourly that no use has been made of his services. I ask him to come and see me and find him disposed to be very critical ; he is especially severe, not only on Messimy and Millerand, but on Joffre, and he says the Commander-in-Chief may be a very good engineer officer, but knows nothing of strategy and very little of tactics. If the Government leaves Paris he wants me to get for him some post about Galliéni, whom he greatly admires. I can only beg Millerand to do what he can for this rather disgruntled politician.

But what a fund of goodwill there is to draw upon ! All the authors want to do something, whether in or behind the firing-line. From Edmond Rostand comes a finely worded letter, the upshot of which is that he will be only too glad to do any secretarial work, however modest. Anatole France, who has swung from dilettante Nihilism to impassioned Chauvinism (though one does not know how long this will last), wants to serve as a private soldier. To-day Pierre Loti writes to me :

" For the last month, without venturing to address you directly, I have done all I can, but in vain, to try and secure some military post, however humble, so as to serve my country again, but I am always knocking up against some cut-and-dried regulations or against the prejudices of two or three lesser authorities who do not forgive me the name I bear.   I am, however, about to approach General Galliéni ; the Académie has this morning strongly repre- sented my case to him, and he seems to think it would be setting a good example if Pierre Loti were to risk his skin.   Would you be good enough to say a word to him, and perhaps another word to M. Augagneur, asking him not to turn me down ? ''

Of course I say the two words and Pierre Loti gets what he wants.   Other men of letters, historians, professors, scholars, philosophers, have joined up, not only to incite the country to a display alike of patience and energy, but to reply to the various slanders which some German pro- fessors have thought well to level against France.   No in- telligent person would think of belittling the great merits of German science.   But when German science lays down that the old legends of our Breton cycle had their origin in part on the right bank of the Rhine, when it is alleged that Gothic art was imported into France from Germany, or when, as to-day, it is gravely stated that the Empires of the Hohenzollern and the Habsburg are not responsible for the war, it may be well, in order to refute these foolish and truculent stories, that there should be in France men of science who also follow the dictates of their conscience.

I learn from Millerand and the liaison officers that we have again had to yield ground on our left, and that there- fore there is no immediate question of resuming the offensive. After a further talk on the telephone with Joffre, the War Minister considers that the departure of the Government and myself from Paris is indispensable and urgent ; he also does not know that Von Klück's army has swerved away from its former objective.   Millerand says that he will not take the responsibility for our remaining an hour longer than to-morrow evening, and that the presence of the Govern- ment in Paris is far too tempting a bait for the Germans ; he will consult Galliéni again, but he is sure that the Military Governor will agree with the Commander-in-Chief.   I still mean to raise objections to this, and shall bring up the matter again in Council.

The War Minister gives me details which are really heart-rending. All our hopes are shattered, and we are in full retreat all along the line ; Maunoury's army is falling back on the fortified camp, and to reinforce him the 4th Corps, which is north of Verdun, may be brought back to Paris.

Millerand has met Lord Kitchener and Sir John French at the British Embassy ; they had both come to see him, and I suggested that, if possible, they should both see Joffre, which is what Kitchener would like. But Sir John, who is fretfully intolerant of Kitchener's authority, and who is also eager, as regards Joffre, to preserve his independence of action, does not think that the rendezvous would be of any use, and as a matter of fact it might be difficult to bring it about without unduly interfering with our Commander-in-Chief's arrangements. Sir John now proposes that the English and the French should only retire, for the time, on the Marne, in which case he will agree for his troops to entrench themselves round Meaux. But he asks in return that Joffre should send a force to defend the Seine below Paris, and that he should reinforce our left wing. The Field-Marshal is, not unreasonably, greatly concerned as to not being cut off from the sea. Joffre's plan is, so far, different. He proposes that the Sixth Army, falling back on Paris, with a cavalry division composed of what remains of Sordet's corps, should be detailed to defend the fortified camp against any German attack ; the other armies are to pivot to the east—from north-east to south-west—until the Fifth Army is completely detached, when all the troops would be able to operate together. Millerand, not being able to get direct telephonic communication with Joffre, who has moved his headquarters to Bar-sur-Aube, has sent an officer to him to tell him what Sir John wants and will agree to, and to beg him to try to come to terms with the English.

While more German aeroplanes are flying over Paris, Colonel Pénélon arrives with a gloomy face and only the ghost of a smile ; there is very much less optimism at Bar-sur-Aube than there was at Vitry-le-François. They are trying to disentangle Lanrezac's army, which is being hunted by nine German corps on its retreat to the Marne ; the movement is not yet over, and there is doubt as to whether it will succeed. We are hard pressed, and the Germans are trying to turn us westwards ; they seem for the moment to be neglecting Paris, and so far have only detached one corps to harry Maunoury's army, which from to-day is being put at Galliéni's disposal, and which consists of four reserve divisions and part of the 7th Corps. The Military Governor has also been promised the 45th Division, coming from Algiers, and the 4th Corps, and with these, Joffre considers, he ought to be able to look after Paris.

But the Commander-in-Chief does not think he can accept Sir John's proposal for the British army to halt on the Marne on condition that the Basse Seine should be defended by our left wing. He prefers that the French army, except the men in the fortified camp, should all fall back and, if necessary, should be led as far as the Haute Seine, making them pivot on their right ; he hopes in this way eventually to resume a general offensive. Except for this difference of plan, Sir John French will continue to co-operate loyally with us, and his troops were heavily engaged yesterday, fighting splendidly and taking ten of the enemy's guns. Millerand urges Joffre to establish a permanent liaison between the two headquarters, and also to keep in mind the necessity of defending Paris, a necessity which is alike moral, political and international. But, Colonel Pénélon says again to me, the Commander-in-Chief still thinks that to give battle now with all our troops, or even with any portion of them, will be a very difficult matter. Even if we were only to set going a fraction of the forces, there might ensue a general engagement, when our Fifth Army would be in a very parlous state, as the slightest check might easily be transformed into a regular rout. Joffre's general orders will therefore run something thus :

"In spite of the tactical successes gained by our Third, Fourth and Fifth Armies in the region of the Meuse and at Guise, the enveloping movement of the enemy on the left wing of the

Fifth Army, not having been altogether checked by the English
and by our Sixth Army, all the troops at disposal must pivot on
their right. As soon as the Fifth Army is secure from the threat
on its left, the Third, Fourth and Fifth Armies will resume a
combined offensive."

Despite the stream of disasters which is submerging
France and flowing Paris-wards, the European Chanceries
have to receive attention. Just when we are offering
Turkey a guarantee for the integrity of her territory, Sazonoff
with his ubiquitous diplomacy, wants to promise the Enos-
Midia line to Bulgaria. He would wish, as we do, that
Japan should send troops to Europe, and he has begged
Paléologue to suggest this to the Japanese Ambassador in
St. Petersburg, who is a real friend to France, but for the
moment Japan only wants to fight in Asia, and the only
help she is willing to give is to sell us 50,000 rifles and
20,000,000 cartridges, whereas we are asking for 600,000
rifles. Sazonoff, more usefully, expends some part of his
ingenuity in trying to find a formula under which Russia,
England and France would agree not to sign any separate
peace. Meanwhile the armies of the Grand Duke Nicholas
are fighting with many ups and downs. Nothing decisive
has happened in Galicia, and in Eastern Prussia the investment of Königsberg is pretty well over. In Western
Prussia, south of Osteroda, the Russian troops on the 27th
and 28th of August were badly checked, although this so
far has been kept secret. The Germans having mustered in
this region all the troops they could lay hands on, and having
reinforced them with the garrisons and heavy artillery from
the Vistula, attacked two Russian Army Corps and inflicted
very heavy losses on them.

From a Berne telegram I hear that brave little Montmédy, one of the towns which I have for so long represented
in the Senate, has had to surrender after an ill-starred sortie
on the part of the garrison in which the Commandant was
made prisoner. Once again I feel that the sufferings in the
Meuse are reflected in the sufferings of our whole country.

In order to appreciate the effect on neutral countries of
our perpetual reverses, one has only to read the reports of

our representatives in Constantinople, Sofia, Bucharest and Athens. Bompard telegraphs to-day :

" The German Ambassador has substituted a very graceful tone for his former haughty manners in dealing with his Italian colleague. The Italian Ambassador, who at the beginning paid very little attention to Baron Wangenheim's advances, now lends a more and more willing ear to them as the German army moves on towards Paris. It would seem that in order to bring Italy to her side, Germany has only to dangle in front of her what she covets in respect of Tunis."

This is the moment which Clemenceau chooses to publish in the *Homme Libre* articles no doubt well intended, the serious effect of which he scarcely calculates. To-day there comes a telegram from Casablanca in which General Lyautey complains bitterly that Clemenceau's remarks about the despatch of Territorials to Morocco are demoralising our troops :

" The violent and ill - informed campaign conducted by Clemenceau at the time of our Taza operations had already prejudiced discipline and my authority. but I had hoped he would anyhow call a truce during the war. It will be impossible for me to exercise my command and to continue to carry out so heavy and so thankless a task if so well-known an individual continues to propagate here disorder and indiscipline. I would therefore formally beg the Government, to whom I am responsible, to stop, as they can under martial law, this campaign which is so injurious to the spirit of the Territorials."

The Government think that unless Clemenceau keeps himself under better control they will be obliged to impose a censorship on him, and it is very unlikely that his unbounded sense of independence will bow to an abnormal régime.

2nd September.—I have asked my good friend, Mr. Myron Herrick, who is still functioning as Ambassador, to call at the Élysée ; I am anxious to tell him how sorry I am to bid good-bye to so staunch and constant a friend of France and to thank him for the way in which he has stood up for the rights of an outraged people ; the tears are in his eyes when he comes into the room, and his face under its attractive thatch of crinkly hair is all puckered up. He means to stay in Paris till his work is finished, and if necessary he will protect our monuments, including museums, under the Star-Spangled Flag, and he will do everything in his power to save the inhabitants here from annoyances and injury. I assure him that France will not lay down her arms, whatever happens, until victory is secured, and I can hope that his presence in Paris will cause the principles of civilised war to be recognised. I agree with him that historical monuments and works of art are in a sense international property and are under the custody of humanity at large One can hope that so long as Mr. Herrick is in Paris the enemies of France will observe the usages of war, and more than this one does not ask. Anyhow, Paris will be defended by her outer forts and especially by the valour of the army within the fortified system.[1]

One last effort I make in Council, anyhow, to postpone the departure of the Government, which would involve my own going away. I could not remain constitutionally *découvert*, and if separated from the Ministers I should be deprived of any means of action.

Colonel Pénélon has certainly said that for the moment the Germans seem to be giving Paris the go-by, but Millerand, in chorus with Joffre and Galliéni, again declares that the hour has come for our leaving. Von Klück was at Compiègne yesterday, and will be at Senlis and Chantilly to-day ; Paris will shortly be under the guns of the enemy.

Maunoury's army is in position on the north front of the fortified camp, with headquarters at Tremblay, and the presence of the Government in the capital interferes with military arrangements. The Cabinet must yield to the arguments which the War Minister urges, and I can only give way with the best grace possible.

It is arranged that we are to leave to-night for Bordeaux, where Millerand has already prepared our lodgings. I dislike the idea of going away by night ; it would have been preferable to leave by day in full view of the people from whom we are perforce to be separated, but the military authority controls the railways, and martial law is incumbent on the

---

[1] Paper relating to foreign relations.

President of the Republic as on the humblest citizen. I can only bow my head and agree to get into the train as I am told. Madame Poincaré begs and entreats that she may remain to go on with her Red Cross duties and other works, but the Cabinet, on Viviani's urgent demand, determines that the wives of Ministers shall accompany their husbands, and I cannot ask for an exception to be made in my case. On hearing this, my wife burst into tears. I have had the courage to be a run-away myself, but she would have loved to let Paris know that in leaving her behind I was not giving way altogether ; even this little consolation is denied us. Viviani shows me a manifesto which he has prepared, and which he wants the Council to see before having it placarded ; it is to explain why we are leaving and is a call to the country. I find the wording a little theatrical, and I ask Viviani to write something a little shorter and less flamboyant. Eventually we agree on a text which runs :

" In order to watch over the national safety, the public authorities are obliged to remove themselves for the moment from Paris. Under the command of a famous General the French army, with all courage and keenness, will defend the capital and its patriotic population against the invader. But the war must go on at the same time over the rest of the land. . . . To fight and to endure must be the motto of the Allied armies. . . . It is for the Government to direct this stubborn resistance, and everywhere Frenchmen will be afoot on behalf of their liberty. But to give to this formidable fighting all that is required it is indispensable that the Government should remain free to act. At the urgent request of the military authorities the Government will therefore for the moment transfer their residence to a place where they can remain in close and constant touch with the rest of the country. The Government do not leave Paris without having insured to the margin of their means the defence of the town and of the fortified camp. There is no need to recommend resolution and coolness to the admirable people who day by day show that they have risen to the height of their great duties. . . . A nation which refuses to perish and which, in order to live, does not shrink from suffering and sacrifice, is sure to conquer."

Galliéni will issue a proclamation, the pithy eloquence of which will compare favourably with ours ; he will simply say that he has received orders to defend Paris, and that he will carry out those orders to the last. To satisfy M. Dubost the Government decides to close the Parliamentary Session, which the Constitution gives them a right to do.

During the day Joffre drafts a new General Order. He confirms yesterday's instructions, but as Lanrezac's army is not yet disentangled, he does not allude to any immediate arrest of our retreat or of a general offensive. He even foresees that, when we have ceased to retire on the Seine and the Yonne, our troops can be supplied from the depôts. He recalls the conditions which still govern his decision, that all the Army Corps should be in their right places and that the English army should be ready to fight alongside them.[1] But as he hopes that these conditions will soon be realised, he recommends everyone to direct their energies towards final victory. Joffre is not yet certain of Von Klück's line of march, but this seems to be more and more obvious, and this morning a scout, Captain Fagolde, has found on the body of a German officer who was killed yesterday a note in which the change of direction is laid down. The decisive hour is at hand, and it is in this hour that we are condemned to leave Paris. It is no use thinking about it, but one's

---

[1] At 2 A.M. on the 1st of September Lord Kitchener hurried to France to dissuade Sir John French from his intention to retreat from the front line. Before leaving Paris that evening the Secretary of State wrote to the Commander-in-Chief :

"*September* 1, 7.30 P.M.

" MY DEAR FRENCH—After thinking over our conversation to-day I think I am giving the sense of it in the following telegram to Government I have just sent :

" ' French's troops are now engaged in the fighting line, where he will remain conforming to the movements of the French army, though at the same time acting with caution to avoid being in any way unsupported on his flanks.'

" I feel sure you will agree that the above represents the conclusions we came to ; but in any case, until I can communicate with you further in answer to anything you may wish to tell me, please consider it as an instruction.

" By being in the fighting line you of course understand I mean dispositions of your troops in contact with, though possibly behind, the French as they were to-day ; of course you will judge as regards their position in this respect.

" I was very pleased to meet you to-day and hope all will go well, and that Joffre and you will make the best plans possible for the future, which you will, I hope, communicate to me. I leave the first thing to-morrow morning.—Yours very truly, K."

grief and humiliation increases with every minute, and by a coincidence, in which one can scarcely help seeing the irony of Fate, the day on which we are leaving our capital is the day which our Russian Allies have chosen to re-christen theirs. A ukase signed by the Emperor has declared that the town of St. Petersburg shall henceforth be called Petrograd. Paléologue says that in abolishing a name which has given so much *éclat* to Russian history, the Emperor has only been inspired by the popular feeling which has pledged itself to implacable hatred of Germany. This way of expressing hatred does seem a little puerile, and one wonders whether, in order not to be suspected of pro-Germanism, we shall have to change the names of Strasbourg, Cabourg, Bourg en Bresse and all the other Bourgs in France.

The hateful moment has come, and we pass along darkened streets to the Gare d'Auteuil, which is very dimly lighted itself. All the Ministers with their wives and the chief officials are on the platform, and the whole concourse mournfully suggests an official exodus, but the exodus is due to military discipline, and through the long night journey our special train constantly stops to allow the passage of troops who are going north, or the convoys of wounded who are proceeding in the opposite direction.

3rd September.—We are back, in mournful order, in the beautiful town where last year Madame Poincaré and I spent such happy and sunny hours. The *vivats* of the people, which, in 1913, sounded so delightful in our ears, are only heard in low tones to-day, but even so I find them out of place, and they make one feel uncomfortable. We alight at the Prefecture where we were lodged last year, but now, in view of a prolonged stay and in order to make room for General Duparge and a little army of officers and officials, there has had to be a regular, and very hurried, *déménagement*, and I am much distressed by all the trouble we have caused.

Before leaving yesterday I begged Colonel Pénélon to telegraph to me one of three coded phrases : (*a*) Lanrezac's army disengaged ; (*b*) Lanrezac's army not disengaged, but not in danger ; (*c*) Lanrezac's army in danger. He first telegraphs to me (*b*), and it would seem that our Fifth Army has not yet succeeded in freeing itself, and I wonder whether it has not suffered a great many more casualties in its painful retreat. But a little later comes (*a*), and one of Joffre's two conditions for calling a halt to the retreat and resuming the offensive has been fulfilled. It only remains for Sir John to co-operate without exacting the transfer of part of the Allied troops to the bank of the Basse Seine. At the end of the day Viviani, Briand and Millerand tell me that a Cabinet Council has been held at the Hôtel de Ville ; Galliéni has telegraphed to the War Minister that all is quiet in Paris and that Maunoury's army has definitely taken up its position. Delcassé has reported a complete Russian victory in Galicia, and Sir Edward Grey has told Paul Cambon that it is impossible to comply with Sazonoff's wish to ask Japan to give us military help in Europe, but that he is insisting that the Tokio Government shall send a squadron to the Mediterranean. Viviani, who yesterday made me sign the closure decree, now thinks we need not promulgate it in spite of the promise made to the President of the Senate ; Briand and Millerand rightly say that if the Chambers remain in session, even without any active work, certain individuals will find favourable soil in which to sow their intrigues. It is therefore decided that the decree shall be published, and I tell Viviani that we ought to have, here as in Paris, a daily Council of the Ministers under my Presidency.

4th September.—The 4th of September . . . on this day in 1870 France was invaded as she is now by German armies, and had just been beaten at Sédan. Paris was not yet threatened, but the news of the defeat sufficed to provoke a revolution. To-day, in spite of the departure of the Government and the approach of the enemy, Paris remains perfectly calm, and the nation is united to support the men who have the heavy task of directing affairs. Ribot, Viviani and Millerand propose in Council an arrangement which would enable us to buy in Spain a large quantity of rifles. As King Alfonso has ordered his friend M. de Léon to accompany us here and to hold himself at our disposition, I beg this delightful diplomatist to come and see us and tell us whether our proposal could be taken seriously. He thinks that it would be impossible to supply the numbers we suggest, but he hopes that the King will authorise a sale of lesser quantities ; he will start for Madrid at once and find out. Joffre has telegraphed that the Germans do not seem yet to have given up their idea of turning our left wing ; their cavalry has reached Château Thierry and has been in contact with Lanrezac's army, but our troops are retiring in good order on the positions chosen for them. Galliéni telegraphs that everything is all right, and adds that a favourable occasion may arise which he will seize. We ask one another what the exact meaning of this cryptic phrase may be ; Galliéni may very possibly be preparing to attack the enemy's flank. We do not know yet that this very morning the Military Governor, informed by the Air Force as to Von Klück's deviation, has advised Maunoury to push out his cavalry reconnaissances between the road to Chantilly and the Marne, to move this afternoon towards the enemy's flank, and to start to-morrow a general movement to the east of the fortified camp. Nor do we know that Galliéni at the same time has telephoned to Joffre that the dispositions of the enemy seem to favour an immediate offensive on our part. News trickles in, and we hear that Joffre has rushed off to see Sir John at Melun and has asked him not to make his co-operation conditional on a useless defence of the Basse Seine ; and having received an unconditional promise of immediate collaboration he returned at full speed to his headquarters and said quietly to his subordinates : " Well, gentlemen, we are going to fight on the Marne."

Galliéni has also been to Melun, and this evening has received a telegram from the English headquarters confirming the promise of support for to-morrow's preparations.[1] Early in the afternoon he has given orders to Maunoury to be on the move to-morrow on the right bank of the Marne and to bring up his front *à la hauteur* of Meaux. Without knowing all the details, the War Minister thinks he knows

[1] See *Galliéni* by M. P. B. Gheusi (Fasquelle). *La Gloire de Galliéni*, by the same author (Albin Michel). " Notes du Général Galliéni," published under the title of *Mémoires*.

enough to draft a communiqué which, among other important items, contains this :

" The Germans are leaving aside Paris and the Sixth Army, and are continuing their movement southwards to the Marne, which the First German Army has reached at La Ferté-sous-Jouarre at eleven o'clock. The Second German Army, marching from north to south, is equally making for the Marne, and has reached Château Thierry. The Guards' Corps has received orders to continue towards the Marne after Rheims was taken about noon. The Third German Army has captured Rheims; the 12th and 19th German Corps are following General Foch's [1] detachment in its retreat."

In order to have a better general view of the impending battle the Commander-in-Chief has decided to shift his headquarters to-morrow from Bar - sur - Aube to Châtillon-sur-Seine. His battle order runs :

" Advantage must be taken of the rash move of the First German Army to concentrate on this army the efforts of the Allied armies of the left. All arrangements will be made during the 5th to begin the attack on the 6th. The arrangements to be carried out on the 7th of September will be (a) all the disponable forces of the Sixth Army to the north-east of Meaux will be ready to cross the Ourcq between Lisy-sur-Ourcq and May-en-Multien in the direction of Château Thierry ; any of the 1st Cavalry Corps in the neighbourhood are to be handed over to General Maunoury for this operation ; (b) the British army, drawn up on the Changis-Coulommiers front, will be ready to attack towards Montmirail ; (c) the Fifth Army (under Franchet D'Esperey who has just succeeded Lanrezac) inclining slightly to the left will be in position on the Courtacon-Esternay-Sézanne front ready to attack north and south ; the 2nd Cavalry Corps will connect the English army with the Fifth French Army ; (d) the Ninth Army (Foch) will cover the right of the Fifth Army, holding the southern debouchments of the St. Gond marches and sending part of the force on to the plateau north of Sézanne ; the offensive will be taken by the different armies on the 6th of September."

5th September.—Viviani reports to the Council he has just seen our Military Attaché at Tokio, who thinks that Japan

---

[1] Foch's force was the one constituted on the 28th of August, and is to become the new, Ninth, Army detailed to strengthen what might be a rather feeble resistance in the centre of the immense line whose methodical retirement Joffre has been able to ensure.

will willingly send us several Army Corps, while our consul, one M. Régnault, telegraphs to us that he has incidentally raised the question with the Japanese Prime Minister, who did not appear at all surprised and quite smiled on the idea. Delcassé is deputed to ask whether the British Government persists in its incredulity on this point, or rather whether they remain unwilling to bring their Asiatic Ally to Europe. Millerand gives the Council all the military details which Pénélon has brought us ; the liaison with the English is closely established and Colonel Lerond will understudy Colonel Huguet, who is attached to Sir John French's Staff, and thus the two Commands will be in close touch. Joffre has willingly recognised the necessity of keeping Sir John French more closely informed, and as a matter of fact the British army has not retired so far as was feared, and is in position south of Melun, between Paris and the left wing of our fighting forces ; General Lanrezac, who, Joffre thinks, is tired out, has been replaced in his command by de Franchet de l'Esperey and placed at the disposal of Galliéni. Our armies are entrenched from west to east on the line drawn in yesterday's Order, that is to say, considerably north of the line which the day before yesterday Joffre thought he would be obliged to take up.

Galliéni telephones from Paris that he will certainly attack the enemy to-morrow all along the front of the Sixth Army ; the detraining of the 4th Corps in the fortified camp is delayed by the block on the railway line and will not be complete till the 7th. But to-day there has been partial fighting, and German patrols have fired on our 276th Infantry regiment, which, without proper scouting, was moving out of the village of Villeroi. Our troops, when attacked, threw themselves on the enemy and lost several Regular and Reserve officers, among others, alas ! Charles Péguy. The 55th and 56th (Moroccan) divisions have nevertheless taken Montgé, Plessis-aux-Bois and Charny.

While the Sixth Army is thus preparing for the great battle which is imminent, an unexpected question crops up. The War Minister had found it impossible to agree to my request as to giving M. Doumer some post on Galliéni's Staff, but Doumer went direct to the Military Governor, with whom he is on very friendly terms, and the latter told Millerand yesterday that, unless he was absolutely forbidden to do so, he intended to give Doumer some civil administrative work. Millerand has told Galliéni that as he is master in his own fortress, the Government will not interfere with any appointment he makes, but several of the Ministers are up against Galliéni's decision, which seems to limit the powers of the Government, and are also urging that it is unwise to confer administrative duties on a prominent politician alongside the Prefect of Police and the Prefect of the Seine, whose prerogatives will be thereby restricted. Millerand agrees with his colleagues and telephones to Galliéni, only to hear from a Staff Captain that the Military Governor might very likely resign if he is not allowed to call on Doumer's services. Viviani, who had already sent one telegram to Galliéni to beg him to give up his idea, now telegraphs again :

" If you consider it indispensable to call upon the individual whom you mention, the Government can only leave you the responsibility for doing so, but they desire that the individual in question shall exercise no authority over the Prefects, who must remain under your immediate orders."

Some of the Ministers think this an insufficient precaution, and that two Ministers should be sent to Paris for duty, but their objections are overruled; after all, if the German armies have followed Von Klück's deflection and have given Paris the go-by, it is perhaps because all the Ministers have left the capital ; and anyhow, as the Government has consented to leave, it only remains to give the Military Governor a perfectly free hand.

Delcassé early in the afternoon receives the text of the declaration which has been signed this morning by the Allies at the Foreign Office :

" The British, French and Russian Governments mutually undertake not to conclude any separate peace in the course of the present war. The three Governments agree that, when the occasion arises of discussing the terms of peace, neither of the Allied Powers shall submit peace conditions without preliminary agreement with each of the other two Allies."

This declaration is published in London to-day; no doubt we bind ourselves, but we also bind the others, and nothing but treason or prevarication can split us. If our own peace conditions are not accepted, we reserve to ourselves to discuss what the others propose, and as we know that our own conditions will be moderate and reasonable, and as we have no thought of any annexations but only of simple restitutions, the advantages of the agreement outweigh the disadvantages.

In the afternoon comes M. Dubost, who seems now fairly easy in his mind and whose *râtelier* has resumed its normal appearance; the President of the Senate, who is really one of the best fellows in the world, has made up, without any further display of temper, his mind as regards the decree of closure. More important, there is to hand a telegram from Joffre who considers the strategic situation excellent. He contemplates resuming the offensive to-morrow, but says frankly that the loss of the big battle he is going to deliver will be very serious indeed for the country, and he hopes that the British army will help him to their last man. He seems to have some slight doubts on this point and begs us to bring diplomacy into play; Delcassé will see Sir Francis Bertie, who has followed us to Bordeaux, and will telegraph to Paul Cambon to make representations in London.

The Generalissimo does not tell us of the complementary and precise instructions which he has sent this morning to the Fourth and Third Armies nor of the fine appeal which he has made to all the troops:

" To-morrow, 6th September, our armies of the left will make a frontal and flank attack on the First and Second German Armies. Our Fourth Army, halting in its southward march, will make head against the enemy, conforming its movement to that of the Third Army which, debouching north of Revigny, will attack westwards. The Third Army will debouch westwards to attack the enemy's left flank marching to the west of the Argonne and will conform to the Fourth Army. At a moment when a battle, on which depends the safety of the country, is to be delivered, it is well to remind everyone that there is no longer a question of looking back; every effort must be made to attack and fling back the enemy. Any unit which cannot advance further

must, at whatever cost, retain ground which has been taken and
perish rather than yield ground.   In the present circumstances
anything like weakness must be banished."

Thus all our armies, from end to end of the line, are
going to carry out a vast manœuvre, and each wing will
have to try and envelop the enemy.   On the left the Fifth
Army will attack northwards, while the Sixth Army with the
British forces will move eastwards on the flank of the German
troops, the one in the direction of Château Thierry and the
other towards Montmirail.   The Ninth Army, under General
Foch, will have to cover the movements of the Fifth Army,
and will have its right behind the St. Gond marshes with its
left north of Sézanne.   On the right the Fourth Army will
try and contain the Germans in front of them, while the
Third Army, facing westwards, will attack them on their
left flank.   If the operation succeeds the German army will
thus be caught in the jaws of an enormous vice, while the
intermediary line will have to resist a great general attack.
We are going to play our part for all we are worth in what
will perhaps be the greatest battle humanity has ever known.

CHAPTER VI

6th September.—To-day from the Meuse to the Ourcq there will be the mighty clash of arms. Being so far away adds to one's anxiety, and my own thoughts turn to the grassy valley of the Ornain where so much of my childhood was spent, and where our Third Army is now ordered to deal with the enemy. In his instructions of the 2nd September Joffre had foreseen that, in order to follow the general retreat, Sarrail might have to fall back, not only on Revigny and Bar-le-Duc, but eventually on Joinville, and thus the greater part of the Department of the Meuse will have fallen into German hands. We have let the enemy take the great Observatory at Montfauçon, cross the forest of Hesse, and remount the valley of the Aire to Beauzée. Our Third Army, which has to operate on the right wing, is therefore obliged to stretch itself from Verdun to Revigny, which becomes the central point of liaison with the Fourth Army and the hinge of the French front. Sarrail has in front of him the Crown Prince, to whom of course there will be confided the flower of the German Army, and if the German march is not arrested to-day, it will be all over with my birthplace.

The new Spanish Ambassador, the Marquis de Valtierra, brings me his credentials after the rather curious episode regarding his predecessor. On the 2nd September King Alfonso, having heard of the possible departure of the French Government, telegraphed to M. de Villa-Urrutia : " I order Your Excellency to remain in Paris whatever happens ".

At the same time the King desired his friend, M Quinonès de Léon, to accompany us to Bordeaux, and Vila-Urrutia, who is a very false friend of France, told his Government that he had come to pay me his respects before we left Paris, which is not true, and that he had said to me : " I am sorry not to be free to follow you. And I am also sorry that my remaining in Paris may be interpreted as an act of politeness to the German Emperor." This fantastic story, which was communicated to the King in Council, surprised as much as it angered the Ministers on account of the twist which M. de Villa-Urrutia tried to give to the King's decision. His Majesty sent word to our Ambassador that " he hoped sincerely that his feeling of great affection for France and esteem in which he held the First Magistrate in the Republic would prevent our taking seriously the silly and senile insinuations of the Marquis de Villa-Urrutia." The latter was at once relieved of his duties, and the Marquis Valtierra, perhaps in remembrance of his having been attached to me when I was in Madrid, has been appointed Ambassador. He is kind enough to tell me this himself, and in my little speech to him I can say truly that I know his feeling for France reflects precisely the feeling of Spain, and that they are in perfect harmony with those of the King himself, who has never ceased to give France proof of his faithful friendship. " France," I could add, " never wanted war and has done all she can to avoid it, but she has now determined to prosecute, with her Allies, the war until victory has been secured and the right has been restored."

Delcassé has heard from Sir Francis Bertie that Lord Kitchener has telegraphed to Sir John French in the terms which Joffre desired ; the British Government want to know when the operations will begin, and we reply that they are beginning this morning. Maunoury's army is at grips with the enemy ; Galliéni telegraphs to Millerand that things are going well and that Sir John French, primed by Lord Kitchener, is giving us all the support he can. Meanwhile Millerand tells us that a carrier pigeon, flying from Maubeuge to Paris, has brought the dreary news that three forts have been smashed, that all the positions are untenable, and that in the town, besieged and bombarded by heavy artillery, the infantry is powerless and the situation is very critical. There are 25,000 men in Maubeuge, of whom several thousands are Regular soldiers ; what would it be if troops were shut up in the old fortifications of Paris ?

M. Paul Deschanel, who is kind enough to come several times a day to the Prefecture, declares that Bordeaux, invaded by Parisians of every kind, has now all the appearance of a pleasure resort, and that some of the Ministers, whom he refuses to name, are setting a very bad example by dining with actresses in public restaurants. No whisper of these scandals has reached my ears, and in the silent seclusion of the Prefecture I know nothing of what is going on in the town. Is it possible that at such a moment Frenchmen can so forget themselves ? The whole future of the country depends on what is happening to-day on the Ourcq and on the Marne ; this morning the Sixth Army has attacked vigorously from Bouillancy towards Acy-en-Multien so as to try and envelop the enemy's right wing, while Sarrail does what he can to make things unpleasant for their left. How can anyone think of anything else than of this far-off fighting ?

7th September.—The liaison officer, Commandant Guillaume, reports that General Joffre is very satisfied so far, that the battle is being fought under the best strategic conditions, but that now it is a question of tactics, and in the last four weeks tactics have too often cheated the hopes of strategy. The Commander-in-Chief reckons that we enjoy, on our left, the weight of nine Corps against seven, and that Maunoury, backed by Franchet d'Esperey and the English, will be able to make a valuable offensive, while at the other end Sarrail will attack towards Argonne. In the centre the Fourth and Ninth Armies have been ordered for the moment to stand still and stand fast. A little later it is known that the 2nd German Corps has had to recross the Grand Morin, that the enemy advance guards have broken back and that our Fifth Army is advancing. Galliéni is asking for 75's and machine guns ; Millerand hesitates as to this ; the Sixth Army has indeed had hard fighting, having taken, lost and

re-taken Basey, Etavigny and other places.   There is no
news of General d'Amade's army, which was to throw itself
against Von Klück's flank and rear.

Of German troops left in the Nord and in the Pas-de-
Calais there are very few, and there is not a single German
soldier at Lille, where two French machine guns arrived
yesterday from Dunkirk to receive a warm greeting.   Joffre
is surprised and annoyed that advantage has not been taken
of this, but d'Amade's army seems to have become a
phantom force.

Doumergue has to report that things are not going so
well in Chari and the Cameroons, where our troops have had
some very sharp fighting, with a good many officers killed.
Germany, who hopes to suck substantial Colonial advantages
from the war, is trying to add African to her European
successes.

During the day come several telephone messages from
Joffre and Galliéni ; the enemy seems to be falling back,
stealing away and refusing to fight. The two Generals
rather fear that they are trying to out-manœuvre us, but
they are determined that the Germans shall not be allowed
to fight at their own option.

At a little dinner this evening in honour of M. and
Madame Bascou, who have so kindly given up their rooms
in the Prefecture to us, Viviani and Briand tell me they are
very much concerned about Delcassé and wonder whether
he is not ill.   He does not seem, so they say, to be *au courant*
with what is going on, and in Council he simply buries himself in his telegrams.   Delcassé has never at any time been
very prodigal of explanations, and even in 1912, when he
was Minister of Marine, he used often to surprise us by his
obstinate silence.   But, anyhow, one gathered then by his
few and far-between remarks that he was thoroughly posted
in what was going on and that he was entirely master
of his department.   To-day he is more silent than ever,
and when occasionally he does speak he seems to lose the
thread of his thoughts.   Viviani and Briand regret that
Doumergue should have been so forward to give him his
place, and I, who have the greatest regard for Delcassé,

must admit that I find him rather under the weather, although I am quite unable to discover what is the matter with him.

8th September.—The news is not bad, and Joffre has telegraphed to Galliéni that the German offensive has stopped altogether and that on our front and on our left we have gained ground. It would seem that the First German Army has fallen back before the English and ourselves, and that their 2nd Active Corps and their 4th Reserve Corps have been pushed back to the Ourcq, while our left wing, moving on, has taken a good many prisoners and machine guns. The German heavy artillery seem to have run short of high explosive, and are using ordinary shell. The 7th Division which Joffre has sent to Galliéni arrived in Paris yesterday, and to get the men as quickly as possible to the Sixth Army, whose left wing is seriously threatened, the Military Governor requisitioned hundreds of taxi-cabs, whose civilian chauffeurs willingly consented to drive them, and have conveyed the troops to Gagny and Tremblay-les-Gonesse. The wireless messages we have intercepted indicate that the enemy are very tired and not a little disordered, and that round Chantilly the French cavalry is warding off any attack on Paris. The Cornulier-Lucienière Division, which has been incessantly engaged since the 5th of September, has been ordered to get in contact, on the Ourcq, with the rear of the enemy, and to advance as far as possible across the forests of Retz and Villers-Cotterets. Unfortunately, there is some little friction between the English and French Commanders-in-Chief. Joffre thinks that Kitchener, as a consequence of our diplomatic appeal, has given Sir John rather too peremptory orders which have wounded the *amour-propre* of the Field-Marshal, who is inclined to be very " touchy " ; to calm him down Joffre has begged Millerand to convey, through the British War Minister, renewed congratulations to Sir John and his army, congratulations which indeed are richly deserved.

By another intercepted wireless we hear of the fall, which was all too probable, of Maubeuge. Independently of the grave check which the capture of this place means, the raising of the siege will liberate two German army corps, who will be hurried to the front on the Marne.

We can only rely on our armies in the field to ward off this near danger, and in view of this future fighting Millerand is considering the formation of a second line army, for which youths of eighteen and men up to fifty-six years old will be called up, but for this guns, rifles and ammunition will be required ; we have only 200 75's in reserve, and there are only fifty not being used in the zone of the armies and these will be immediately required ; fifty batteries of 75's are on order, but the factories require four months to finish the first eight. All this is quite insufficient for the requirements of the Field Artillery, and in respect to heavy guns we are almost barren. I have told Millerand that I do not think the armament officials are sufficiently alive to these shortages ; Millerand, on principle, defends his subordinates energetically, but he fully shares my anxieties. He hopes to be able to buy batteries in Portugal and Spain, and 1400 rifles of the '86 pattern are being turned out daily, a figure which will be increased after the end of September. We expect 50,000 rifles from Japan, and at St. Étienne they will be able to transform every day 1000 1874 rifles into the 1886 model. All this is very far from what we really require. The grievous lack of material, which through indiscretion has leaked out, is serving as a pretext, in social and political quarters, for a new fit of " defeatism ". Sir Francis Bertie is very much put about, and is disposed to pessimism as regards our military operations. He even said to Ribot to-day that Joffre's plans were wrong, that the Commander-in-Chief didn't know what he wanted, and that if he, Sir Francis, were in his place . . . Who would guess that the Ambassador conceals under the embroidered uniform of an irreproachable diplomat the vocation of a soldier ? But perhaps after all he is only the smiling interpreter of Sir John French's spasm of ill-humour which Joffre is trying to dissipate. M. Albert Thomas has come from Paris with eyes flashing through his eye-glass and his hair tumbling about his forehead. He has found a regular staff of civilians in uniform around Galliéni, and he says that the *Guerre*

Sociale, directed by Gustave Hervé, has a friend in M. Lichtenberger, Paul Doumer's secretary; he suggests that the newspaper is going for the Ministers and the Parliamentarians and is beginning to advocate a sort of dictatorship. I foresee the moment when, frightened by this story, some of the Ministers, including Viviani, will be in dread of a military *coup d'état* or a pronunciamento. To my mind nothing is less likely, and Galliéni's character is a sufficient guarantee against any rash action, but what is really wanted is the return of the Government to Paris. . . .

The evening is an anxious one, and it is not till late at night that Joffre's telegrams are deciphered, and we know fighting is going on generally, but that we have been held up everywhere except on the Petit Morin. Maunoury has been violently counter-attacked and has had to retire at several points, and to prop him up Galliéni has sent the 62nd Reserve Division to Montgé and Dammartin. The telegrams end with an inexplicable phrase, " Attack on Nancy ". Maubeuge has certainly fallen and most of the garrison are prisoners, but 600 men are said to have escaped through Belgium and made their way to Lille. D'Amade's army has at last been found, but, composed as it is of Reservists and Territorials, there is considerable difficulty in reconstituting it. It transpires that too many regular officers are not making themselves felt as they ought to do with our reserve units, whom they regard with fine contempt and believe to be almost useless, although evidence goes to show that these are becoming more and more the vital substance of the armies. In Lille, Arras and Amiens there are only " details " of the Landwehr; we have allowed these towns to be occupied, and the people to be terrorised, and we have watched the Germans take away wounded prisoners and requisition provisions. A few thousand Frenchmen could have dealt with these scattered patrols; they could have harassed the rear of the enemy and co-operated effectively with the Belgians, who wanted 25,000 English or French soldiers to assure the land communications between Antwerp and France. All that the Government of the Republic can say is that we have no troops to dispose of, but that we will fight until the last inch of Belgian territory is evacuated. A division of reservists would be better consolation for our Belgian friends. A telegram from Lille announces that in some of the towns, and especially at Douai, the inhabitants of military age have been forced to appear before the German military authorities with their certificates, and have been sent under military escort to Aix - la - Chapelle. Even in the towns where they did not halt the Germans did not waste time, as they took away any men who might a little later on have served with the colours.

General d'Amade, having pulled his army together as well as possible, has been told to proceed to Beauvais.

9th September.—Hope comes back to us under the familiar features of Colonel Pénélon, who arrives radiant from General Headquarters at Châtillon-sur-Seine, and says that everything is, strategically, going well, and that the Germans are very much as we were after Charleroi, as they are outflanked by our two wings. If our tactics do not break down, the Germans will have to retire on the Marne and then on Rheims ; their plan of campaign will then have been altogether upset. The only fly in the ointment is the approaching arrival in the theatre of war of the two corps which were before Maubeuge and which no doubt can be railed to the front, as the Germans hold the Hirson-Soissons, and perhaps the direct Maubeuge-Soissons line. To cut their communications some of our cavalry, under General Conneau, are trying to get to Soissons, but a late telegram from Joffre says that Maunoury has still in front of him and on his left—that is, in the direction of Soissons—large enemy forces.

Our Fifth Army is moving slowly on towards the Petit Morin, which the 18th Corps has crossed, although the right has had to retire before the German Guards. The Ninth and Fourth Armies are doing well all along their front, and before our Third Army fighting is going on from Nubécourt to Vassincourt and Revigny ; Nubécourt, where my father and mother sleep side by side in our little cemetery; Revigny, where died my beloved grandmother, whose death was my first great grief. But what are these little personal sorrows in the immensity of public suffering ? Contrary to what we were led to suppose by yesterday's telegram, Nancy does not seem either to have fallen or even to be threatened.

Briand again offers to go and represent us for a few days in Paris, and Marcel Sembat has the same idea. The Government decide that they will make a voyage *de conserve*, partly to let the population know that we are looking after them and partly to examine certain questions, such as the evacuation of he *banlieue*, which Galliéni wants settled in view of the estment he still thinks possible, as also the relations of Paul Doumer with the Prefect of the Police, and, it is seriously suggested, the matter of the *Guerre Sociale* with M. Lichtenberger, as if it were not already certain that the former Revolutionary, M. Gustave Hervé, has been transformed into an ardent patriot by a war which is in no way tinged with Socialism.

M. de Léon has returned from Granja, where he has seen the King, who says that he would gladly sell us rifles, but that the Spanish army have scarcely enough for their own use. Trouble might suddenly break out any day either from Carlist movements or internal rioting, and this would have to be repressed. All the suggestions which reached Lefèvre and Millerand as to purchases in Spain have either melted into mirage or were of suspicious origin ; anyhow these prospective provisions have disappeared, and all we can do is to intensify our own manufactures.

In the afternoon Joffre telegraphs :

" Our action is proceeding all along the line and there has been fresh fighting round Montmirail against the enemy's rear-guard."

Rear-guard ! The word alone fills one with hope and suggests the enemy in full flight with our men following close on their heels. In the evening another telegram from headquarters. Our left wing has in the last three days advanced forty kilometres, the English have reached the Marne, and we hope to be there ourselves to-morrow, although we have had a slight set-back near La Ferté-Gaucher. Under the shadow

of Paris in the valley of the Ourcq Maunoury's army holds
good.   Altogether things seem satisfactory.

Somewhat comforted by this news, one can pay a little
more attention to what is going on outside France.   The
Russian armies are fighting with considerable success, and
have advanced west of Lemberg and along the Vistula.   Progress has also been made in Eastern Prussia, and they are
anyhow keeping busy a large number of Germans, who would
otherwise be on our front.   If they do not represent the
" steam-roller " which many newspapers dreamt about, they
are anyhow giving valuable help to France in a critical hour.
Germany apparently recognises that her great plan of attack
has boiled over, and Count Bernstorff at Washington is taking
a good deal of trouble to bring about American mediation.
He has sounded the Secretary of State, Mr. Bryan, who has
talked the thing over with President Wilson.

" I have not concealed from Mr. Bryan ", Jusserand telegraphs, " that the chances of success as regards intervention are
infinitesimal as each day swells the list of German crimes and adds
to the general indignation.   As at one moment he alluded to a
return to the *status quo*, I replied that we would accept this if the
Germans, in order to re-establish it, would restore life to our dead
soldiers."

With his accustomed versatility M. Sazonoff continues to
negotiate with the Balkan States, and telegram follows telegram, but the result is nil.

10th September.—Galliéni's telephone message this morning is not highly coloured :

" Situation not bad without being so good as we should like it
to be."

Joffre is more cheerful.   Maunoury did not do very much
yesterday, and even, after losing Betz and Nanteuil-le-Hau-
douin, had to retire on Silly le Leng.   But the First German
Army has been obliged to recross the Marne north of La
Ferté-sous-Jouarre and Château Thierry, while Bülow's
Second Army has crumpled up under Franchet d'Esperey's
blow.   The Third German Army has had to give ground to
our Ninth, under Foch, which had to ward off violent attacks

along a front of thirty-five kilometres. Foch was obliged at all cost to prevent the enemy from crossing the St. Gond marshes, and his men had to stand up against a succession of attacks ; his 11th Corps, which was the most highly tried of all, was obliged to evacuate Fère Champenoise, while the Ninth, threatened with being taken in reverse, was obliged to retire, allowing the enemy to get near the Château de Mondement, whose old tower dominates the plain and which is the key of the marshes. In the thick of the fighting Foch was obliged to ask his neighbour, Franchet d'Esperey, to help him to re-place the 42nd Division, which was exhausted after three days' fighting. Franchet d'Esperey at once placed at his disposal whatever fresh troops he could spare, and Foch immediately threw himself against the flank of the 10th German Corps, but while his reinforced left was pushing on, the Prussian Guard succeeded in driving back the gallant Morocco Division and seized the Château. One more turn of the screw and the enemy would open the breach, but Foch has always said that to be conquered you must believe yourself to be conquered.[1] Instead of being the least frightened of being submerged under the advancing flood, he told the Morocco Division that whatever happened they must get the Château back ; he then urged the 42nd Division—which he had slipped up behind the front line from north south-wards—to march on Corroy and told them to attack facing eastwards. The division, breathless and pretty well worn out, pushed its way to the front to bring the needed help to the threatened troops, and the Germans, even more exhausted than ourselves, with the deployment of these new forces, hesitated, shook their heads and began to go back.

It is under the impression of these happy events that I see Tittoni. He is not effusive but only exquisitely polite, though he has evidently been inspired by the military news

[1] " The story runs that at that critical hour you sent to the Commander-in-Chief this delightful message : ' Hard pressed on my right, my centre must give way, impossible to move on, situation excellent, I attack.' Serious authors have treated this text as authentic, and I have not the courage to undeceive them ; if you never actually wrote this optimistic message it was anyhow in your thoughts and, better still, you translated it into action." (Reply to Marshal Foch's speech at the reception given to him by the French Academy, 5th February 1920.)

which has filtered through the diplomatic quarters of Bordeaux. His amiability seems to me of good omen . . .
Multos numerabis amicos.

Delcassé, who came to speak to Viviani and myself with
regard to Turkey, Greece and Bulgaria, suddenly burst into
tears ; when we asked him what was the matter he excused
himself, and, still sobbing, told us that his son had been
wounded and taken prisoner, and that he feared that the
name of Delcassé, which was so hated by the Germans, would
mean every sort of misery for the unhappy boy. We console him as best we can, but his fears are more than likely
to be well grounded.

In the afternoon Millerand and I inspect a brigade
from Morocco and a battalion of *tirailleurs* who have just
landed in France and are being sent to the front. They are
fine troops and very well turned out, and do nothing to make
one regret the Protectorate Treaty of 1912 nor the " Moroccan Expedition " which Clemenceau thought would prejudice
our mobilisation.[1] On the way to and from the camp the
crowd give vent to most kindly greeting, but at every *vivat* I
think of the soldiers who are fighting and falling on the field
of battle, and the first thing I hear when I get back to the
Prefecture is that Nancy, which one thought was immune
from injury, has received its baptism of fire. The town was
heavily bombarded for a whole hour ; six women or girls
have been killed and there are a large number of wounded
civilians. Yet Nancy is an open town and the German
officers have no shadow of excuse to try and destroy it ; it
would seem that their idea of what is right and wrong in war
has, since 1870, become more inhuman instead of accommo-
dating itself to the laws of civilisation and of moral progress.

German propaganda, however, insists on inverting our
characters, and is ladling out the most absurd stories which
state that we are using dum-dum bullets and that at Longwy
there was even found machinery for making them ; nothing
could be more monstrously untrue, but a fable like this once
let loose travels widely. The Kaiser has telegraphed to the
President of the United States to assure him that this odious

[1] See *Le Lendemain d'Agadir*, p. 92 *et seq.*, and p. 117.

invention is true, and to register a protest, in the name of
virtue, against the crimes of the French ; I am obliged to
cable to M. Wilson myself so as to give the lie to a story to
which the Kaiser has set his imprimatur. A sheaf of telegrams from abroad interrupt for a few minutes the thoughts
which otherwise obsess one. The Turkish Government has
taken upon itself to abrogate the system of capitulations,
the suppression or reform of which they so earnestly asked
us to bring about ; no doubt the Turk thinks now that he
has nothing to fear from a split-up Europe. From Copenhagen we learn that the German General Staff has published
a notice, reproduced at once in Denmark, which announces
that, in spite of the Geneva Convention, the German troops
will for the future use dum-dum bullets, as the French and
English have set the example ; what the Kaiser evidently
wanted was a pretext which would enable him to employ
methods of barbarism. Jusserand informs us that his British
and Russian colleagues have received instructions to refuse,
for the time, any attempt at American mediation, Sir Edward
Grey having telegraphed to Sir Cecil Spring-Rice that the
English people are most certainly partisans of peace, but only
of a peace with such guarantees as will secure its being kept
and which will prevent any recurrence of deeds, such as the
violation of Belgian neutrality. Such a peace, Sir Edward
added, is scarcely likely to be signed. From Sofia comes the
news that the Russian successes in Galicia, the waiting attitude
of Turkey and the check to Austrian advances at Bucharest
have produced a good effect on the Bulgarian Government
and on King Ferdinand himself, and that to-day Bulgaria
favours a prudent neutrality. The telegram from Russia is to
the effect that the converging attack by the Russian armies
against the Austrian troops of the centre from Zamostre
to Rawarusska has forced the enemy to retire, and that
on the right bank of the Vistula, south-west of Lublin, the
Austro-German forces have been dislodged from their fortified
positions and are retreating southwards. The Serbians are
engaged with forces which are of course numerically superior
to them, and sharp fighting has taken place round Semlin,
which the Serbians have seized this morning. From Berne

comes an extraordinary item. According to the *Dernières
Nouvelles de Munich*, the internment camp at Lechfeld, where
the French prisoners are assembled, has been surrounded by
wire, and the public is allowed in at a charge of 20 pfennigs,
the money to go to the help of the families of German
soldiers. Our unhappy captive compatriots are therefore
being shown like wild beasts shut up behind bars in a zoo-
logical garden. The Prefect of the Seine et Oise telegraphs
that German cyclists have blown up the railway from Paris
to Dieppe at two points, while the Prefect of the Seine
Inférieure throws light on the inaction of d'Amade's army ; a
German troop of six or seven hundred men has arrived at
Amiens from Doulens and set up a command there. But the
news from headquarters is what one anxiously awaits, and is
to-day more and more comforting. The public is to be fully
informed as to the great battle which has taken place since
the 6th September from the Ourcq to the Meuse, and which
will be known in military history as the battle of the Marne.
From the beginning of the fighting Von Klück's army,
which on the 6th had reached the region north of Provins,
has been obliged to retire before our threat of envelopment.
By a succession of skilful and rapid movements, Von Klück
managed to disentangle himself, and attacked, with the
larger part of his forces, our enveloping wing north of the
Marne and west of the Ourcq. But the French troops at this
point, substantially helped by the British army, inflicted
really heavy losses on the enemy and gave the necessary time
for our offensive to develop elsewhere. The Germans are in
retreat towards the Aisne and the Oise, and in these last days
have gone back in some places seventy-five kilometres. Meanwhile the English and French troops operating south of the
Marne have steadily advanced, and parties, some from the south
of the forest of Creçy and others from the north of Provins and
the south of d'Esternay, have debouched from the Marne to
the north of Château Thierry. There has been bitter fighting
from the beginning in the environs of La Ferté-Gaucher,
d'Esternay and Montmirail, and the left of Von Klück's
army, as well as Von Bülow's, have had to yield to our forces.
The bloodiest struggle has been in the region between the

plateaux north of Sézanne and Vitry-le-François, where, besides the left of Von Bülow's army, the Saxon army and part of the army commanded by the Prince of Würtemberg were posted ; again and again the enemy tried to break our centre, but in vain. Our successes on the plateaux north of Sézanne enabled us to take the offensive in our turn, and last night the enemy broke off the battle on the front which extends from the St. Gond marshes to the region of Sommesous, and has retired west of Vitry-le-François. So much for the Marne. On the Ornain the fight is still swaying against the forces of the Prince of Würtemberg and the Crown Prince, and to-day our 6th Corps, west of the valley of the Aire, has had to deal with a desperate onrush of the Germans, who wanted to cut our lines and to surround Verdun. But the chasseurs of St. Mihiel were more than ready for them,[1] and Joffre declares that the German situation, whether from the strategic or the tactical point of view, has completely altered within these last two days.

A final telegram confirms the impression.

" Everywhere ", the Commander-in-Chief says, " our soldiers have shown themselves beyond praise," and he adds, " I have so far been chary of giving you news until I could be absolutely certain of results. To-day I can announce these to you. In front of our left the enemy armies, in full retreat, have been thrown across the Marne by Sir John French and Franchet d'Esperey, who have secured, in four days' fighting, more than sixty kilometres. Maunoury has withstood quite admirably the great efforts which the Germans have made to disengage their right, and his troops, who have been under a long and continuous fire from heavy guns, have been able to repulse every attack and have just resumed their own movement northwards following up the enemy. This morning the German centre has begun to give way. Foch is moving towards the Marne and finding everywhere traces of the very hurried retreat of the enemy, whose Army Corps, and especially the Guards' Corps, have lost heavily. On our right we are vigorously withstanding violent attacks, and everything encourages us to hope that our success will be furthered."

11th September.—I submit in Council the letter of congratulations which, according to custom, the President addresses

[1] See *Les Chasseurs de St. Mihiel et la Guerre dans la Marne*, by P. Jolibois, instituteur, Imprimerie Comte Jacquet, Bar-le-Duc.

to the troops even after a review in time of peace. To the
expressions of deep admiration I add words of encouragement and my earnest wishes for the welfare of the troops,
but I am careful to allude to the success which has just been
secured, not as a decisive victory, but as a pledge of future
results. The Ministers quite agree with me that we must
not nourish ourselves with any illusions that the end of the
war is in sight, but they—and not the least the two Socialists
—are as overjoyed as I am at what has happened. Never have
French Ministers been so closely bound together, yesterday
by heavy trial, to-day by an accession of happiness ; there
is perfect unanimity, and the one thought is for France.

Briand telephones me from Paris, and in his deep voice,
which vibrates on the instrument, I can perceive an un-
accustomed emotion. His going, together with Marcel
Sembat, to the capital—according to the arrangement made
a day or two ago that two Ministers should proceed there—
has had the best effect on Parisian opinion. Everything is
quiet, and Galliéni is very satisfied with the military operations.

The liaison officer tells me that Joffre is determined to
continue his forward movement and to drive the enemy back.
The Germans have strewed their line of retreat with rifles,
ammunition, papers, maps and every sort of thing. At
Fère Champenoise they looted the cellars and pillaged the
houses, and, besides indulging in every sort of orgy, they left
behind them in the basements dead-drunk soldiers of the
Imperial Guard. Our troops have retaken Epernay, Châlons-
sur-Marne and Vitry-le-François, while the Crown Prince
is being pushed back northwards, through Laheycourt, by
Sarrail ; the Prince is setting fire to places through which
his army passes, but he must give up the idea of reaching
the valley of the Meuse to the south of Verdun.

Late in the afternoon Joffre telegraphs anew that our
success, on our left and centre, is assuming the character of
a real victory ; our 1st Cavalry Corps, in the command of
which General Bridoux has replaced General Sordet, is trying
to cut the enemy's line of retreat.

Our Belgian friends are delighted, and well may they be.

M. Klobukowski this morning met the gallant King, who was just coming from his headquarters, and said to him: " This battle is a proof of General Joffre's vision : he ordered the offensive at the precise moment when it was likely to succeed. The Belgian army is making now a supreme effort to co-operate with the French and British, and our immediate rôle is to harass and, if possible, hold up the enemy's communications. We shall do our very best."

12th September.—Now that things are a little easier I learn that these last weeks, without knowing it, I have been the object of bitter, and often contradictory, criticism in certain political quarters. To-day the tone is different. But yesterday I was responsible for everything, for what I knew of, as well as for what Ministers allowed me to ignore; for what I had done in 1912 as President of the Council as for what had been done, or left undone, by the Governments in which I had no part or lot. Insufficiency of armament and equipment, absence of heavy guns, corruption in certain branches of administration, inexact or insufficient communiqués, all these in the dark hours were used as recriminations against myself. Some politicians, who represent themselves as respecting profoundly the Constitution, have gone so far as to blame me for not assuming a dictatorship and for allowing myself to be muzzled by the Government; others, on the other hand, have alleged that it was I who did everything, good or bad—especially the bad— under the cloak of the Ministers. What would it have been if Von Klück had not made his sudden switch, and if Joffre and Galliéni had not in such masterly manner availed themselves of it to take the offensive? Supposing our armies had not fought with such magnificent courage? On my head would certainly have fallen to-day all the reproach, and to-morrow, if the slightest reverse should occur, the thing will begin over again, and my *métier* is, I suppose, to attract the thunder on my own head so that it shall not fall on too many people at once. One is compelled to the reflection that the Jewish people were very happily inspired when on the Day of Atonement they used to hunt the poor scapegoat into the desert; this innocent beast would be very suitably placed in the sheepfold of Rambouillet, near the President's château.

M. de Kerguezec, whose wife belongs to a great Roumanian family, comes to see me on his arrival from Bucharest. He has had a talk with our friend Také Jonesco, who said to him : " If Italy were to come in, Roumania would certainly do likewise, but for Italy to come in, France must promise her something, Tunis, for example." Jonesco is too level-headed to have made this suggestion of his own accord ; he must have been inspired to do so, and the suggestion itself exhibits a state of mind which must be sedulously fostered, whether at Rome or Bucharest.

According to what M. Lahovary has confided to Delcassé, King Carol remains entirely under the influence of Germany and Austria. The Kaiser seems to have guaranteed him the possession of Bessarabia, if Roumania can manage to conquer it, and there is an Imperial promise of the annexation of Transylvania at the end of twenty years, that is to say, just when Austro-Hungary will have begun to break up. The German Emperor, who declared war in the hope of warding off Austro-Hungarian dissolution, now seems to consider this as inevitable.

The Grand Duke Nicholas has telegraphed to Joffre :

" *12th September*.—The battle in Galicia, which has lasted for ten days, has ended in a great victory for our army, and on the 8th, 9th and 10th of September we took 200 guns with 30,000 prisoners, including 200 officers. The Austrian armies are retiring all along the line. I am indeed happy to give you this news on the very day when I hear of the successes gained by the valiant French and English armies."

This is all very well, and we can warmly applaud the Russian victory, but it appears that in Eastern Prussia the Germans have got their own back again, and that Russia, contrary to our repeated requests, is making her chief effort against Austria as if the surest way to beat Austria were not to begin by beating Germany.

13th September.—At the Council this morning I say again that I am determined to go as soon as possible and visit headquarters, the front line, and the devastated areas.

I am rather annoyed by the " put-off " replies which I get, and I say bluntly that if there is any further delay in confirming my project I shall waive the precedent under which one or two Ministers must always accompany the President on an official journey, and shall go where and when I think right without authority or Ministerial consent. This threat of a microscopic *coup d'état* does not raise any protest if it causes some surprise and a little embarrassment.

Viviani, Ribot and Thomson submit a very important financial note. The Treasury wants money and cannot simply ask the Bank of France for an increase of paper circulation ; nor can there be any augmentation of taxes, which the Government think it would be very difficult to collect, especially at a moment when so many taxable persons are at the front. Ribot thinks the only way will be to issue short-term Bills ; the sum of Treasury Bonds at this moment is not more than 350,000,000 francs ; a larger amount could easily be reached. The Minister proposes to issue Bonds to which all Frenchmen would be invited to subscribe, and to entitle them Bonds of National Defence.

Joffre telegraphs that

" Our victory is pronouncing itself as more and more complete and brilliant. The enemy is in full retreat even in front of our First and Second Armies (Lorraine and Vosges), whom for so many weeks they have resisted. Everywhere the Germans are abandoning prisoners, wounded and material, and our advance guards are treading on the heels of the adversary without giving him a moment to pull himself together. On our left we have crossed the Aisne below Soissons, gaining more than 100 kilometres in six days' fighting ; the armies of the centre are already north of the Marne ; the armies of Lorraine and Vosges are arriving at the frontier. . . . The Government of the Republic may indeed be proud of the army which they have put into the field."

I have hung two German flags, which Colonel Pénélon brought to me, in the Prefecture, and now General Gouraud —who is burning to go to the front—brings me two Moroccan flags taken from the rebel tribes who have given in their submission. He speaks with enthusiasm of the victory which our troops have secured, but at the thought that he was not there himself his blue eyes become a little dim.

14th September. — Senators and deputies continue to angle for official missions. M. Ferdinand Dreyfus wants to go to Italy to inquire into the state of public opinion there ; M. Jonnart has been allowed by M. Ribot to make an economic inspection in the Nord, the Pas-de-Calais and the Somme and has just given an account of his tour ; M. Albert Thomas, whose leisure hangs very heavy on his hands, says he will do anything anywhere, if only he could be given something to do.

Millerand explains to the Council that General d'Amade was inexcusably precipitate in ordering the evacuation of Lille ; he had no doubt received a telephone message from Messimy which authorised him to consider Lille as an open town, but he had no instructions as to immediate evacuation, and the troops were taken away with no thought of carrying off rifles, munitions or provisions : the War Minister is going to inquire particularly what part General Perçin, Governor of Lille, played in this unfortunate affair.

Delcassé gives us an account—not too clear—of external affairs. The German Minister at Athens has told Venizelos, who has just taken over the Foreign Office, as " a piece of good news ", that Turkey and Bulgaria were preparing as Allies to attack Serbia, but that they entertain nothing but friendly dispositions towards Greece. M. Venizelos brushed aside this clumsy attempt to sound him and replied that Greece would take up arms against any country which attacked Serbia. At Constantinople engineers and mechanics, German-sent, are putting the *Goeben* and the *Breslau,* whose boilers have been damaged, into working order.

M. Eugène Lautier, who is on the staff of the *Temps,* has let me know that a certain number of Hungarian civilians have been interned at Bordeaux, notably a Francophile deputy, one Michel Karoly, with two of his colleagues and a well-known sociologist, one Nordau, who in point of fact has often spoken of France in unjust and spiteful terms. Karoly came to Paris in the month of June to get some backing against his political adversary, Count Tisza, who eventually, despite his earlier hesitations, took on himself a large share of responsibility as to the war. Lautier thinks there is something paradoxical in keeping Karoly in captivity, and the Government decides to set free all the Hungarians, including Nordau, and to send them to Spain ; a gesture on our part which may scarcely be appreciated either at Budapest or at Berlin.

The King of the Belgians has added to the general order of yesterday a fine paragraph which runs :

" In the event of attack the utmost resistance is to be shown. The successes gained by the Anglo-French army impose on our own army the duty of co-operating to the margin of their means towards final victory, and this by compelling the enemy to send against us the maximum of men."

The King has conveyed personally this message to each divisional commander, and, when talking to our Military Attaché, alluded to our victory as " the finest military operation in modern times " ; to myself he telegraphed in the same cordial tone.   But the German General Staff have their own way of paying respect to truth.   The Wolff Agency in this morning's issue glibly says :

" The operations of last week, of which the details cannot yet be published, have led to another battle, the development of which is favourable to our arms.   The unfavourable news which the Allies have taken every means to spread abroad is false."

How well informed Germany is !   What the Wolff Agency does not state in its communiqué is that the German armies have to-day halted in their retreat, and are profiting by a few hours' rest which has been given to our men—a pause which, in spite of inevitable and terrible fatigue, it might have been far better to postpone for a little while. The Germans have taken up their position on a line running from the north of the Aisne, between the Oise and Berry-au-Bac, to the hills north of Verdun.   This line on the east touches the approaches to Rheims, and on his new front the enemy is already making preparations to stand fast.   The German right wing seems to be uncovered, and our Sixth Army with the English have been told to deal as roughly as possible with it and to try and get round it by Puisaleine and Carlepont.

15th September.—The *Indépendant des Pyrénées orientales* published yesterday an article which contained this specimen of journalism :

" At Bordeaux they are drinking champagne, smoking and joking, while yonder our soldiers are risking their skins in order to save the skins of the people in the town. Not only are there orgies in the restaurants, but on Sunday Ministers, who had spent an agreeable day at Arcachon with some ladies, were seen going about the streets of Bordeaux in automobiles full of flowers and driven by the military."

The *Indépendant* has been suspended for a month on account of this paragraph by the General commanding the 16th Region, but Millerand and Malvy are going to reduce the suspension to a few days. All the Ministers, however, are furious about such tittle-tattle, and Malvy tells me that the only possible foundation for it is that, being rather unwell, he spent Sunday afternoon at Arcachon with one of his friends, and that on leaving, one or two of the local associations gave him some flowers. He assures me that nothing else happened, and, of course, nobody but himself has suggested that he was the Minister designated by the article.

Telegrams of congratulation, which we reciprocate, are to hand from the Prince Regent of Serbia, as well as from the Czar, but we are more and more wishful that Russia would be active against Germany. Paléologue has made further representations as to this, and the War Minister, General Soukhomlinow, who impressed me very unfavourably each time I spoke to him, has told our Ambassador that the Russian troops cannot be pushed farther in Eastern Prussia towards Berlin, and that it might be better for them to be busy in Silesia and Posen. He even added : " We lost 100,000 men at Soldau when trying to help the French armies at the end of August ". Paléologue should have answered : " We would have made the same sacrifice to help the Russian armies, but it isn't our fault if the faint-heartedness of one of your corps commanders suddenly left the flank of the Russian army in the air ".

M. Denys Cochin, who has been appointed Inspector of Powder Factories, has come back quite satisfied with his first tour ; he is an eminent chemist and is quite competent to carry out the duty entrusted to him. Marcel Sembat and Briand have come back from Paris, and Galliéni, who is always a conqueror, has easily made a conquest of these two. The Socialist Minister speaks of the Military Governor with enthusiasm, and his effusive praise, which, as far as I am concerned, is quite superfluous, will I hope put an end to the malevolent hypotheses of which Clemenceau and some of the Ministers have been the dupes. Not only is Sembat open-mouthed in his confidence in the loyalty of Galliéni, but he now thinks that the Military Governor was quite right to secure the services of Doumer, whose force of character and astounding capacity for work are of the greatest help in the civil administration of the fortress. " Galliéni ", Briand declares, " is quite perfect in his attitude. He does not seek for popularity and only thinks of doing the work. Sembat and I visited the northern sector, where immense improvement has been made in organising the defence. The General wants the Marine Artillery to be sent to him, and I have spoken to Augagneur, who will do what is wanted as quickly as he can. The guns will be so disposed as to enfilade the railways, which are indispensable to the Germans to carry their 420 howitzers, and it may thus be quite possible to prevent these howitzers being put in position. Galliéni thinks that with this precaution Paris could hold out for at least four or five weeks. I also went with Sembat to the front and saw Maunoury's army ; the turn out of the troops is excellent, and their supplies are admirable ; the fields are still strewn with German corpses. I am delighted, M. le Président, that, in agreement with the Government and Galliéni, you insisted that Joffre should reinforce the army of Paris. The Military Governor was able, with the help of the taxis he requisitioned, to transport troops he had received to the field of battle and place them at the disposal of Maunoury. This supplementary force most certainly contributed largely to ultimate success." Doumergue, as Colonial Minister, has been told by the Government to reorganise the supplies in the liberated areas of the Seine and Marne, of the Marne, and of the Aisne and Oise, and the programme which he confides to me seems very admirably conceived. Then Delcassé, who is still very anxious about the fate of his son, has a further word to say about Turkey and Bulgaria. He has an interesting despatch from Klobukowski who, as the result of a conversation with Baron Beyens, the former Belgian Minister at Berlin, writes :

"The Austro-Serbian War", so the distinguished diplomatist said, "was a *coup monté* by Germany, the torch which was to light the fire, the sought-for occasion for action against France. The Kaiser, who for a long time showed himself as a sincere friend of peace, finally gave way before the assaults made on him by the Camarilla, which have never ceased to breathe the spirit of Bismarckism. For two years he has been visibly depressed, and his health, always rather precarious, has been impaired by the preoccupations brought upon him by the constant suggestions of the people around him. Although intellectually rather tired out, he could still see the terrible import of a Franco-German War, but it would seem that an initial mistake concealed the immediate repercussions. He thought that Russia, who was setting her military house in order, would not forcibly interfere in a Balkan conflict, and that England, paralysed as she was by internal dissensions and generally unwilling to take part in any Continental war, would abstain also, while Italy would go in with her two Allies, and that Germany, with her enormous contingents, which had been for so long trained for the field, would have only France to reckon with. France, by reason of her numerical inferiority in troops and conflicting political opinions on military matters, did not seem a very dangerous adversary, and the Kaiser thought that the moment had come to bring about, by force of arms, German hegemony. Among his entourage there were many partisans of war, but it was especially the Crown Prince, nominally anyhow (for his intellectual capacity is very limited), who was the leader of the party which was thundering against France. For some time this party had been seeking a pretext, no matter what, to embroil things, and the Germans, as one knows, have never far to seek for a quarrel. Hence the origin of the Austro-Serbian squabble."

King Albert had also talked openly with Klobukowski and had said to him :

"To act on the defensive is the only possible way, in view of the powerfully organised masses of troops against us, and I am very glad that the French Commander-in-Chief is resisting so methodically and so vigorously. To fight and to endure is the formula which inspires, or ought to inspire, France as well as Belgium. Germany could only count on success if she were not checked in her first rush ; her plan of campaign has failed at its outset, and it is a great honour for Belgium to have contributed to this result. Hence the intense irritation of the Emperor William against us, and against myself, and this irritation is even greater than people think. In very truth this way of making war deserves universal reprobation, but there is nothing which ought to surprise us in the conduct of a military oligarchy, which is as presumptuous as it is boastful. These people are envious, unbalanced and ill-tempered, jealous of our fine monuments, of our pretty towns, of the charm of our country-side, as well as of our industrial activity ; our cathedral at Malines has been bombarded, simply because it was beautiful ; our Library at Louvain, which the very iconoclasts respected, has been deliberately set on fire, because it was unique. The old Emperor William, who was a simple character, would have resisted the suggestions of a narrow-minded and brutal entourage, but his vainglorious grandson admires what is superficial and theatrical ; he is too fond of playing to the gallery to be insensible to the flatteries of men, who have dangled before his eyes the realisation of the grandiose dream with which he has always been haunted ; to be the great Emperor, the ruler of the world, before whom everyone and everything is to tremble and bow."

As if to correct by a more flattering touch these life-like portraits of the Kaiser and his heir-apparent, the Wolff Agency states that the Crown Prince's army is besieging and bombarding Verdun ; Joffre telegraphs this item of news is quite untrue and begs us to contradict it. But our contradiction will not be accepted in Germany, and everyone there will credit the Crown Prince with a blazing success. The truth is that the Fifth German Army has failed in all its attempts ; in the first days of the month they tried to over-run the left wing of Sarrail's army and cut it off from the Fourth, but Sarrail slipped into the gap the new 15th Corps, and the Crown Prince could not get on. On the other hand, on the right of our Third Army some of the Verdun forts have been bombarded, and German units, coming from the Woëvre, have neared the Troyon fort, which they have twice assaulted without being able to take it. On the 10th Sep-

tember the Crown Prince again attacked our Third Army
and again failed, and three days later the Fifth German
Army was hurriedly retiring : to-day the 5th German Corps,
which was occupying, in the environs cf the Troyon fort,
the right bank of the Meuse, has gone back in the plain
of the Woëvre. But what devastation the enemy has left
behind him in this once happy country-side, where there is
not a village or a watercourse or a wood that is not familiar
to me.

16th September.—Our pursuit, begun after the battle of
the Marne and unfortunately interrupted by a short respite,
brought us into touch yesterday and the day before with the
German rear-guards, who have halted and faced about and
are now reinforced by the bulk of the German army. A new
pitched battle must ensue on the line which the enemy has
rapidly put in a state of defence, a line which extends from
the Oise to the Argonne through the region of Noyon, the
plateaux to the north of Vic-sur-Aisne and of Soissons,
Laon, the neighbouring heights of Rheims and the environs
of Ville-sur-Tourb. The German positions, which are already
prepared, stretch to the east of the Argonne from Varennes
to the Woëvre north of Verdun. The ground in front of
Lunéville and St. Dié is pretty well free of the invader, but
are our troops fresh enough, and have we enough guns and
ammunition to speak effectively these coming days with an
enemy who has scientifically dug himself in ? Joffre, in a
telegram of yesterday, put it to our armies to take methodical steps and make good by degrees the ground we have
won ; he does not want any recurrence of the earlier illusions
and blunders. But if the Germans entrench themselves
and fortify themselves as they are doing, have we what is
required, besides courage, to dislodge them ?

Anyhow, we want Russia to do something to relieve the
pressure on us, and once more Paléologue has been instructed
to urge this on Sazonoff, who, after an audience with the
Czar, has declared that as soon as the Austrian armies of
Galicia have been crushed, a direct attack will be made,
with all vigour, against Germany. But when are those
Austrian armies of Galicia going to be crushed ? Doubtless

the Russian troops have crossed the San and are following up the Austrian left wing which we are told is routed ; no doubt the centre and right wing of the Austrian army have been thrown back on Przemysl ; no doubt—according to to-day's telegram—the Austrian armies are evacuating Galicia, leaving behind them 250,000 dead and wounded, and 100,000 prisoners, while the German corps which came to help them are themselves in retreat. But if this be so, why must Russia await any further crushing of Austrian troops in Galicia before dealing a direct blow against Germany ? For the moment the First Russian Army has entirely abandoned Eastern Prussia, and there is no further whisper as to an investment of Königsberg.

Our successes anyhow have encouraged some of our friends, and in Roumania there have been great manifestations in honour of France, M. Philippesco, sometime Minister for War, having put himself at the head of this popular movement. Our Minister even thinks that before the end of the week the Roumanian Government will decree mobilisation and declare itself on our side, and that the King will either have to sign or abdicate. M. Lahovary entertains the same hope, but some of us are very much afraid that they are mistaking the wish for the deed.

17th September.—Colonel Pénélon is again all smiles and comes in with an armful of good news. I am a little surprised to hear that General Headquarters have now been established at Rheims, which I thought would be under the new line of fire, and the Colonel himself thinks that we may have gone a little quick in choosing a town so near to the enemy and where it will be difficult to keep the offices of the Command ; of course nobody thought that the Germans would face about so suddenly, and Rheims is bombarded by batteries from forts to the east of the town.

Joffre inclines to the idea that the Germans had no option but to accept battle, and it is our vigorous pursuit which compelled them to do it. They are, it is true, too strongly entrenched for us to dislodge them by counter-attack, but we are planning to turn their two wings. The 13th Corps, from Dubail's army, detrained yesterday on our left to reinforce Maunoury, and Castelnau is manœuvring to the east to get round the German left. The fight will last for two or three days, but Joffre is full of hope that we shall win, for he thinks that the German Command have had their hands forced to fight by the Kaiser, whose masterful impatience will be satisfied with nothing less than immediate revenge.

If our success in the field has not knocked out the enemy, it has, anyhow, largely cheered up the Belgians. They have just made a very useful offensive movement; the defence of Antwerp is being quickly organised; Western Flanders and part of Eastern Flanders, the province of Antwerp and Limberg are no longer in German occupation. The same cannot be said for Hainault, Brabant, the provinces of Liége, of Namur and of Belgian Luxembourg, where many of the towns have been destroyed or injured and where the country has been devastated. Belgium, like ourselves, is paying a heavy price for victory.

CHAPTER VII

A letter from Pope Benedict XV.—The front line is stabilised—The enemy bombards the Cathedral of Rheims—Towns and villages devastated—The capture of St. Mihiel—Antwerp threatened.

18th September.—While France was escaping, in a battle without historical parallel, from what might have been irreparable disaster, there has been elected at Rome a new Vicar of Christ. Jacomo, Marquis de la Chiesa, Archbishop of Bologna, has been proclaimed Pope under the name of Benedict XV. A cardinal only since last May, he is an aristocrat by birth and a diplomatist by calling. It is difficult to foresee what his policy will be, but he has chosen for his Secretary of State Monsignor Ferrata, who has largely contributed to his election and whose attitude towards us has so far been wholly favourable. Cardinal Amette, who has just returned to Paris, writes to me :

" When leaving Rome our Holy Father, Pope Benedict XV., graciously charged me to convey to you the accompanying letter in which His Holiness announces to you his election to the Sovereign Pontificate. Your absence from Paris, necessitated by the requirements of national defence, prevents my having the honour of delivering this letter to you myself in an audience which I should have asked of you. I should have been indeed happy at the same time to thank you for having been good enough to respond to my request and to have caused yourself to be represented at the service held at Nôtre Dame for the repose of the soul of the late Sovereign Pontiff : this act on your part has been appreciated, as it deserved to be, in France and at Rome. I would also have taken the opportunity to tell you how entirely France may congratulate herself on the election of the new Pope, on whose benevolence she can rely. Pray accept, M. le Président, together with the prayers which I never cease to make towards the throne of God for the success of our arms, the expressions of my dutiful homages.—Léon Adolphe, Card. Amette, Archbishop of Paris."

With this letter, which breathes patriotism, was enclosed one from the new Pope :

" Perillustri viro Galliarum reipublicae Praesidi Benedictus P. P. XV. Perillustris vir, Salutem. Inscrutabili Dei consilio ad suscipienda Ecclesiae gubernacula vocati, munus impositae dignitatis Tibi nunciare properamus, eidemque atque nobilissimae Gallorum genti omnia fausta feliciaque adprecamur. Datum Romae apud S. Petrum die III septembris anno MCMXIV Pontificatus nostri primo. Benedictus P. P. XV."

One would have thought that, after receiving these two letters, the right thing to do was to reply as quickly and as courteously as possible. But the Churches are legally separated from the State, and we have also—without one justifying the other—broken off diplomatic relations with the Vatican. To correspond with the Pope outside the Government would be a step on the part of a President which the more susceptible Republicans would certainly condemn ; it would be a sort of *secret du Roi* which no constitutional king would to-day entertain. In all correctitude, therefore, I communicated the two letters to the Government ; there was no question as to my replying, but it was decided that, from the very character of the correspondence, my replies should be prepared by the Minister for Foreign Affairs, and to Philippe Berthelot, I think, the task was entrusted. The two drafts sent to me ran :

"To His Eminence the Cardinal Amette Archbishop of Paris.— Monseigneur, In acknowledging the letter in which you inform me that His Holiness the Pope has been graciously pleased to notify me of his elevation to the Sovereign Pontificate, I would beg you to be so very good as to forward the letter herewith enclosed. Greatly appreciating as I do the sentiments you have expressed and the prayers which you are offering for the success of our arms, I beg Your Eminence . . ."

" To his Holiness the Pope.—Most Holy Father, I hasten to acknowledge the notification which Your Holiness has addressed me with regard to your elevation to the Holy See. In thanking Your Holiness for your prayers for the prosperity of the French nation and for myself, I beg you to believe in my earnest good wishes for Your Holiness and for the 'grandeur' of your Pontificate." [1]

I would willingly have signed these two letters, although they seemed to me to err rather on the side of dryness, but it was laid down that they should be examined in Council, and the Government decided that we ought to suppress the word " grandeur ", which rather shocked some of the Ministers. There was no objection to my expressing my goodwill for the Pope and his Pontificate, but they did not like the idea of my wishing the Pontificate to be great.   What miserable small-mindedness !   As a set-off they let pass the words " *sensible aux sentiments* " to correct, no doubt, by this double affirmation, the coldness which politics seemed to enjoin, and finally it was thought well that, in order not to render the Cabinet officially responsible, my letter should be sent under Delcassé's countersign.   I agreed as to all this, but not without thinking that these trumperies are not very pretty.

We are beginning to ask ourselves the meaning of the silence at General Headquarters, and what is really happening at the front.   We were told that the enemy had halted against his own will and that we were sure to dislodge him ; we are now told that there will be nothing decisive for two or three days and that the situation remains about the same. What is the mystery ?   Yesterday Joffre, in an order to Maunoury, said " It seems that the enemy is slipping troops north-west under the cover of the defence organised all along his front : a force must be got together on our left, not only to deal with this movement of the enemy, but also to ensure our own envelopment of them."   Our left wing has

---

[1] " Son Éminence le Cardinal Amette, Archevêque de Paris.—Monseigneur, En vous accusant réception de la lettre par laquelle vous m'avez transmis la notification que S.S. le Pape a bien voulu m'adresser de son élévation au Souverain Pontificat, j'ai recours à votre obligeance pour vous prier de faire parvenir à destination la lettre ci-jointe.   Très sensible aux sentiments exposés par Vous et aux vœux que Vous formulez pour le succès de nos armes, je prie Votre Éminence de croire à ma haute considération." " A Sa Sainteté le Pape.   Très Saint Père, Je m'empresse d'accuser réception à Votre Sainteté de la notification qu'Elle a bien voulu m'adresser de Son élévation au Saint-Siège.   En la remerciant des vœux qu'Elle forme pour la prospérité de la nation française et pour moi-même, je prie Votre Sainteté d'agréer mes souhaits pour Elle et la grandeur de Son Pontificat."

accordingly made some slight progress, but has done nothing like enveloping the German right wing, and it will be a ding-dong fight as to which outruns and envelops the other. But on each wing, as in the centre, we are faced with troops solidly entrenched. On the Marne the trenches which the Germans have abandoned are, however improvised, admirably organised; and there is no doubt that they have not halted without having a position thoroughly prepared by the troops who had remained in rear of the fighting-line.

England had proposed a few days ago to disembark men at Dunkirk so as to make a diversion in the north of France and in Belgium. Joffre quite approved of the idea, but wondered whether the British contingents would suffice to allow of this manœuvre being carried out soon. Although the British Dominions and India have, with quite extraordinary rapidity, come to the help of the Mother Country, the great distances compel England to wait for some time before she can receive active co-operation. The troops from Hindustan are on their way, but cannot reach Marseilles for another ten days, and the reinforcements from England herself have been already sent up to Sir John French, so that there only remain for the moment, for the Nord and for Belgium, the new contingents which Kitchener has put into being and is training.

Another Russian initiative, which is not any the happier because it does not emanate entirely from Sazonoff's fertile brain. The Grand Duke Nicholas Nicolaievitch has addressed a manifesto to the peoples of Austro-Hungary inviting them to shake off the yoke of the Hapsburgs and to realise at long length their national aspirations. In like manner the Russian Government invites the Roumanian Government to occupy Transylvania, and suggests that they should share with Russia in the occupation of Bukovina. Whatever one may think of these proposals, they are entirely coloured by politics; they involve important questions and may prejudice the conditions of peace. Russia ought not to do this sort of thing without first consulting England and France.

19th September.—The Prefect of the Meuse telegraphs that

the Germans in their retreat have burnt most of the villages
which they occupied during the battle of the Marne, and that
at Triaucourt, where my brother always spent his holidays,
twenty-nine houses have been systematically destroyed and
ten people shot for no reason whatever ; only the South of
the Department has been spared devastation.

Sir Francis Bertie tells us that the English are going to
land at Dunkirk 3000 men, of whom 2400 will be Marines
and 600 Regulars, together with 60 armoured cars. These
will suffice to police the Department of the Nord, but will
be nothing like enough to make any serious diversion to the
rear of the enemy. According to what one of the liaison
officers says, Joffre hopes anyhow to be able to use in this
same region what was d'Amade's army, the looking for
which had sorely tried our patience ; this force has at last
been re-formed and entrusted to General Brugère, who has
defied Time even before defying the enemy, and is as fresh
as ever, although he figures on the retired list ; he has entrenched his Territorials and Reservists in front of Amiens
so as to support, if necessary, the movement of our left wing.
There is no longer any question of doing anything very
serious on our right, and activities have been translated to
the other end of the line. Castelnau, in moving forward
recently across the plain of the Woëvre, came up against
enemy forces so strongly entrenched that he had to give up
any idea of getting round them, and even if this could have
taken place it would have been a false move and would have
interfered with the larger operation. The Germans have
quite evidently reinforced very powerfully their right and
are preparing to deliver their heavy stroke against our left.
Castelnau's army will therefore move away from the
Lorraine, on the soil of which they have for six weeks poured
out their blood, and will be railed westwards, leaving on
their old ground one corps which will come under Dubail's
orders. The 14th and 20th Corps will be transferred to
somewhere between Amiens and Noyon and, with the 13th,
4th and Conneau's Cavalry Corps, will come under Castelnau.
They will attack the enemy's flank and take the lines north
of the Aisne, which the Germans have made good. Three

days, so Joffre says, will be required to transport the troops, and the " decisive " action, which was thought to be so near at hand, is again postponed ; in other words. it was a mistake to think that we should get the enemy to fight under conditions favourable to ourselves and at a place and hour of our own choice. The enemy has settled down on our ground, and it is more than possible that he will now reinforce his right wing, as we are reinforcing our left, and that Castelnau, moving westward, will find in front of him the same Sixth Army which he has been fighting in Lorraine. To what tortures of Sisyphus does our victory condemn us !

G.H.Q. continue, however, to draft daily communiqués so buoyantly optimistic that if Millerand did not correct and water them down, public opinion might be nourished day after day with mere illusions. The War Minister is also very anxious about the state of our artillery and ammunition ; there has been a quite startling consumption of every class of projectiles, particularly of the 75's, and manufacture is far from being on the same scale. Something must be done and done at once. I ask Millerand to give me as quickly as possible a detailed statement showing exactly what equipment we want of every sort and what we have in hand (a) for the Regulars, Reserves and depôts of the First Line, and (b) for the Territorials and their Reserves of the Second Line ; also I want on paper precisely what steps are being taken to supply the crying deficiencies, what is being bought in France and what outside, and how soon the articles in each category are likely to be forthcoming. As the war seems likely to drag on, a whole host of new arrangements have to be made for providing material ; at the present rate the ammunition for the 75's will not last out more than a month. Joffre, however, says all is well and that the situation remains satisfactory. We have taken another flag south of Noyon, and on the plateau of Craonne, where Napoleon beat the Allies just over a hundred years ago, we have tried to repeat history, and, as the result of a sharp fight, we have taken a good many prisoners from the 12th and 15th German Corps and the Imperial Guard. The enemy has a little worn himself out in vainly attempting to retake Rheims, and has wreaked his revenge in bombarding the town ; his malevolent intentions have been specially directed on the old basilica, as if he derived an unholy pleasure in renewing the outrage done to the cathedral at Malines ; Joffre has of course withdrawn his headquarters and is at Romilly-sur-Seine.

20th September.—Our troops are marking time and have not been able to get on farther in the wooded region near Noyon ; confused and fruitless fighting is taking place in the Vosges. We have taken the wooded slope of Pompelle, near Rheims, but have had to give up the Brimont height ; the bombardment of the town has been intensified to-day, and the cathedral, which has already suffered badly, is obviously marked out for destruction ; the library of the Archbishop's palace is in ruins, the Sous-Préfecture has been set on fire and one of the Deputy Mayors has been killed. Delcassé has circularised by telegram all our diplomatic agents, denouncing to the civilised world these acts of vandalism ; but up to now the civilised world seems to have neither eyes nor ears for us.

Meanwhile the hopes of G.H.Q. have been again doomed to disappointment. We are not getting forward, and it is the enemy who has made a violent attack on us and on the English north of the river Aisne and above Soissons. In the neighbourhood of Craonne, where at first fighting was in our favour, the crest of the Chemin des Dames and the farm at Heurtebise have been taken, lost and retaken over and over again at the point of the bayonet. Across a century come back the well-known names of battles, and our leaders can remind their men of those Marie Louises[1] who also, in March 1814, carried the fortified farm where the whistle of the bullet rivals the whistle of the breeze.

In the Est the enemy, emerging from Metz and taking advantage of Castelnau's departure, has pushed on towards the line on the heights of the Meuse which, on the right of the river, interposes between the south and the north its wooded hills, narrow necks and many defences.

The Grand Duke Nicholas, who is not unreasonably rather disturbed by our immobility, has told General Laguiche

[1] The term given to a class of Napoleon's recruits.

that he must know, as soon as possible what Joffre really proposes to do to follow up our victory of the Marne. He asks whether we are going to content ourselves with throwing the enemy out of France, or if we intend to push him back into the heart of Germany and there to dictate terms of peace. The Grand Duke's plan seems to hinge on one of these alternatives, and only in the second case would he arrange to march with every available man on Berlin as soon as Austria is knocked out. This is rather going back from what he originally said, and Paléologue and Sir George Buchanan have concocted a note to Sazonoff in which it is emphasised that, as the Allies have agreed not to conclude any separate peace, the question put by the Russian Generalissimo is coloured by politics rather than by strategy and is dependent on the three Governments. The two Ambassadors add of their own accord that the hour has come for the Allies to decide on their final goal and that with the Austrian armies *hors de combat* in Galicia, it only remains to annihilate the German forces in order to institute a new European régime which would guarantee peace for many a long year ; Sazonoff replied that the goal aimed at by Russia was precisely the régime indicated and that the Emperor entirely endorsed the Grand Duke's ideas. Delcassé having read these secret telegrams to us in Council, all the Ministers present agreed that the Government could not look on the war as finished merely when the invader was expelled, even from Lorraine, and that we are just as decided as Russia is to have done, once and for all, with the hegemony of Prussian militarism.

President Wilson has just replied to my protest against our being accused of using dum-dum bullets, and the great arbiter is careful not to compromise himself.

" I entirely appreciate the honour Your Excellency pays to the United States in turning to us at this critical hour as to a nation which holds in horror inhuman practices running clean contrary to the usages of war. In this respect your confidence in the people and the Government of the United States is not misplaced. The day will come when the great struggle will be over and when the truth can be irrefutably established ; when that moment has come, those responsible for having violated the rules of war between civilised people, if such violations have taken place, and who have brought false accusations against their adversaries, will have to bear the weight of the world's judgement."

But on what evidence will this judgement be given, and who is to say whether a lying propaganda, examples of which we are daily receiving from our diplomatic agents, will not end by leading astray the opinions of that world whose disinterested verdict President Wilson so placidly awaits. The *Tag* published on the 10th September a photograph of parcels of cartridges found at Longwy and submitted by the Germans as containing dum-dum bullets, and it was the finding of these packages which furnished a pretext for this particular German campaign of lies. But the simplest scrutiny of the design proves that the cartridges are without any penetrative power, and that they were made for use on the ranges and were quite useless for the field of battle. As soon as the German authorities saw that the illustration in the *Tag* gave the lie to their allegations they at once climbed down and had all the numbers of that issue destroyed, but a copy of it has been sent to us by our Consul-General at Geneva ; Delcassé is notifying the incident to our diplomatic representatives, and President Wilson will therefore hear of it himself from Jusserand.

Count Sabini, the Italian Commercial Attaché, who some few weeks ago gave himself a great deal of trouble about Clemenceau and myself, has been to see M. Barrère in Rome, and hinted to him that he was " in the know " as to secret Italian negotiations with Vienna and Berlin. According to Sabini, Austria has promised the Trentino and predominance in Albania to the Marquis de San Giuliano if Italy will remain neutral, while Italy would certainly emerge from her neutrality if France would consent to rectification of the Tunis frontier. Our Ambassador thought Sabini was a little vague as to what was really meant, and has only pigeon-holed the information.

M. Bratiano, who champions Roumania's immediate intervention, has gone to Sinaïa to have one more try with his Sovereign, who will welcome him but will promise him nothing. The United States, Italy and Roumania are neutrals who will choose their own hour to do what they please, and it is far better not to importune them.

21st September.—" Why ", I ask the Ministers, " do we remain at Bordeaux ? Paris is, of course, not immune from some further enemy attack, but the immediate danger is over and there is no longer any reason for prolonging our stay here." " That may be so," says Millerand, " but Joffre prefers us to remain here." Joffre, I shrewdly suspect, is not alone in his view, as the officials, especially the War Office officials, have settled down at Bordeaux and want to defer as long as possible another move. I am therefore condemned to possess my soul in patience while the unfortunate liaison officers are obliged to make these fearfully long motor journeys in order to maintain contact between Government and G.H.Q.—not very satisfactory working conditions.

Colonel Pénélon appears again, deputed as usual to tell us that " all is going well " ; he is quite aware, however, that there is a three days' delay in the programme which was at first drawn up. The Chief of the Staff, General Berthelot, wanted the big manœuvre to be made on the right, and this was found impossible. It was hoped that the 13th Corps would suffice to attack on the left wing, but the thing was badly done and everything has to be begun again, while three more days must now elapse before the other troops are in position. When they are ready, Joffre will try to sweep the Germans westwards.

With Beaudemoulin's cavalry on their flanks, Brugère's 60,000 Territorials, now entrenched near Amiens, will move on Cambrai as soon as Castelnau is ready to fight ; Castelnau's force is made up of the 4th Corps with one Moroccan division, the 13th Corps with another Moroccan division, the 14th and 20th Corps with two cavalry divisions. The 14th Corps will detrain at St.-Just-en-Chaussée and the 20th Corps south of Amiens ; they will then slip up in the direction of the Oise to catch the enemy in the flank. But three days are an eternity and, in the meanwhile, the Germans may have some fine surprises in store for us. Joffre has telegraphed to Millerand that the Germans seem determined to make a great effort in the forthcoming battle, but he would prefer, he says, that this should take place on the Aisne rather than in the Est, because if the French armies were to push the enemy as far as the Meuse, the destruction of a good many roads and bridges would make the transport of troops and of supplies less easy for us.   For this reason, and because G.H.Q. thinks the strategic situation favourable, Pénélon says again that Joffre congratulates himself on having "compelled" the Germans to halt on the Aisne; the Generalissimo, however, thinks that our troops are still inferior to the enemy, both as to training and shooting, and have only their constant courage and keenness in their favour.

Our Adriatic fleet has just landed at Antivari two batteries which are to be hauled up to the top of Mount Lovchen, and as soon as they are in position they will open fire on the Austrian warships now lying in the bay of Cattaro.   We have told Italy about this, and she is not likely to be displeased.

22nd September.—The Prefect of the Meuse sends further details of the ravages which his unhappy Department has suffered since the beginning of the war.   Several towns and more than twenty villages have been partially or totally destroyed, and the list does not include the communes of the Nord or Est.   Most of the *arrondissement* of Montmédy and the largest part of that of Verdun are in the enemy's hands; ruin abounds there and Étain no longer exists.

The Prince of Monaco, who has lost some of his illusions about the Kaiser, telegraphs to me from Monte Carlo :

"The criminal act perpetrated at Rheims by France's savage enemy constitutes a provocation to the civilised world while it characterises an army, a nation and a reign.   My consternation is no less than that of the truest French patriot."

Doumergue gives me an account of his tour of the Marne, the Oise, and the Seine and Marne ; Senlis is partly destroyed ; several towns are terribly damaged, and whole villages have been set on fire.   But such country-folk as have not been mobilised have got back to work, and the country itself has resumed its ordinary appearance ; the high roads have not been badly injured, and the general outlook on the invaded territory is less mournful than one

might have thought, while the supplies for the civilians are
all right. Doumergue has seen General Foch at Châlons
and is loud in praise of his extraordinary calmness and clear-
headedness.

General Headquarters has heard to-day that the enemy
are detraining troops at Cambrai and seem to be getting
ready for fresh operations. Joffre has asked Castelnau to
push north two corps of the left of the Second Army to
outmanœuvre the enemy's right, but at the same moment
the 13th Corps, which forms Castlenau's right, is fighting on
the wooded massif of Lassigny, where it is entrenched without
being able to get out.

23rd September.—The Indian troops are disembarking in
the next two days at Marseilles, and the British Government
have asked us to provide trains which are to stop on the road
for three hours to let the men wash and another hour to let
them cook their rice. But this does not mean that they will
ask for the same interlude on the field of battle. Galliéni
has written two letters to Millerand, one official and the other
private, to ask for three further army corps and 72,000
Territorials for the eventual defence of Paris. The War
Minister thinks this demand very exaggerated just when
Paris is under no threat, and when every man available is
required for the front line. It seems to me more and more
necessary that we should inform ourselves on the spot, and
I again urge this on Millerand, who now raises no objection
to our paying a visit in the near future to the General Headquarters and to the armies.

M. Bratiano has come back from Sinaïa a little dis-
concerted; he no longer thinks the moment favourable for
any immediate action, but he still agrees with Jonesco as to
a possible abdication of the King.

Serbia begs us to send mountain guns, but the bareness
of our own cupboard prevents our dispensing goods to our
friends with liberality.

24th September.—Joffre has telegraphed to Millerand asking
for authority to appoint Foch as assistant to the Commander-
in-Chief, with eventual succession to himself. Each time
that Pénélon speaks of Foch, he says that he is the genius of

the war,[1] and he is certainly the one of all of Joffre's subordinates in whom those who know him lodge their highest hopes. But by an arrangement which has not been made public, Galliéni is designated as Joffre's successor, and the Military Governor of Paris holds too high rank to make him immediately subordinate to the Commander-in-Chief.   Galliéni and Joffre are about the same age, and in the Colonies the latter was under the orders of the former, whose personality scarcely fits him for a subordinate post—and if Foch were to receive at once a promise of succession, Galliéni would consider himself deprived of an eventual right, which has been admitted, and he could scarcely be other than dissatisfied.   But Joffre, who is shouldering a crushing task, is certainly in need of an assistant, and it would as certainly be impossible to find a better man than Foch.[2]

From my friend the Mayor of Commerçy comes a telegram which is mournful reading :

" Our unhappy compatriots of the villages which have been set on fire and destroyed have found refuge and help at Commerçy and St. Mihiel ; they beg me to convey to you their thanks for the gifts you have sent them and to assure you of their entire confidence in the Government of national defence.   Vive la France ! "

What wonderful fellows, to think more of sending us encouragement than of asking us for help in their extremity !

In the evening we learn that a battle is going on between Noyon and Péronne and that Castelnau is busy from the Oise to the Somme.

25th September.—Colonel Pénélon comes to see me in the morning, by no means so confident as a day or two ago. Our people still hope to win the battle, which was to be

---

[1] " C'est le dieu de la guerre."
[2] A few months later Joffre and Foch were motoring to Furnes, to see the King of the Belgians, when an accident occurred, the Generalissimo being somewhat severely hurt and having to return immediately to his Headquarters.   Foch wrote to the Government to inquire what would have happened had the Commander-in-Chief been more seriously injured and placed *hors de combat*; he received no reply for about two months, when he was informed that the official letter of " succession " was in Galliéni's pocket.—G. A.

forced on the enemy under our own conditions, but no very great results are now expected from it ; it is only reckoned that Castelnau will take St. Quentin and thus hinder communications between the Germans and Belgium ; the enemy would thus retire, not to the Meuse, as was hoped, but on the canal behind St. Quentin and to the east of the town. At the most we shall have gained a very slender advantage.

On our right Sarrail has, according to G.H.Q., made a bad blunder. He ought to have moved up northwards and forced the lines which Castelnau had not been able to cross ; he has not succeeded, and as he only left on the Hauts de Meuse, to the east of St. Mihiel, one reserve division, the Germans have pushed on to the approaches of the town. The smooth things which G.H.Q. said to us yesterday have once more been traversed by facts ; my poor country of the Meuse has been more and more invaded from the east as it has been from the north.

In Council the question arises of who is to be "adjoint". We all recognise that the choice of Foch, whether as immediate collaborator or as eventual successor, is excellent in itself, and that we cannot brush aside the Generalissimo's proposal, but most of us think also that we shall have to tread delicately as regards Galliéni. How can we take away from him without wounding him the official letter which he holds, and further, if Paris should in the near future be quite unthreatened, how can we leave so important a soldier simply as Governor of Paris ? Millerand thinks the best thing will be to talk the matter over with Joffre and Galliéni, and consequently he now admits that he and I ought not to postpone any further our visit to Headquarters.

There is bad news from our left wing, where we have lost ground. A wireless from the German cavalry shows that a battalion of our 14th Corps has been surprised and a large number of prisoners taken, although the remainder of the 14th Corps and the 20th have been able to continue northward their appointed march. Joffre still thinks that they will succeed in effecting the turn south-eastwards, but he is reckoning less and less on any important results.

At the end of the day the Prefect of the Meuse sends me a telegram which fills a cup of bitterness :

" Germans are masters of St. Mihiel and the Roman camp."

My wife and I are tortured with thoughts of the lovely little town with all its works of art, and of all the friends we have left there, and we ask ourselves how the enemy was able so easily to seize the fortress of the Roman camp which G.H.Q. thought would be sure to hold out for some days. But we have scarcely conjured up these thoughts before we learn that our batteries, our cupolas and our casemates, if they have not served any great purpose for ourselves, are, on the other hand, going to be useful to the invader.

" The Germans", the Prefect telegraphs to us, " are bombarding Sampigny from the Roman camp."

They will never have a better line of direct fire, as from the camp of the Romans they can see the peaceful village where my parents, my wife and I have passed so many happy days. Oh, those happy days which, in the middle of this fearful general disaster, I have no right even to think about.

26th September.—The communiqués to the Press still continue to conceal reverses, as I think, wrongly. There is no allusion to the surrender of the Roman camp, but we are told that we have retaken Berry-au-Bac and Ribécourt, although we were never told that we had lost these places. Once more I urge on the military authorities that we should be told the truth, and I ask why it is that one of our *forts d'arrêt* has so quickly given in. We are unable to dislodge the enemy when he is entrenched in open country, and yet on the Hauts de Meuse we cannot defend a fortified position for half a day. The Germans have violated Belgium because they were afraid of our forts of the Est, and now they have accounted for these bugbears almost without striking a blow. If the Roman camp had been smashed by the 420 shells, as Badonvillers was, one could understand its having been taken in a few hours, but we are not even told that it succumbed to a bombardment of heavy artillery. I

am determined to have light thrown on who is responsible
for this occurrence, and Millerand says, not too pleasantly,
that the question only affects the responsible Minister. I
reply that I have a right to know, and several of the Ministers
back me, and the Council agree that I am right. The
members of the Government are indeed conscious that they
are left far too much in ignorance of military operations,
and Viviani says that no one tells him anything. He has
gone so far as to say to Ribot : " I know nothing of what is
happening with the Armies, and I can get no information ;
when Parliament meets I shall plead guilty and resign."
This was, of course, only a little bit of sulks, but it goes to
show how intensely annoyed the Prime Minister is by the
secretiveness and silence of our G.H.Q. In the evening
Millerand tells me on the telephone that the usual " All is
going well " has come in ; the enemy, it would seem, has
attacked all along the Front and has been repulsed with
heavy losses. That's all very well as far as it goes. But
yesterday Pénélon told me that it was we who were going
to attack their centre, whereas to-day it seems that we
are being attacked and have to defend ourselves. Our left
wing seems to have crept on a little bit, but the enemy has
yielded next to nothing, while on our right the " situation is
unchanged ", that is to say, the Germans, who have crossed
the Meuse from St. Mihiel by the big bridge, have not even
been thrown back into the town. What on earth has
happened over there that such a dent has been made all
of a sudden in our Front which seemed to be so strongly
fortified ?

With the post comes a telegram :

" TROYES.—Germans at Nubécourt (Meuse) have made the
burial allotment for the Poincaré family into water-closets and
have sacked any house in which there is a Poincaré portrait."

This news is not so far confirmed, but I hear for certain
that the Germans have taken away from my brother Lucien's
house at Triaucourt my pictures and photograph, and at
Nubécourt have forced open the locked door of our little
cemetery in order to bury their officers just where my wife

and I are going to lie, near those we have loved and who have gone before.

The Government has asked the Belgian army to co-operate in the movement which Joffre wants to set afoot in order to free our Departments of the north and Belgium itself.   Klobukowski has found M. de Brocqueville as energetic, as full of confidence and as decided as ever, and the King likewise, and he telegraphs :

" I have received the best possible impression as to the action which is being strenuously prepared for, and in which the Belgian army will participate with all keenness."

While we and our Allies are making these fine projects the Germans continue their bombardment of the cathedral at Rheims, and, to excuse themselves, their propaganda has invented a new fable.   The German Minister at Copenhagen has handed in to the Danish Government a Note which throws on France the responsibility for setting the basilica on fire.   It is alleged that the reason why the enemy has fired on the towers is because we had set up a signal station there, and that for the defence of the German army it was necessary to destroy this observation post.   General Head-quarters denies this statement categorically, but the Danish Government is in such mortal fear of the Empire of the Hohen-zollerns that they allowed almost all the Danish Press to comment favourably on this pitiful attempt at self-justification.

27th September.—The " decisive move ", according to G.H.Q., may now be put off till the 30th.   Once more our left wing has been opposed by the enemy in greater strength than we expected, and we shall no doubt be obliged to move fresh troops to the Somme ; the 11th Corps, taken from the Ninth Army, has gone into the line to-day but is not suffi-cient to ensure the success of the operation.   As they want the battle to be finished before our visit to G.H.Q., Millerand and I must postpone going until 1st October.

The English are quite methodically completing the conquest of the German Colonies, and the port of Frederick William, the capital of German North Guinea, has been occupied by Australian forces.

28th September.—Things drag on, and Millerand acknowledges, *en tête à tête*, that he is very anxious. He is quite
right to conceal, as I do, his anxiety before the public, but
what I object to is that he is as secretive with me as he is
with strangers. Anyhow it is quite certain that we cannot
make any way against the reinforced German right wing,
and an even more serious state of things is to be found in
our shortage of armament, which now is known to be much
worse than what Messimy and Millerand were led to believe
by the incomplete information furnished to them. It is
not true, as was said, that we are turning out 500 1886
rifles every day, nor is it true that we are altering daily a
thousand 1874's into the 1886 pattern. No 1886 rifles are
being directly made, only carbines to replace the rifles
which the Custom House officers and foresters are using,
and which will be taken from them for the troops ; the
alteration of the 1874 rifles into the 1886 cannot be begun
as yet. The shortage of ammunition for our 75's is more
alarming ; our reserve of these guns is exhausted, while our
mobilisation plans did not envisage the manufacture of any
new guns.

As to aeroplanes, at the beginning of August we had only
twenty-four squadrons, each comprising six aeroplanes
manned and equipped, besides some spare aeroplanes with
lorries and transport. Since war broke out twelve new
squadrons have been brought into being, and we have six
dirigibles *en ordre de marche*, one of these has been destroyed,
another is being repaired, and a third is useless ; four more
are being constructed, and thus our inferiority in aviation
is terrible. The same deficiencies are painfully obvious in
clothing, boots, camp equipment, blankets, warm clothes and
single tents. We have bought in England, Spain, America
and Canada, but what an infinity of things is still lacking.
The war has certainly taken us by surprise at a moment of
something like penury, while the Germans could gather from
our last Parliamentary discussions what was our position.
Millerand is faced with a formidable task which will claim all
his immense capacity for work as well as all his stores of
sound common sense.

Colonel Pellé, a distinguished artillery officer, has been sent by Joffre to give me further news about armaments. He is not quite so pessimistic as General Gaudin was, but he recognises that munitions for the 75's are sadly lacking and it will be impossible to maintain the expenditure at the present rate. It will not be a question of speeding up production ; it will be absolutely necessary to limit the artillery firing and if necessary to reduce the batteries to three or even two guns. What will be the consequence of this ? Pellé tells me that Joffre himself has only just been informed as to the amount of stuff that has been fired away, and there is no doubt some battery commanders have been much too extravagant, especially young officers who have suddenly, owing to their seniors being killed, succeeded to commands without sufficient experience.

29th September.—Colonel Pénélon, who reflects what is felt at G.H.Q., becomes more and more disillusioned every day. He fears now that no decision will be arrived at, and that we may be doomed to carry on a long siege warfare against an entrenched enemy ; we have further reinforced our left wing. The 2nd Corps is trying to make its way to-day into the region of Thiépval but is finding itself up against the promontory where the Germans are settled, and is stopped short. The 10th Corps, which has been taken from the Third Army, has just been moved to the left of the 2nd Corps, and other reinforcements are arriving or will arrive, Barbot and Fayolle's reserve divisions, the 8th Cavalry Division, and in a little while the 21st Corps will be there. As the Second Army is now strung out along a considerably increased front, General Maud'huy, a *chasseur à pied* who hails from Metz, is in orders to command, under Castelnau, a detachment of this force. The Germans are strengthening their right also, and are solidly entrenched in positions north of the Somme and between the Somme and the Oise.

Joffre has agreed as to sending the troops on the flank of the enemy by Dunkirk and the north ; Millerand will ask for the batteries which are at Havre and the 30,000 Territorials who are doing nothing there to be sent up.

As an interlude I receive the deposed Sultan of Morocco,

Abd el Aziz. I saw him two years ago at the Quai d'Orsay when his visit to France was marked by escapades which were little short of scandalous. He is a Moroccan, very brown in complexion, with white teeth and a heavily scented skin, and seems to be a blend of cleverness and trickery ; he brought with him his smooth-tongued and very wideawake interpreter, Ben Ghabrit. General Lyautey does not want Abd el Aziz to go back to Morocco, where his presence might encourage disaffection ; but we shall have some difficulty in keeping him in France by persuasion, and more substantial arguments will have to be used.

In the evening Millerand telephones again : " Situation unchanged." G.H.Q. thought this morning that the German corps which is occupying St. Mihiel, and which has debouched on the left bank of the Meuse, at Chauvancourt, has been very rash, and that we might be able to surround them, but on the contrary it is the Germans who are attacking us in this sector as they are attacking us in Woëvre and in the faubourgs of Rheims. Patience has indeed to be our motto.

30th September.—The month is over and we are still at Bordeaux, Heaven knows why. This morning Klobukowski telegraphs that the American Secretary of Legation at Brussels, who has come to Antwerp through Holland, says the Germans have arrested M. Max, the burgomaster, whose courage and devotion have been alike more than admirable. The only thing that can be alleged against him is that he has been too firm, and too astute, in standing up for the rights of his fellow-citizens. The Prefect of the Nord reports that he found Orchies, which the enemy set afire on Friday, a cinder-heap. Out of 1200 houses only 100 have been spared, the Hôtel de Ville and parish church being destroyed.

The Belgian Minister, very much overwrought, calls on behalf of his Government to implore our aid for Antwerp, which is seriously threatened. We had been forewarned of this yesterday and to-day by Klobukowski : and it would seem the Germans are attacking again the Waelhem and Wavre St. Catherine forts, and the attack is extended south-east as far as Lierre. Neither of the two forts can withstand heavy artillery, and if the first stronghold is forced, the Belgian Government will retire to Ostend with the field army, about 65,000 men, leaving the garrison to hold out as long as possible.

We agree—Viviani, Millerand, Delcassé and I—that we cannot ask Joffre to spare any men just when, man for man, we are slightly inferior in numbers to the enemy facing us, who is, moreover, likely to be stiffened very soon with fresh contingents; but we must give a helping hand to Belgium, who has shown herself as brave as she is loyal. The question is whether we can send from Havre to Ostend the Territorial division under the command of either Pau or Lanrezac, or even under a British General ; one thing is certain, England must be asked to join forces in this matter, and Delcassé will see Bertie, who is at Bordeaux, at once, while Millerand will talk to the two generals who are also here.[1]

1st October.—This morning General Joffre has not sent the Ministerial bulletin, for fear, he says, of indiscretions, nor has the messenger who left Headquarters last night brought any special message. But a little later comes a telegram from the Generalissimo to Millerand to say that in order to husband the ammunition for the 75's, he must give up at several points the proposed offensive ; he adds that the last official report as to the manufacture does not agree with what was said earlier, and he gives the impression of having had an ugly surprise. Truth to tell, G.H.Q. should have had more precise knowledge of the average daily consumption of munitions and should have warned the War Office as to how far demand was exceeding supply. What has been needed is closer and more regular correspondence between the General in the field and the Minister in his office. Perhaps also the " sprinkling " the enemy's front, as apart from actual artillery preparations, has been a little overdone, and perhaps also a little more economy altogether might have been judiciously observed ; anyhow, it is annoying that the administrative centre should not have been better, and earlier, informed.

Millerand says that after the evacuation of Douai by the Germans, 100,000 empty shells for the 75's were found in the

[1] Cf. *Le Déblocus d'Anvers*, by Major Menzel.

town, all of which could perfectly well have been used : there seems to have been some unaccountable neglect.

The War Minister has consulted Joffre as to whether we can send the Territorial division from Havre to Ostend or Antwerp. The Commander-in-Chief deprecates the idea and thinks no good will come of it ; anyhow he opposes giving the command to Lanrezac, who, he thinks is responsible for the sets-back at Charleroi and Guise. But Delcassé has already announced the despatch of this division to the Belgian Government, who are profuse in thanks, and we must ask Joffre to give way on the point, and allow us to make an effort to save Belgium from the impending disaster which, as Millerand telegraphs to G.H.Q., will have a serious moral as well as military effect.

It is put to Joffre whether his objections would fall to the ground if part of the Belgian army, retiring from Antwerp, were to be posted in the neighbourhood of Ghent alongside of our own people and of a division which we are asking England to send.

Joffre proposes as a compromise that the whole field army should come out of Antwerp, leaving there only the garrison necessary to defend the place, that the French troops should go from Dunkirk to the neighbourhood of Courtrai to link up with the Belgian army if these are obliged to retire on Bruges and Ostend. A considerable French force, including a large number of cavalry, is being formed round Arras and Douai, and a strong English contingent, part of which will land at Boulogne, will move on Lille ; with this combination the Belgian army should be safe. As soon as this plan has been carried out, the Belgian army would be on the left of, and in contact with, the Allied armies. Joffre tells Millerand that the plans must be kept absolutely secret, and that for the moment no one in Belgium should know about it but the King. But the matter presses, for to-day again the Belgian Government say that the fall of Antwerp might be really imminent, and General De Guise, the Governor, declares that he cannot answer for anything in view of the fearful effect of the German heavy guns.

Clemenceau is obsessed with the idea that, if only the Government had taken the trouble, it would have been possible to have obtained the co-operation of the Japanese army, and he so harps on this idea that Delcassé has decided to resume conversations at Tokio. But it is more and more obvious that Japan is reserving her forces, or anyhow her land forces, for the Far East ; Sir Edward Grey and Paul Cambon are perfectly aware of this and are occasionally a little sarcastic in reminding us of the fact.

The Serbians have suffered terribly in their attempt on Semlin. The Serbian army seems to be in a great tangle ; the units are attenuated after their heavy fighting, and the troops are beginning to show signs of depression.

2nd October.—There is further complication as to Belgium and her difficulties, and we are told that with Antwerp it is only a question of hours ; also the English Government will only send one division unless we send trained Regular troops. It is eventually decided that our Territorial division from Havre shall be sent to Ostend and Ghent in any case, and that we shall tell London that we are doing this without prejudice as to the future ; Millerand is to ask Joffre again if he cannot possibly spare a Regular division either from the troops at the Front or from the garrisons at Paris or Belfort ; we also suggest that General Pau shall be sent to Antwerp to study the situation on the spot. Joffre answers that he still has no faith in what the Belgians will do in this matter, but that he agrees to the Territorial division being sent from Havre to Belgium so as to create a moral effect ; he thinks anyhow that one of the Territorial divisions from Paris should be sent with the one from Havre by sea. He sees no objection to General Pau being sent on a special mission to Antwerp, but he thinks that the command of the two Territorial divisions should be given to Brugère, who is in charge of the Territorial army of the Nord. Augagneur and Delcassé will do the necessary, but if it is a question of hours, shall we be too late ?

3rd October.—We know from a secret and trustworthy source that there is a Convention between Italy and Roumania, and that neither of them will emerge from their neutrality without reference to the other ; we must leave them time to make up their minds.

Another troublous day ; Pénélon has left Joffre in despair, as a result of a conversation with General Gaudin, who has told him it is impossible to let him have for some weeks the 50,000 daily rounds for the 75's. Joffre declares that the strategic situation has never been better, but that the shortage of munitions paralyses him, and it has been decided that of the 450 rounds apiece which remain, only 300 shall be used up to the 10th of October. There will then only remain 150 rounds per gun, plus the 10,000 from daily manufacture, plus the 100,000 shells cast for artillery schools for their use in practice, plus the 60,000 shells picked up here and there, plus—if the Germans have not gone back to Douai since yesterday—the 100,000 shells which apparently were so strangely forgotten in that town. All this put together leaves us still very short.

Joffre also has told Millerand that the situation at Arras is very serious, because one of the regular corps there was badly deployed ; also, near Roye, we have been violently attacked and have only just been able to hold on. In the evening our news is a little brighter, and so day by day we oscillate between substantial fears and slender hopes.

The Belgian Government has decided to withdraw to Ostend to-day ; the King will move with his Field Army. Antwerp may hold out for eight days more, and we are again entreated to do anything we possibly can, either to relieve the place by some prompt movement or to help the Belgian army in their retreat. But our own arrangements are again changed, and Joffre, by a sudden and happy inspiration, now prefers to send, instead of the Paris Territorial Division, a brigade of Marine Fusiliers who, so far, have not fought at sea and are sure to fight as well on Belgian soil as on far-off coasts.

The Portuguese Government has made an offer to England to send us a division here, with artillery, to be at the disposal of Sir John French, but some time must elapse before they can arrive.

Suddenly there arrives from Antwerp, marked as

" Extremely Urgent ", a new telegram. The First Lord of
the Admiralty, Mr. Winston Churchill, whose intelligence is
of a piece with his impetuosity, has arrived there and has
seen the King and the Ministers, from whom he has obtained
a provisional consent to let things remain where they are ;
the Field Army will therefore not retire for the moment. Mr.
Churchill has promised to furnish within three days 7000
men in addition to the 2000 Marines whom he has already
brought to Antwerp. Seven days later the British Government will send 60,000 more men, including two cavalry
divisions,[1] which, with the two French divisions detailed,
will bring this Allied relief force up to about 100,000 men.

A talk with General Gaudin leads me to the belief that
our situation as regards munitions, poor though it is, is not
quite so dangerous as Joffre thinks, if only manufacture is
speeded up ; Gaudin is going to make an exhaustive inquiry
in every Department as to establishments which can undertake to execute immediate orders.

At last, after daily and lively representations, the Government and General Headquarters have granted my exeat,
and it is arranged that I am to go to-morrow with Millerand
to the armies. Hitherto a President of the Republic has
never travelled, in his official capacity, without being accompanied by a Minister as by a shadow, and I have determined
to pay respect to this custom on this occasion. But if later
I meet with further difficulties on this score, I shall waive an
arrangement which, after all, is not constitutionally imposed.
It will remain for another Chamisso to write of my adven-
tures, if he so wishes.

[1] The 3rd Cavalry Division only was intended.—G. A.

CHAPTER VIII

4th October.—A very short Council and a very hurried breakfast to enable us to get away in time. Millerand and I occupy a military motor-car, on the box of which there is a reservist chauffeur, who is none other than the son of M. Morel, Governor of the Crédit Foncier, and by his side a good-looking Captain of Spahis, one Captain Doumayrou, who is attached to the War Office. Viviani, with General Duparge, follows in the second car, while in the third there is M. Richard, Director of the Sûreté Générale, and one or two of those officials whom I designate my guardian angels.

We drive rapidly across Angoulême and Poitiers, which are teeming with Territorials, who try to look as soldierly as possible, and with young recruits ; at the entrance to every town we are stopped by sentries who verify our *laissez-passer*. In these places life seems to be following a more normal course ; if it were not for the coming and going of men in uniform, there is little to remind us that we are at war. At Tours the liaison officer meets us with the report that the situation at Arras is still serious, if not critical. As was feared, Douai has been retaken by the Germans ; to help the town the 21st Corps had been moved to the region of Lille to try and get the better of the German force at grips with Maud'huy, but they had to stop short at St. Pol, Merville and Armentières, and almost immediately were obliged to retire southwards towards Lens, and are now on the heights of Nôtre Dame de Lorette. It would seem, therefore, that the German sweep north-westwards and seawards has begun, and an intercepted wireless runs :

" His Majesty desires that the cavalry shall be to-morrow, 4th October, on the rear of the enemy."

To-day is the 4th of October, and one can only wonder how far the Imperial order has been carried out. We leave Tours at eight o'clock in the evening and, under a glorious starlit night, make our way to Orleans, where we are the guests of the Prefect. The drive gives an opportunity for a long and confidential, if anxious, talk with Millerand, who for the moment speaks his mind to me, as he used to do, and throws aside the secretiveness in which he likes to wrap himself when in Council.

5th October.—We leave Orleans at seven o'clock in the morning and pass through Pithiviers and Fontainebleau to reach the quiet little town of the Aube, Romilly-sur-Seine, where General Headquarters are installed in a large school building.

Joffre seems to be in splendid health, both physical and moral ; he is just as one has always known him, imperturbable, unruffled, with a smile on his face, and making his points with gentle obstinacy. It does one good to see the tall massive figure, the serene face, the great white moustache and the light blue eyes shining out from under the thick eyebrows. Every word he says gives the impression of balance and coolness, and suggests that with him lodge the precise military merits essential for the uneasy hours in which we are living. What would have happened on the morrow of Charleroi with perhaps a more imaginative but a fretful and impulsive Commander-in-Chief ? One shudders to think of it. Almost the first consideration is the supplies of munitions, and it seems impossible to reconcile the calculations of General Headquarters with those of General Gaudin; we have to ask Joffre to verify anew the figures of his experts, but anyhow a vast effort must be made if manufacture is to keep anything like step with requirements, and it is possible that, to have a sufficient output, we may, sooner or later, be compelled to recall to the factories some of the skilled workmen who are at the front. Needless to say, this way out of the difficulty does not attract G.H.Q. Joffre gives me a detailed note with regard to the movements of British troops. Sir John French has asked that his army shall resume its former place, that is to say, on the extreme left ; but this position is a little altered by the creation of Maunoury's army, by the change of place of Castelnau's army, and by the even more recent formation of Maud'huy's detachment. To-day, the English army holds, on the right bank of the Aisne, a front line between the Fifth and Sixth Armies, and agreement has been come to with Sir John that, without for the moment any definite change of position, his 2nd Corps may be taken out of the line here and sent north, a move which is taking place and will be completed by the 9th. Sir John now asks that his 3rd Corps shall follow the 2nd, but these successive moves will mean that for ten days the British army will be split into two parties, and during that time we shall not be able to reinforce Maud'huy's detachment on our left. The Generalissimo insists that the current manœuvre has for its chief object to overrun and overthrow the German right wing, and that it is therefore of the utmost importance that the troops moving to the left, whether English or French, should act all together as soon as they are detrained ; failing this, the success of this flank march may be seriously compromised. General Wilson has come to our headquarters to tell Joffre what is in Sir John's mind, and says that his Chief wants to wait until all his forces are together before attacking ; unfortunately, it is only too likely that in the interval the enemy will not leave us alone. If he should attack it may mean, so Joffre says, a regular battle, and it would be a great pity if this were to take place when a certain number of British divisions are to all intents and purposes immobilised. Joffre has said all this to Sir John in a letter which he sent him the other day ; and of which he gives me a copy ; he now asks me to arrange for the French Government to approach Lord Kitchener and urge that the British divisions shall take the field as soon as they detrain without waiting for their rendezvous. As regards Galliéni, Joffre agrees it would be awkward to take away the official letter with the reversion to command in the field, and he will appoint Foch as his " assistant " without giving any definite promise as to his succession to supreme command. Foch, who was sounded as to this yesterday, is quite willing, and he has now been instructed to look after the defence of the region of the north and to hold up the Germans if they try and outrun us and get round our left in the race to the sea. Foch is to start immediately and, after seeing Castelnau and Maud'huy, will probably make Doullens his headquarters.

The military situation, we are told, is serious, but need not give rise to serious anxiety. The worst feature is the shortage of munitions, which for some weeks, if not for some months, will paralyse or, anyhow, impede us in our course. With his finger on the map, the Commander-in-Chief explains in detail all the prescribed movements of troops, and then, amid the hurrahs of the inhabitants, takes us to the little house where he is lodging and entertains us to a breakfast which is as excellent as it is simple. Joffre has a few words to say about Lanrezac, whom he considers an excellent theoretical soldier, but out of place on the field of battle, and whom he charges with serious mistakes ; I have heard the very same thing from an officer on Franchet d'Esperey's Staff, who told me the other day that when under fire Lanrezac seems to lose his head a little. Joffre is going to say to Millerand : " You have entrusted Lanrezac with the preparation of the Second Line Army ; nothing could be better, but the day when the army is ready to take the field, you must find another Commander ".

Early in the afternoon we take leave, and on our journey make a slight detour to cross the fields at Sézanne and Mont-mirail, where the other day our victory of a hundred years ago was repeated, the German wave having been broken at a village which, curiously enough, bears the name of Allement. All up and down the place the houses have been demolished by shells or burnt out by fire, but the peasants have come back, and in the ruined country they are doing what they can to resume their agriculture.

Then a visit to the Château of Mondement, which the Moroccan division took from the Prussian left, and where the

enemy officers were feasting gaily, when one of our batteries
moved up in the night and fired on them almost point-
blank, the walls toppling down on the heads of the tipplers :
hundreds of empty bottles and the débris of hundreds of
others strew the courtyard as witnesses to a Germany orgy.
Near by, in the country-side, we can recognise a French
grave by a little wooden cross and a newly made mound on
which are some *képis* and some autumn flowers, and where
two poor women have come to pray and weep ; a few steps
farther and, on the outskirts of a wood, we find the scattered
remains of a German battery which has been annihilated by
our 75's.   A wheel, some parts of an ammunition waggon,
some blood-stained linen, some boots in holes, paper and
French post cards on which German handwriting is traced ;
again a little farther, and ground, recently dug up, is covering
German corpses.

Just before reaching Fère-en-Tardenois, the British
Commander-in-Chief's Headquarters, we meet a long line
of supply waggons, and it would certainly seem that the
British soldier is well fed.   Sir John is awaiting us with
Prince Maurice of Battenberg,[1] the Queen of Spain's brother,
whom I saw in London last year, and who seems very
pleased to be fighting alongside our men.   A guard of
honour, composed of Englishmen and Irishmen, gives the
salute, and we find the French mission installed in the
garden belonging to the house which shelters the Field-
Marshal, who has a big fire burning on his hearth, although
the weather is by no means cold.   I have a long and quite
cordial talk with Sir John, who says there is no need to
approach Lord Kitchener, as he is quite in agreement with
Joffre, and promises that his troops shall take the field as
they arrive.   Sir John does not appear to be very much in
sympathy with his Minister for War, whom he blames for
not establishing any liaison between British Headquarters
and the British troops who are to co-operate with the
Belgians and ourselves in the defence of Antwerp.   Sir
John begs me to ask the British Government to put
an end to conditions which he thinks conflict with unity

[1] Killed a fortnight later.

of action,[1] and this evening at Epernay Millerand will telegraph to Delcassé.

A glass of champagne in honour of the British army and we bid Sir John good-bye, to cross at nightfall the woods where, according to Joffre, there still lurk Uhlans, who come nightly to prey on the neighbouring farms.

At Epernay we are lodged in the house of a great champagne manufacturer, M. Chandon ; during the battle of the Marne our host had to entertain General von Bülow, whose map is still pinned on to the door of his dressing-room, and my room, full of bibelots and beautiful furniture, is the one which the German General occupied ; somehow the reversion to it makes me feel a little uncomfortable.

Late at night one of the liaison officers arrives at Epernay and tells us that Lille has certainly been retaken by the Germans, who are also in Lens, that nothing is yet known as to how our cavalry fared in the fight going on north of Arras, and that towards Roye we have been shifted back a little : in a word, the day has been far from satisfactory. Maud'huy's detachment now becomes an independent army and will be numbered the Tenth.

6th October.—Very early in the morning we start for Romigny, the little village north of Châtillon-sur-Marne, where Franchet d'Esperey has his headquarters. The line for which he is responsible extends from Poissy, north of the Aisne, to Neuvillette, north-west of Rheims ; on his right he has what remains of Foch's army, which has to-day been broken up, and on his left are the English.

---

[1] Sir John's dissatisfaction at the 4th Corps not being placed immediately under his orders, and his complaint to Joffre on this score, were premature ; on the day after the fall of Antwerp (10th October) Kitchener wrote to Sir John :

" . . . I hope you do not think I was unduly interfering with your operations by not putting the special force it was proposed to send for the relief of Antwerp under your direct orders. My reasons for doing so were, in the first place, that the Cabinet would not allow the 7th Division, etc., to leave the country for more than a rapid movement on Antwerp, with the intention of bringing it back here when the blow had been struck there. I only got this decision altered yesterday, and at once placed them under your orders ; secondly, we were in such close touch by telegraph and telephone with Ostend and Antwerp, while you were engaged in moving and more or less cut off. . . . I am doing all I can for you and for the sake of the main operations which I never lose sight of."—G. A.

Franchet d'Esperey is a sturdy little man, keen and refusing to be depressed, burnt by the African sun and toughened by one expedition after another into *Le Sud Oranais*, Tonkin, China and Morocco. He is rather fretful as to not being allowed for the moment to go forward, Joffre having forbidden this, partly from lack of ammunition and partly from fear of letting our left be exposed ; the General, who knows the Balkans very well, thinks that if we settle down into trench warfare in France, we must think out a way, in agreement with the Serbians, of turning the enemy in the Near East. Among his staff officers whom he introduces to me is the hereditary Prince of Monaco, now serving as a volunteer with the French army.

While the General is telling us what he is doing, the guns never cease booming in the direction of Rheims ; his trenches are in certain places only thirty or forty yards from the Germans, and the barbed-wire entanglements are sometimes common property. A wounded German remained for some days between the two lines without his comrades coming to take him away, and every night the French patrols found him in the same place, and as he was not in a condition to be moved, they arranged for him to be fed. As soon as possible the man was brought in to our lines, and was delighted with the way in which he had been treated by our people. Meanwhile the enemy, under pretext of shortening the war by a system of terror, were burning the villages and shooting the peasants, but there is no reason why, even in a bitter struggle like this, Frenchmen should forget their obligations to humanity.

The General takes us to Jonchery, where he proposes to move his headquarters, and where we see a casualty clearing station and a hospital ; so that I can inform myself at first hand as to the sanitary and postal arrangements in respect of which I receive almost daily complaints. Things have been improved, but if much has been done, much remains to be done.

After breakfast at Château Thierry we move on to Villers-Cotterets, where Maunoury has the headquarters of the Sixth Army. The gallant artillery officer, who fought in

1870, is an old friend of mine, as I knew him as Governor of Paris in 1912 ; he had reached the age limit and was only recalled to duty on the 20th of August on the very eve of the battle where he played so valuable and brilliant a part. Like Franchet d'Esperey he is eating his heart out at not being able to attack and is loud in praise of his troops, who only want to be allowed to fight again. On leaving Villers-Cotterets we make a brief halt at Senlis ; the lovely little town on the grassy banks of the Nonette now offers a spectacle of horror and desolation ; the Rue de la République has been deliberately destroyed, and nothing remains of the fine Palais de Justice or the Sous-Prefecture, but happily the cathedral has only been slightly damaged ; the Mayor has been taken as hostage and shot.

7th October.—We reached Paris late last night and arrived at the Élysée without anyone recognising us. The *Bulletin des Armées* announces to-day my visit to General Headquarters, and Millerand puts out, perhaps a little pompously, the reasons why this visit did not take place earlier. It would seem that my visit was deferred because the official presence of the President of the Republic might be something of a nuisance and hinder operations. That may be so, but is it necessary to give so solemn a complexion to a simple visit to the troops, and is it not possible to do this quite quietly, without getting in the way and without attracting any attention ? Anyhow this is what I propose to do in the future.

Galliéni takes Millerand and myself to see the fortress, and he shows us, with quite justifiable satisfaction, the improvements that have been made in the last week ; sixty-five summers and rough Colonial experience may have done something to impair Galliéni's health, but they have done nothing to enfeeble his intellect or his brain, and one has only to talk to him for a few minutes to know that one is in the presence of a real leader of men. He discourses on military events shrewdly and quite impartially, and has only one criticism to offer, that the front is now too long for one command ; he would like two distinct armies to exist, one of which would be under his orders, a splitting up of authority which would probably have more drawbacks than advantages.

Toward midday Colonel Pénélon once more brings me rather a better account, as we know at least from intercepted wires that General de Marwitz and his cavalry are standing at bay. Round Roye, north-east of Montdidier, our 4th Corps has unfortunately given ground to the 21st German Corps, and Castelnau has sent a rather uncomfortable telegram to General Headquarters to which Joffre has replied that he must hold on at any price and that he will send him fresh troops. Our 11th Corps is going to make an immediate counter-attack, and Foch is in position ; otherwise there is nothing. On the Hauts de Meuse we are making very, very slow progress, and our troops have been obliged to bombard my dear St. Mihiel, in which the Germans are sitting.

In the afternoon Viviani and I visit an English hospital sumptuously installed in the Hôtel Astoria at the corner of the Rue de Presbourg which the Germans built in the form of a "skyscraper", quite indifferent to the inconvenience caused to the inhabitants in the Place de l'Etoile ; the hotel is now confiscated, and I hope that after the war its insolent head will be decapitated. Then we go on to another hospital at Neuilly, even more luxuriously arranged by the American colony, where we are received by kind Mr. Herrick, who warmly congratulates us on our victory of the Marne ; the people who recognise us here, and during the drive, give us a sort of " prodigal son's " greeting.

In the evening M. Klotz, in his uniform of chef d'escadron, and Paul Doumer come to the Élysée full of praise for what Galliéni has done and with an account which is delightful to hear, of the calm demeanour of the Paris population.

8th October.—At eight o'clock in the evening we arrive back at Bordeaux, and to my great distress I learn that Colonel Jouffroy's car, which was following mine, knocked down a poor old woman, who was killed on the spot. The Colonel assures me that no sort of blame can attach to the chauffeur, and I can do nothing but send sympathetic messages and some substantial help to the poor woman's

family, but the incident puts the finishing touch of sadness
to our return here. This is accentuated again when late
at night comes a telegram from the Mayor of Sampigny, who
says that forty-eight German shells have fallen on our little
town, and that the object evidently was to destroy my
house. In this the Germans have been completely successful,
as from what I can learn, the place is practically in crumbs.

9th October.—The Commander-in-Chief telegraphs thus
as to the bombardment of Clos:

"To pillage and vandalism have succeeded acts of black-
guardism. It did not suffice for the Germans to destroy the
Cathedral of Rheims; a little while ago at Nubécourt they
desecrated the family burial-ground of the President of the
Republic, and yesterday, from the heights of the right bank of the
Meuse, near St. Mihiel, they fired systematically and at long range
on the personal property of the President at Sampigny. There
was not the slightest military reason for this, the proof of which
is that only the President's house has suffered, and one might
almost think that the rest of the village had been spared by
authority."

The day is spent in going through a mass of papers which
had accumulated. A Council of War is being held at
Antwerp with the King as Chairman and in presence of
Mr. Winston Churchill. The situation is recognised as little
less than critical, and the enemy with 200 guns can account
for the place pretty well when they like. It has been decided
that the Field Army with the King shall make its way
towards Ghent, the move which Joffre advised and which
was suspended at the request of the British Minister. The
bombardment of Antwerp actually began yesterday in
the evening, and it has gone on ever since, but most of
the forts are still holding out and the evacuation of the
Field Army is proceeding fairly satisfactorily. General
Pau has arrived at Ostend, and thinking it better not to
bring our Marine Fusiliers there, has sent them also towards
Ghent, while Joffre has ordered the 87th Territorial Division
to proceed to the neighbourhood of Poperinghe so as to join
hands with the Marine Fusiliers and Belgian troops, and thus
to facilitate the sortie of the Field Army. M. de Brocqueville

reckons that 50,000 Belgians have been killed since the beginning of the war.

A telegram from the Governor of Tahiti tells us that Papaete was attacked on the 22nd September by two German cruisers, but which happily, owing to measures taken, were not able to enter the Roads and were obliged to sheer off after having fired about 150 shells and burnt the commercial quarter. What will Pierre Loti think ? " C'est bien Papaete cependant : ce palais de la Reine, là-bas, sous la verdure, cette baie aux grands palmiers, ces hautes montagnes aux silhouettes dentelées. . . ."

Paléologue has again spoken to Sazonoff about what Russia is going to do in the matter of taking the offensive. The battle should have been in full swing yesterday, and is likely to last at least a fortnight. If the Russian army be victorious one may calculate that they will arrive at, if not north of, Breslau about the 6th of November, but General Bielaïef, the Chief of the Staff, is careful to insist on all this being hypothetical. The Czar has left Tsarkoïe-Selo for the theatre of war to show that the operations against Germany have entered on a decisive phase ; he will not take actual command, but will only inspect the whole front line to encourage his troops. So at last Russians really means business ; up till now the delays in their concentration have only allowed them to make spasmodic efforts, but anyhow they have beaten the German army at Augustovo and forbidden them to cross the Niemen, while in the Carpathians they are still on the heels of the Austrian rear-guards.

10th October.—While I have been away Count Albert de Mun has died suddenly of a heart attack ; he has been ailing for some time, but no doubt the happenings of these last weeks have done much to precipitate the end, but up to the last he seems to have lost nothing of his admirable gifts. If he could no longer mount the tribune in Parliament and deliver one of those wonderful speeches from which even his adversaries could not withhold their applause, he could publish day by day either in the *Écho de Paris* or the *Gaulois* articles in every line of which was breathed pure patriotism. Here was indeed a great man, a fine soul, whose character was scarcely revealed to any but the innermost circle of his friends. His devout Catholic convictions did nothing to hinder him from rendering full justice to those who were opposed to him ; he was before all things a Frenchman, and whenever national interests were at stake he would always be found on the side of the responsible Government. I only wish I could have been present at the solemn Requiem which the Presidents of both Chambers and almost all the Ministers attended.

On account of this sad ceremony our Council was postponed till this afternoon, when we heard of the fall of Antwerp. The enemy pushed his way quicker than we thought he would ; the Escaut forts are still holding out, but the town has been fearfully knocked about, and many of the inhabitants have embarked on the river for Holland or England ; they went off shouting loudly : " Vive la Belgique ! "

Joffre proposes that the English troops, including the new arrivals, who are to operate on the terrain Belgium still enjoys, shall come under the command of Sir John French, that the Belgian troops shall remain under the orders of King Albert, and that the French troops in Belgium and in the North shall be assigned to Foch, who will thus make good the liaison with the Allied armies. Unfortunately the cavalry has had to retire on Béthune to cover the disembarkation of the British infantry, and the attempt to join hands with the Belgians is therefore either strangled in its birth or anyhow postponed.

From Prince Ferdinand of Roumania comes an unexpected telegram :

" M. LE PRÉSIDENT POINCARÉ. It is with profound grief that I announce to you the sad news of the death of my beloved uncle, King Charles. FERDINAND."

I at once express my sympathies to the Prince and to Roumania, but the death of a sovereign who in life was so ultra-Germanophile can hardly plunge me into woe.

11th October.—At last one hears the real reason of the occupation of St. Mihiel. The Germans were bringing to bear double pressure on our front round Verdun, to the west

towards the Argonne and south-east towards the Hauts de
Meuse, probably with the idea of surrounding and investing
the place. Our 8th Corps, which was at, or near, St. Mihiel,
had been hurriedly sent off to the rescue of the Argonne,
and there only remained, on the right bank of the Meuse,
between Vigneulles and St. Mihiel, one reserve division.
The Germans were easily aware of this and at once slid up
to, and into, the town without firing a shot. The fortress
they attacked from the rear and carried after considerable
bombardment. G.H.Q. does not think that any blame
attaches to General Sarrail, who was obliged to face both
ways at the same time without sufficient troops, but Joffre
considers that we allowed ourselves to be taken by surprise
on the flanks, and that the consequences may be very disagreeable. The railway from Lerouville to Verdun and the
canal running alongside the Meuse are both cut in parts,
and communications between Verdun and the Paris-Nancy
line have become impossible. We have good cause to fear
that sooner or later the Germans will attack from the north-
west and try to cut the railway from Châlons to Verdun, so
as to try and isolate the latter place ; the fall of Antwerp
will enable them to bring up their big siege guns, and the
Verdun fortress will no doubt be very soon under a heavy
bombardment. M. Couyba telegraphs from Sampigny that
the Germans keep on firing on Clos, and that the only
object on the *rez-de-chaussée* left intact is a bronze Pro
Patria, which my townsmen gave me the other day. The
symbol which has enjoyed this exceptional treatment may
console me for the loss of so many other souvenirs.

From Ostend the news is indeed unhappy. The Field
Army has moved to Western Flanders, and 60,000 men have
been able to get away. But General Pau, who has remained
in Belgium with the King, thinks that Ostend is no longer
a suitable seat of Government, and M. de Brocqueville has
telegraphed to Klobukowski asking if France would offer
hospitality to the Belgian army :

" The Belgian Government begs France to help them to
provide what is necessary for their army to resume the fight
vigorously and with as little delay as possible. . . . Further,

the Belgian Government cannot, without compromising national interests, find themselves at the mercy of the enemy, and they must establish themselves where, without interfering with military action, they can watch over the requirements of the Belgian soldiers of to-day and to-morrow, to whom France is already giving shelter. Having in view our most friendly relations with England and that country's resources which we can draw upon, especially in the matter of military material, the Belgian Government is very anxious to be where communication will be easy with their English friends. The Belgian Government therefore ask France whether, in these dark hours, she would give them lodging in a seaport town such as Havre. The Government, who have experience of the French nation's infinite courtesy, have no doubt but that, during their stay on French soil, the French Republic will do everything to help them in the fulfilment of their duty."

To this declaration a Supplementary Note was appended :

" It would be well for the Belgian Government to secure in France a position which would show clearly that in leaving Belgian territory they retain in their entirety all their sovereign rights. The formal recognition of these rights and of ex-territoriality for that part of the territory which they will occupy will be among the proper means to attain this end. The Government will be accompanied by their Ministerial services, and the numbers of officials, their rank and the relative importance of their functions will be indicated as soon as possible. A contingent of gendarmes will follow the Government."

Of course we can do nothing less and nothing else than accord Belgium the hospitality she asks and conform everywhere to her wishes. As it would be unwise to telegraph in clear, Baron Guillaume is to cipher a message of welcome to which I can add :

" I am anxious to tell Your Majesty personally how proud my compatriots will be to offer, until the hour when our common victory is assured, the hospitality of the town which Your Majesty has selected."

King Albert's reply to me, if couched in formal terms, underlined his sense of genuine friendship for ourselves, and of loyalty to the common cause.

An aerolite falls into my room in the shape of Charles

Humbert, my former co-representative of the Meuse in the Senate. To employ his rather exuberant activities Augagneur told him to go to America and buy, among other things, ammunition, horses and equipment; he has done a large number of deals which he considers very advantageous, but which Millerand views quite differently, and the Commissioner has been recalled from America and mobilised as an Infantry Captain. Humbert is burning with indignation about this, and I arrange for him to see Millerand and give an account of what he thinks he has done so well; I also ask the War Minister for an inside story of what has happened; from this it would appear that our envoy, on his own responsibility, entered into a large contract with the Chairman of the Bethlehem Steel Corporation, the results of which may be open to doubt.

12th October.—Joffre advises that the Belgian army shall, until further orders, remain on its own territory, while keeping touch with the English and ourselves, but of course part of their reorganisation must take place on our soil, Dunkirk being their base : the Belgian Government is to embark to-morrow morning for Havre with the various officials, but the King remains at the head of his troops. Our Marine Fusiliers, who arrived at Ghent on the 8th of October, were in action during the next two days, and gave an excellent account of themselves.

Galliéni and the Prefect of the Seine complain of the frequency of " Taube " raids and of incessant air attacks, and after inquiry as to the precise conditions of our Air Force, I am asking General Hirschauer, who has just been placed in control of the Air Force, to have the squadron sent which Galliéni requires for the protection of the town.

G.H.Q. telephones : " Violent attacks at several points; we have gained ground in many places and lost none." That is all very well, but from what Pénélon said yesterday we were to have attacked to-day with the English on the left ; Franchet d'Esperey and Maunoury were to have attacked in the centre, and an attack was to be made on the Hauts de Meuse. The weary warfare goes on and decision seems something of a will-o'-the-wisp.

13th October.—M. de Brocqueville and his colleagues have landed at Dunkirk *en route* for Havre, but we can only greet them with very scanty news of what is happening, as we seem to be fighting everywhere without any appreciable result. On our Eastern front the Germans are within fifteen kilometres of Warsaw ; the French colony has had to evacuate the town, and the Russian civilians have also left, and thus the hopes which the Grand Duke Nicholas inspired in us have begun to fade.   At Bucharest the new King Ferdinand has just taken the constitutional oath to Parliament ; the rapturous greeting which followed some of his declarations, and notably the one in which he promised to serve his country as a faithful Roumanian, have given our Minister the impression that the representatives of the nation do not wish to part with the dynasty, but will insist that the dynasty shall be guided by the interests and the wishes of Roumania.   Queen Marie, who is English by birth and who avowedly favours the Triple Entente, has been the object of enthusiastic manifestations, altogether exceeding those which the King has so far enjoyed.

14th October.—We anxiously await further news from Russia, but only hear from Paléologue that fighting is going on with heavy losses on both sides.

"I regret ", he telegraphs, "that I cannot give you more precise information as to the general action which seems to be taking place from Sandomir to Warsaw, as the secrecy imposed by the Grand Duke Nicholas is extended even to the General Staff at St. Petersburg."

The British Government, who know no more than we do, are no less anxious than ourselves.

15th October.—The days seem very grey and very sad.   I cannot get the Government to decide as to our return to Paris; some Ministers favour this, but Millerand and his subordinates have settled down and dislike the idea of another move.

Once more from G.H.Q. comes the most meagre intelligence, but a telegram from our Minister at Copenhagen leads us to fear for a moment that the Germans, in order to

engineer a success for the Crown Prince, are preparing a great
attack on Verdun. The Queen of Denmark has received a
telegram from her brother-in-law at Stenay :

" I am in high delight at having received the order to attack
at Verdun."

M. Bapst has heard of this from someone to whom the
Queen read the telegram, but he is not sure whether it may
not be a trick to throw us off the scent, especially as the telegram was sent in clear, and our Minister's suspicions seem to
be the better grounded as the Germans are certainly preparing to attack in Flanders. Three times they have tried to
get round us, and three times they have failed : west of Roye,
west of Bapaume, and west of Lille they have been on the
point of enveloping us when their attempts broke down. We
have not been able to turn their right, but they have not been
able to turn our left, and their one great chance is to resume
operations in Flanders. If they can succeed there they will
not only outflank us but they will get to the coast and cut the
British communications with England : it would seem that
they are pouring troops towards the Lys and the Yser.

According to our Minister at Stockholm the *North German
Gazette* alludes to a sensational discovery which the Germans
have made in Brussels. They have found in the archives of
the Belgian War Office papers which indicate that so far back
as 1906 the disembarkation of an English Army Corps in
Belgium had been arranged in the event of a Franco-German
war ; the whole Imperial Press pronounces that " British
hypocrisy" is hereby proved to the hilt, and that Germany's
conduct towards Belgium is fully justified. One of the
Swedish Liberal newspapers, however, remarks very aptly
that these papers only prove that Belgium was afraid, not of
French but of German violation of her territory.

16th October.—I am beginning to be deluged with letters,
mostly anonymous, which accuse me of cowardice ; I am said
to have left Paris in a fright, and that fright prevents me from
returning. No doubt the Taubes have upset some of my cor-
respondents, but precisely because the population of Paris is,
as a whole, so little disturbed by any fears, the Government

and myself ought to be where they are. No one can now for
a moment pretend that our presence in Paris would draw the
Germans on the capital, while the dragging on of the war and
the infinitesmal successes we have scored these last weeks are
doing something to depress people who, on the morrow of the
Marne, hoped and believed that victory was within sight. An
old friend of mine writes to my Secretary-General :

" Both Joffre's and Poincaré's stocks are very much down,
because it was thought that Poincaré would report victory from
headquarters."

The " telephone " from G.H.Q. is as laconic and windy as
before. We have gone a few steps forward on the slopes
which lead up to the Roman camp and we have also made
a trifling advance near Rheims, as again between Lens and
Béthune, while on the other hand a heavy blow has fallen, in
that the Germans have walked into Ostend.

17th October.—The students of the University of Glasgow
wish to elect me Lord Rector ; so far this honour has been
conferred on no foreigner and only on men like Lord Beacons-
field, Lord Rosebery, Mr. Asquith and Mr. Balfour. The
only duty involved is to pay a visit to the University and
deliver a speech ; I accept at once the offer and thank the
young Scotchmen for their very touching thought of me.
But when shall I be able to go to St. Andrew's Hall and
express orally my gratitude ?

18th October.—Germany announced the other day that she
had taken 63,000 French prisoners, but she now alludes to
115,000 ; whether this is correct or not one does not know,
but apparently we have only taken 40,000 German prisoners,
and the discrepancy is awkward to explain. North of La
Bassée canal the French troops have taken Givenchy, Fro-
melles and other places, but the Germans have wrested from
the Belgians Westende, Leke and Keyem without being able
to force the passage of the Yser.

19th October.—Our Military Attaché at Madrid reports an
interview with the King, who appeared very much cast down.
His Majesty is always and eagerly looking for a great victory
on our part, but he is surrounded by people, even in his own

household and Government, who disfavour France altogether, and he complains bitterly of the line they take.

Paléologue and Sir George Buchanan again tell Sazonof
how important it is that the General Staffs of the Allied
armies should be informed as to operations in Poland, and
the Grand Duke has promised to let Joffre and Kitchener
know what is going on. But the telegram which our Commander-in-Chief has received is lacking in anything like precision, and he can only gather that the Russian concentration
on the right bank of the Vistula is not yet complete, and that
a long time must elapse before the Russian army can move
on Berlin.

20th October.—North and south of Arras our troops have
fought continuously for ten days to gain a few yards of ground,
while a big battle is developing on the Yser and round Ypres :
our 4th Division has come from Rheims to support the left of
the Belgians at Nieuport, while their right is backed at Dixmude by our Marine Fusiliers. Lorries are bringing the 31st
Infantry Division to Ypres, and the 9th Corps with a Brigade
of Senegalese sharpshooters are hurrying to lend a hand there
Our forces are in groups of armies and under the orders of
General d'Urbal. Flanders is evidently to be the theatre of a
great struggle.

21st October.—General Pau, who was present at the evacuation of Antwerp and Ostend, tells me that the King behaved
magnificently, nor can he say too much about M. de Brocqueville, but at one moment there was a good deal of " *pagaye* "
about, which at first made things more difficult for the
military commands. Everything, however, was all right
at the finish, and the retreat of the troops was well
carried out.

Augagneur, who has been to Havre to superintend the
installation of the Belgian Government and who went thence
to Furnes, the Belgian Army Headquarters, tells me also that
he finds the King as cool and as resolute as ever but very
anxious as to the future of his people. " Will France ", he
asked, " defend Belgium to the very end ? " " Yes," was
Augagneur's answer, " precisely as she will defend herself."
All along the coast our Minister for Marine met Belgian

refugees, men, women and children, carrying their furniture and effects on carts and wheelbarrows ; the Belgian army is now in position behind the Yser, and is flanked on the right by our Marine Fusiliers, while one of our Territorial Divisions forms the rear support.

I read between the lines of a G.H.Q. telegram that we have lost Varennes, and the Germans must have got near the railway between Ste. Menehould and Verdun ; if they go much further they will be able to cut the line which brings Verdun's supplies.

At night the Russian Embassy lets Delcassé know that a telegram from Petrograd speaks of a great victory near Warsaw, and that the Germans are in full retreat.

22nd October.—Briand and Sarraut have been to Verdun, and found out that the Douaumont fort has been bombarded these last days without G.H.Q. telling us a word about it. A great discussion in Council, when I again insist that we ought to return at once to Paris. Viviani and Augagneur support me, but Ribot thinks that we ought to wait till the end of November, and somehow I cannot get a majority in my favour. I therefore say that I shall go to Paris myself next week, that the decrees ought to be signed where I am and not where the Ministers are, and that I claim the right of returning to the Élysée without discussion on the part of the Council. The answer I get is that the duty of the Council is to watch over my safety, that I am the " Queen Bee ", that it is I who appoint the Ministers, that Members of the Government can be changed, but it would be a disaster if any accident happened to the Chief of the State. I reply in turn that there is no probability of anything happening to me, but that if any accident should occur, the Cabinet would enjoy full powers until my successor would be named, and that if there be some shadow of danger in my going back, there is all the more reason for my not delaying any further my return. The discussion ended a little uncomfortably ; Millerand will ask Joffre if he sees any special reason why the Government should not return to Paris, and will add that they propose to go there on the 15th of November. I repeat that personally I shall not wait until then, and anyhow I have quite made up my mind to spend some days in the capital next week.

After the Council, I come to terms with Viviani and Millerand that we shall go in a few days to the Belgian armies and also pay a visit to Maud'huy and Castelnau.

23rd October.—Pénélon's report to-day suggests nothing important or immediate ; and I want to go as soon as I can to the armies of the Centre and the Est. where I could not possibly be in the way as, at the moment, interest centres in Ypres, where Foch has just ordered a general attack. Joffre is complaining rather bitterly about French, who is not very easy to move and who, according to our Commander-in-Chief, could have taken Lille the day before yesterday without striking a blow. The Generalissimo is even afraid the Field-Marshal, who is very anxious about his naval bases, and especially for Calais, may retire on that town, and I think he would be very pleased if Sir John were replaced by General Wilson, on whose services Foch places very great value.

The news given by the Russian Embassy is confirmed, and the Germans are moving quickly back south-west of Warsaw as well as west of Ivangorod and Novo Alexandria; fierce fighting is still going on in Galicia.

The garden in which Madame Poincaré and I take a short daily walk is this afternoon guarded by a detachment of cyclists, as the police have information that the Germans who are domiciled in Barcelona have hatched a plot to assassinate me. To be thus protected is like being in prison the Queen Bee must not leave her hive.

24th October.—Millerand, Viviani and I pay a visit to the camp at Souges where we find Territorials and young recruits of the 1914 class in tents pitched in the middle of a pine wood on a very picturesque site. The men look very well, but their drill leaves a good deal to be desired, and General Legrand treats the officers to a pretty sharp lecture.

25th October.—We were outnumbered in our attack at Ypres and the Germans have been able to cross the Yser between Nieuport and Dixmude ; in their wireless they even flatter themselves of having taken Armentiéres and Bailleul.

There has been an unpleasant incident regarding Caillaux, who is serving in the Army Pay department. He was recognised by some people in a Paris restaurant yesterday, and was only rescued by the police from being roughly handled by a crowd who had gathered. It would seem that Caillaux rather brought this on himself by the way in which, even when in uniform, he has spoken of the Government, and has declared that everything is going wrong.

26th October.—The Germans who got across the Yser have not been able to push forward, while to the west of the Vistula and north of Pilica they have been pushed back on Lovicz and Rava ; France, Belgium and Russia can therefore for the moment breathe again.

27th October.—To avoid further disagreeable incidents Millerand has taken Caillaux's name off the Army List and attached him to the Finance Minister ; to satisfy Caillaux's thirst for active employment M. Thomson, the Minister of Commerce, thinks he will be able to send him on a mission to the further shores of the Atlantic.

The Belgian Government, in order to contain the Germans on the Yser, has ordered all the land between the river and the railway embankment to be flooded. The locks at Nieuport have been opened, and the water will quietly bar the road to the enemy.

28th October.—Briand and Sarraut, on their return from their little tour in the Est, have spoken plain words as to the discontent in Paris about my being stationary outside the capital. The Government are now quite willing that I should leave this evening for Paris, where Millerand will join me, and we will go together to Dunkirk and Furnes.

Joffre has written again to the War Minister that he thinks a premature return of the Government to Paris might interfere with military operations and wants us to wait until the 20th of November. No thank you, I have waited quite long enough. I have let the Belgian Government and King Albert know of my forthcoming visit, and Millerand and I are also to meet Lord Kitchener, together with Joffre and Sir John at Dunkirk on the 1st of November (Sunday) ; Joffre has given up all idea of asking for French

to be replaced by Wilson, an idea which would certainly
never have been realised.

General Headquarters telephone :

" Dubail's army has made real progress in the Leprêtre and
Ailly woods and in the Apremont forest ; the enemy has bombarded violently round Sampigny, Mécrin and Marbotte."

What will be the fate of those unhappy communes of the
Meuse whose inhabitants have been obliged to leave and
whose houses are close up to the line of fire ? They are
doomed to suffering and ruin. Marbotte, Mécrin, Sampigny,
what will there be left of the villages with which my life has
been bound up, and where I have tasted such happiness.

Paul Cambon telegraphs that the students of Glasgow
have unanimously elected me Lord Rector of the University.
I shall go and thank them one day when England and
France have secured victory.

CHAPTER IX

29th October.—I arrive in Paris this morning and have
early visitors in Galliéni and the Prefect of the Seine. The
Military Governor is inclined to be a little critical, but
everything he says is deserving of attention. He thinks
our front is too strung out and that our screen of troops is
a mere fringe, and he is sure that the Germans will bring
up further large forces. When I tell him that we are
obliged, so long as the Allies cannot put more men into the
field, to hold the line from the sea to Switzerland, he replies
that we ought to be quicker in forming our Territorial
Divisions, and that they could be sent to him in Paris
where he would have them trained and forwarded to the
front as asked for. He is very down on what he calls the
slackness of the military bureaux.

M. Delanney, the Prefect of the Seine, tells me—and
seems rather to like doing so—that there is something like
a campaign against me conducted by the conservative
bourgeoisie and in particular by the Palais de Justice; there
is nothing definite alleged against me, but it seems that I am
in bad odour, and this due to the economic troubles, the
prolongation of the moratorium, and stagnation in public
business, rather than to the miseries and emotions of the
war ; the feeling is voiced by a discreet, but continuous,
whispering against the " Government of Bordeaux " per-
sonified in myself.

Joffre, who had been informed by the liaison officers of
my arrival in Paris, comes to spend an hour with me and is,

as far as one can gather, quite unperturbed by the delays and the uncertainties which wait on his operations ; he still thinks that the Government ought not to return yet awhile to Paris, but the reasons which he adduces for this do not seem substantial, and I have no hesitation in telling him so. While he is happier about material and munitions he has been very anxious about happenings in Belgium, but thinks now that he has duly reinforced Foch, the danger is over ; he will come with me on Sunday to Dunkirk and on Monday to Furnes, and Lord Kitchener has let me know how glad he will be to meet him with Millerand and myself.

This afternoon, in order to feel the pulse of this *bourgeoisie boudeuse* as to whom the Prefect of the Seine is eloquent, I pay a visit to the Académie Française with my friend Eugène Brieux, who is going to the United States, and to whom I must give a letter of introduction to President Wilson. He has told me that there is to be drawn up to-day a reply to the manifesto of the ninety-three German " Intellectuals " who have tried to throw upon the Allies the responsibility for the war, and several of my colleagues want to have my opinion as to the proposed text. I have no observations to offer, and the draft, the work of Ernest Lavisse, is unanimously adopted. Marcel Prévost, in his uniform of an Artillery Captain, takes the chair at the meeting, and Pierre Loti, who, thanks to Galliéni, has resumed his uniform, represents the Navy at this pacific meeting.

Some of the Academicians have thought that, in the present circumstances, the election to membership of a Belgian writer, such as Maeterlinck, would be very popular, but Lavisse tells me that some of his colleagues are opposed to the idea ; they think that Maeterlinck represents the German rather than the French spirit, and they remember— perhaps this is their chief objection—that some of his books have been placed on the Index. If Maeterlinck's election cannot be *nem. con.* it would be better to give up the notion altogether.

30th October.—The day is spent in visits to the regulating railway stations of Noisy - le - Sec and Pantin, and to the military cemetery at the latter place where families in deep mourning are praying at the graves, to the Beaujon Hospital, the ambulances installed in the Grand Palais of the Champs Élysées, and to the central post office, the last in order to go into the matter of the existing postal arrangements for soldiers no less than for civilians. On emerging from the last place a large number of passers-by greet us with extreme warmth, and from similar demonstrations which one received during the day it would not seem that the people of Paris bear us any special grudge for our long absence, although the flood of anonymous letters continues in which the Ministers and I are dubbed as runaways and " funks "— and this because the Government thought it right to yield to the insistence of the military authority.

31st October.—Galliéni, who takes me to-day over the fortified system, still thinks that Millerand is not quick enough in getting ready the Territorial Divisions. He takes me beyond Meaux and shows me the trenches which the Germans dug when they were checked by the battles of the Ourcq and of the Marne ; although improvised, they are of admirable depth and constructed with consummate skill. Galliéni then shows me the trenches which he has himself had made the last two months, and I can congratulate him on the rapidity with which the work has been executed. " A close study ", he explains to me, " of the first happenings of the war has enabled us to get away from the original precepts as laid down, and we have tried to make the line of resistance as far as possible from the town by organising the battlefields which may be occupied either by the mobile garrison or by the Field Armies. Hence the line we have drawn from Thérain to Automne ; on the left this line rests on a *tête de pont* north of Beauvais, and to the right it stretches as far as Longpont and the Savières valley. It is flanked by the defences we have prepared all along Thérain below Beauvais, along to the Oise between Crei and Verbrie, and along Automne to the northern outskirts of the Villers-Cotterets and Retz woods. This work has been entirely done by the garrison troops, and we are now making a line further out which would have its left on the Epte and its right on the Ourcq. As you will see, this is very well forward, and besides the garrison troops we have employed 15,000 civilian workmen who were unemployed." Everything that Galliéni says, and his further explanations as to precisely how the trenches should be constructed, go to show that he is as methodical as he is scientific.

In the afternoon I receive at the Elysée M. Lamy, the Secretary of the Académie Française who tells me frankly that the reason why he opposed Maeterlinck's candidature was his fear of annoying the Belgian Government which is so profoundly Catholic. M. Massard, the editor of the *Patrie*, who is wearing the uniform of a Territorial Captain, tells me rather sadly that Paris is discontented with the Government and myself; there is a good deal of disaffected talk in public conveyances, the newspapers are complaining of the censorship, suffering abounds, and trouble is to be feared when the grants to the families of mobilised soldiers are withdrawn; I tell Massard that these grants will not be withdrawn until peace is signed, and then it will be gradually done; but to balance his budget Ribot will have to tax all his ingenuity, the more so as he thinks it will be difficult to impose fresh taxes on men almost all of whom are serving at the front.

1st November.—A little after eight o'clock Millerand arrives from Bordeaux and he, Ribot and I start at once for Dunkirk; as the railway line is reserved for military transport, we make the journey in War Office motors, with Ribot next me as far as Amiens. He is to-day quite in his old form and opens his mind to me, criticising the military bureaux no less severely than Galliéni does; he thinks, as several other of the Ministers do, that the War Office is displaying too much masterly inactivity which Millerand is always excusing, and that something must be done to alter this.

Joffre comes to meet us at Amiens and, after breakfast at the Hôtel du Rhin, we resume our journey through St. Pol and St. Omer. It is All Saints' Day and everywhere people are carrying flowers to the cemeteries, while near St. Pol an enemy aeroplane drops a bomb a hundred yards from the car immediately behind the one in which Joffre and I are seated, but happily without any accident. All along the road between St. Omer and Dunkirk there are bulking convoys of English, Belgian and French supplies.

Since the 23rd of September Dunkirk has been protected against a German invasion by inundation, the natural defence she has so often used. The waters of the Yser have been brought into the region of the Moëres, while those of the Aa have been equally poured over the plain ; round the town, as round Bergues, there is a great sheet of water which extends over a surface of about 8000 hectares. The town during the last fortnight has received continuous attentions from the enemy Air Force, and several of the inhabitants have been killed, while three days ago two shells fell on the Hôtel de Ville where Baron de Brocqueville, the Belgian Prime Minister and War Minister, has his lodgings.[1]

We arrive at Dunkirk at five o'clock in the afternoon to find Lord Kitchener, who crossed in a destroyer from New-haven to Boulogne last night, accompanied by our Ambassador.[2] He is a man of considerable height, with energy written on every line of his face, piercing eyes under well-defined eyebrows, the nose a little short and inclined to be retroussé, heavy moustaches well brushed up, and a strong chin very carefully shaved. He is clad in a simple khaki uniform without any decorations and greets us cordially and with perfect simplicity. We at once go into the different subjects at issue, and Kitchener tells us that their Artillery has in hand about 600 rounds per gun, but that up to now they have only manufactured 20,000 rounds per week for about 480 guns, and he would like us to be able to lend some cannon to the British army ; after due consideration and agreement with Joffre, Millerand promises 300 of our 90's.

Kitchener thinks that the German offensive in Flanders is very formidable and likely to develop with new enemy resources. " I am afraid ", he says without circumlocution, " that the British army, which is still far too small, might be bent under a heavy assault. We rely on you to

[1] See *Dunkerque, ville héroïque*, par Henri Male, Perrin et Cie, 1918.
[2] See *Life of Lord Kitchener*, by Sir George Arthur, vol. iii. p. 74.

reinforce us." Joffre has told us that the English have been
obliged to give ground a little; they are courage itself, but
when they were worsted two or three days ago, they had to
be relieved, and the enemy took advantage of this to renew
his attacks. This is the precise complaint of Foch, who has
also come to Dunkirk to confer with Kitchener and myself.
Since the 4th October Foch is Second-in-Command, and a
week ago he shifted his headquarters from Doulens to
Cassel. Just when he took over his new duties the Germans
were trying to outrun us to the sea, and to get ahead of them
our troops moved gradually towards the Somme and the
Pas-de-Calais. Sir John French, who had wanted to bring
his force nearer to his naval base, concentrated in the
Hazebroucke and St. Omer zone troops whose efforts it
became more and more necessary to co-ordinate with ours
and the Belgians. It was to Foch that this delicate task
fell, the first timid attempt at unity of command. But
anyhow the lesson of this experience will not be lost, and a
day will come when English and French alike will remember
it.

Faced by the vast plain of Flanders, the cockpit of so
many centuries of fighting, Foch had for his first idea to
throw in the French and British troops against Menin and
Courtrai. But the fall of Antwerp, on the 9th October,
compelled him to give up this tempting project and, instead
of an attack, he had to prepare to stand on the defensive
and to assure the retreat of the Belgian army. The enemy
was already creeping over the sands of the dunes towards
Nieuport, and by a master-stroke Foch immediately brought
into line the 42nd Division, the same which he had so boldly
handled at the marshes of St. Gond during the battle of the
Marne. The division travelled straight through to the
Belgian frontier, and was deputed to support our Allies at
Nieuport and the Yser; the six Belgian divisions were hard
by, and had preserved the strip of territory left to them,
where they had settled themselves down as a token of
national independence. The Allied front in Flanders was
thenceforward more solidly constituted with the English on
the right, the French in the centre, the Belgians on the left

and our 42nd Division on the extreme left near the sea
where the British monitors and destroyers kept guard. Our
troops had been successively reinforced by the 11th, 16th,
32nd and 20th Corps, and on the 22nd of October Foch, agreeably with our Belgian and British Allies, had ordered an
attack in order to forestall and spoil a great German attack
which he knew to be more and more threatening ; thus
began the battle of the Yser which was to be soon followed
by the battle of Ypres.

At the beginning we were stopped by the Germans, who
managed to construct eleven foot bridges across the loop of
the Yser ; it was at this moment that the Belgian engineers
opened the locks, and the enemy could make no further
headway against the water.   Foch gives me all these details
with perfect simplicity and taking no credit to himself, and
he also told me that on the evening of the 30th October
he suddenly learnt that the Germans had broken through
the British cavalry screen and taken Ramscapelle and
Hollebecke.   It was midnight, but he dashed to French's
headquarters and woke him up with the question : " Have
you any reserves ? " " Unhappily, none," was the Field-
Marshal's reply.   " I will send you some," was the re-
joinder, " hold on till you get them."   Sir John said he
would do all he could, and Foch hurried back to Cassel, and
at 2 A.M. gave orders for troops to reinforce the English.
But the British Corps was almost exhausted, and Sir John
again contemplated retiring his heavy Artillery and making
a general retreat.   Foch dashed to Vlamertynghe where he
found the Field-Marshal and said to him : " If we show any
weakness we shall be blown away like straws ; at any cost
your 1st Corps must remain where it is ; I shall attack
myself from right to left with all the troops I can bring."
He took a sheet of paper from a desk, scribbled on it four
lines to explain what he meant, and handed it to Sir John,
who read it, reflected for a moment, and then summoned
an orderly officer and said to him : " Take these orders."
Thus disaster was warded off, and although we lost Messines
and Wytschaete yesterday, the enemy has been checked.
Foch is loud in praise of the English, but they seem to him

still to be inclined to look upon war as a great sport and suppose that they are free to choose the hours for fighting and the hours for resting. The enemy does not recognise this sort of thing, and it is high time that the English either change their habits or that they be relieved by fresh troops. Kitchener himself, in spite of his perfect sang-froid, says again that he is not without considerable anxiety as to the fate of the little British army. Foch promises him the whole support of the French troops, but adds : " Do send us your new divisions as soon as possible." " You will have a million men in eighteen months," is Kitchener's calm statement. " Eighteen months," ejaculates Foch. " I should prefer fewer men arriving a little sooner." But the British War Minister replies that he is obliged to look far ahead ; the Germans might still try to land in England and some forces must be kept at home; besides, before sending recruits to the front it is essentially necessary that they should be thoroughly trained ; he has found the cupboard at the War Office entirely bare, and he has been obliged to improvise everything. He is renting ground here for two years, and he promises that before the expiration of that period British soldiers will be poured in, and that meanwhile those who are already in the field will do their utmost to back us in the struggle against a common enemy. " Two years," Ribot murmurs to me, " does he really think the war is going to last two years ? " M. de Brocqueville, the Belgian Prime Minister, who prefers to remain nearer the King and the army rather than go to Havre, is quite a different type from Kitchener. There is nothing military about him ; he is a man of the world, beautifully groomed, with dark complexion, black eyes, an expressive face, fluent in speech, and with a smile on his lips, but, as with Kitchener, one feels that here also is a man as strong as he is resolute, and burning with the fires of energy. He seems, if anything, less pessimistic than his British colleague, and Foch, who, like me, fears that Kitchener is not too sure as to our " staying " powers, keeps on saying to him : " We shall hold on all right ; we shall hold on all right." The British Minister seems gradually to be more reassured as to our future course; under a quiet and apparently almost casual exterior there lies an inflexible will which, lacking though he be in anything like vivacious enthusiasm, he will exercise whole-heartedly in the common cause.

Lord Kitchener, M. de Brocqueville, the Ministers, the Generals and the Mayor dine with me, and we seem to gain confidence with one another and to grow quite genial as the evening draws on. At midnight Lord Kitchener re-embarks for England, and he will be back in his room at the War Office to-morrow morning.

2nd November.—The Day of the Dead; but every day now is the Day of the Dead. The Germans are still fighting fiercely to try and get Kemmel, but they are not making any more headway.

Very early in the morning Millerand and I set off, and find the road to Belgium congested with carts, waggons and charabancs loaded with fugitives of all ages, who are carrying their furniture, their old clothes, their eatables and all their household goods with them; a sorry sight, and the misery of these poor people is heart-rending to witness. Every-where are soldiers, French, British and Belgian, some marching to and from their duties, others " resting " in their billets, and after crossing the Belgian frontier, military and civilians in their hundreds seem to be floundering about in the mud. With his wonted graciousness King Albert comes to meet us on the threshold of his territory; he is in service kit, and on his black dolman there is fastened, as his only decoration, his French Military Medal. Very kindly and very quietly, indeed almost timidly, he thanks me for my visit, while he renders the highest praise to our armed forces, especially as regards the 42nd Division and the Marine Fusiliers, who have been respectively on the left and right of his own men. He does not hesitate to say, and says it quite charmingly, that it is our people who enabled him to forbid at least one strip of his territory to the Germans. I can tell him in reply that what Belgium dared and did enabled us, taken aback as we were by the German attack, to concentrate our army and put them steady on their feet. Such is the first conversation which, in a little muddy

Flemish village, without any fuss or formality, is held between the representatives of the two peoples.

The King takes me in his open motor along the Flemish dunes to the little villa on the sandy shore of La Panne, where Queen Elizabeth has just taken up her abode for the war. What the Belgians on the coast here call a *panne* is a sort of parabolic depression which, under the dual action of sea and wind, protrudes itself here and there, the centre reclining farther and farther backwards towards the land, while the two arms stretch out to the sea. Here in this very modest lodging the Royal Family of Belgium await the future of their gallant country. In a sitting-room, furnished with extreme simplicity, the Queen, who is dressed in white, receives me with all her exquisite charm ; frail and delicate, one would think a breath of wind would blow her away and that anyhow she would be broken by the storm which is raging around her, but she has nerves of steel and a soul which no Kaiser will conquer. She lives only for her people and her country, and, after inquiring about Madame Poincaré, Paris and France generally, she speaks of little else than the war and speaks with a firmness which nothing will shake. The young Princes and the little Princess are in England, where they are being looked after by Lord Curzon ; their mother telegraphs to them every day by a cable, for the care of which she acknowledges herself most grateful to our Territorials. There is something really very fine as well as plucky in the attitude and the action of these unhappy personages ; to witness their courage is to make one take fresh courage oneself. When I am about to say goodbye the Queen asks me to let her take a photograph of the King and myself in front of the villa in the middle of the dunes, and the copy which she says she will send me I shall always cherish as a souvenir of these terrible times. Joffre and Millerand arrive just as the King and I are about to start, and I present them to the Queen, to whom Joffre speaks of his sure and certain hopes of victory. The King and I next make our way to the old town once sacked by the Vandals and which seems likely enough to renew the ugly experience. Furnes was bombarded yesterday, but although two or three Taubes fly overhead and seem to keep a sinister watch, no shell comes to disturb the greeting which has been arranged for me. On the picturesque Place de Hôtel de Ville there is drawn up on one side a squadron of our mounted chasseurs, a platoon of infantry and one of our bands ; there is no other French military display, as our men are all in the fighting-line. A rather larger party of Belgian soldiers in on parade, and on our arrival their band plays the " Marseillaise ", to which ours replies with the " Brabançonne ". After a rapid review of the handful of troops the King takes Millerand, Joffre and myself up the old winding staircase into the big Council Chamber of the Hôtel de Ville, when he tells us how Furnes has become a sort of provisional capital of Belgium where the old national traditions of the kingdom are being maintained, and where the plans for avenging the country are being prepared. The King then insists on accompanying me back to the frontier, and after taking leave of him there we hurry on to Cassel, where Foch has taken up his headquarters. On the way we pass the Algerian contingent, fine, brown-skinned men, dressed in grey velvet and wearing turbans, who are en-camped in an enclosure surrounded by large farms. They do not seem to have suffered overmuch from the autumnal weather or the French climate, and the Military Medals which I have to distribute are greatly appreciated, as well as the Cross of the Legion of Honour which is awarded to their Colonel, Bujonchet.

Foch has breakfast ready for us at Cassel. It is im-possible to imagine any finer observation post, and from the window where our table is laid we have a splendid outlook over the Flemish plain stretching at our feet, dotted by thirty-two towns which, century in century out, has been the constant theatre of battles of every sort and size. What Foch does not know is not worth knowing about the victors who have preceded him at Cassel, Robert le Frison, Phillippe de Valois and the duc d'Orléans ; he has military history at his fingers' ends, and his talk is brimming over with souvenirs and comparisons, which show his extraordinary knowledge of things past as well as present. During breakfast an officer comes to bring the morning report, from which it would seem that the Germans are attacking vigorously but that we are holding on. Joffre, who is still with us, says that he has no wish to have Sir John French replaced, and that Foch has gained a happy influence over the British Field-Marshal, and has also established a permanent liaison between the two armies, this last thanks largely to General Wilson, the English officer who seems best to understand French methods; things are going as well as possible with our Allies, and there would be no advantage in swapping horses in mid-stream. One cannot help lingering some little time in the old Hôtel de Ville of Cassel with Foch and his subordinates while the General explains in masterly detail the operations of yesterday and to-morrow with the aid of large maps covering the tables and hanging on the wall.

In the afternoon we add an item which has been omitted from the programme, and, recrossing the frontier, pay a visit to General d'Urbal at Vlamertynghe. Troops are being moved towards Ypres, and there seems one long string of lorries and cars filled with men who cheer us enthusiastically, and make one think that a Chief of the State may do something to encourage soldiers fighting for their country by going among them. Some of the men in billets even give vent to loud hurrahs, and when I suggest to Joffre that this seems scarcely " regulation ", he murmurs in his creamy tones : " That is all right : they are behind the line, and they mean far too well for anyone to blame them."

Uniform abounds everywhere, English, Indian, French, Belgian ; the nations of the world are standing to arms. At Vlamertynghe, General d'Urbal is to receive the cravate of a Commander ; he is a fine Dragoon officer, who, from the first day of fighting, has made his mark both at Verdun and round Arras ; his command in Belgium now comprises the 42nd Division under General Grossetti, some Marine Fusiliers, de Mitry's cavalry corps and two Territorial divisions. In the course of conversations with officers and men who are the very reverse of depressed, they ask me if the English will see it through. Kitchener had his doubts about us, and these fine fellows have had their doubts about him, but I have only to tell them what the Field-Marshal said at Dunkirk yesterday in order to reassure them completely on this score. Bailleul and Béthune are in semi-darkness as we pass through on our way to Bruay, where we are to spend the night with one M. Elby, a friend of Ribot and Léon Bourgeois. But there is activity, not to say bustle, all along the road, and one is especially glad to note the excellent turn-out of the artillery of the 20th Corps who are making their way northwards to lend a hand in breaking down maleficent German efforts.

3rd November.—Before resuming our tour we don miner's kit and descend one of our host's mines, where I am asked to handle a pickaxe, and acquit myself very awkwardly. The miners are very few, as most of them have been called up, and those remaining are often working under fire ; they give me a very hearty welcome, and I slip my offering into their box, an act which will probably result in my having to stand godfather to innumerable children, and in a correspondence which will know no end.

We find General Maud'huy at St. Pol, a little town in the Pas-de-Calais which Charles V. once destroyed, and over which Spaniards and French struggled so bitterly. Maud'huy indeed has his heart in his work, as he well may ; he springs from Metz, and was thirteen years old when Metz was torn from our side ; he and I are old friends with many recollections in common, not only because we served together as chasseurs à pied, but from being country neighbours, as he commanded a brigade at St. Mihiel before the war. The hospitals here are full of maimed and mutilated men, not one of whom utters a murmur of complaint, and it would almost seem as if pain had become a second nature for our people. A detachment of cyclist chasseurs, splendid fellows, are drawn up on the Place, and one of them, who has been terribly injured, is led forward by two comrades ; the man has distinguished himself brilliantly under fire, and as the Cross of the Legion of Honour is being pinned on him, he shouts out, " Vive la France ", while the crowd gathered on the pavement behind the cyclists applauds vociferously.

Maud'huy goes with me to Haute Avesnes, one of his

command posts, whence we make our way on foot to Mont
St. Eloi, a place which occurs again and again in official
communiqués, and which is tirelessly and mercilessly bombarded by the Germans.

4th November.—After spending the night at Abbeville
we journey on to Cagny, near Amiens, which is Castelnau's
headquarters, but we find the General himself at his advanced headquarters on the plateau of Santerre in the
Villers-Bretonneux district. Despite his sixty-three years,
Castelnau has all the fire of youth, and although below
medium height, he seems to be as active and strong as a
Cévennes mountaineer. He tells us that our 4th Corps took
Quesnoy yesterday, and is pushing on to Andéchy, and that
Lignières is under fire, but as I am very anxious to congratulate the Commander of the 4th Corps, whose quarters are
there, on the brilliant success of his troops, we extract from
the General permission to go as far. On the way we find a
squadron of Air Force ; the men these last days have done
some splendid flights, but for the moment are standing by,
as rain is forbidding any reconnaissance. A little farther
on a waggon crosses us, carrying back men wounded an hour
ago, who call out : " Do not worry, M. le Président, we will
shift the Boche," a nickname which our men have just
begun to give to the Germans. Castelnau, who always
carries a large supply of cigarettes in his motor-car, gives
out handfuls of them to the wounded, and from Lignières
we can see our 75's in action, the houses at Andéchy on fire,
the bursting of the German shells, and yonder below our
feet infantry emerging from a wood and moving forward
under fire; in the foreground there stand out a peasant, who
is pushing his wheelbarrow along, and a woman, who is
picking beetroots : Life is defying Death.

Our way back to Paris is through Montdidier and Creil,
where the finger-marks of the enemy are very evident.

5th November.—The day is spent in Paris and the Prefect
of the Seine comes to tell me, rather vaguely, that Galliéni is
intriguing against Joffre, while the President of the Chamber
of Commerce submits proposals for propaganda which are to
furnish answers to German allegations in neutral countries.

Before leaving for Bordeaux I let the Press know that I shall be back in Paris in a few days, and that I shall then pay a visit to the armies of the Est, which, through no fault of mine, I may seem to have neglected.

6th November.—Early in the morning I am back at Bordeaux, and having got rid of the railway dust, preside over a Council where it transpires that, in spite of the objections raised by Ribot, Briand and myself, the Government has definitely agreed as to the Mission to be entrusted to Caillaux, who is to proceed to Brazil and there study the question of cables and of economic relations between that Republic and ourselves. However important these studies may be, nobody can really suppose that they will satisfy Caillaux's appetite for activity and ambition. I ask what has been going on in my absence, and Delcassé's is by far the most important budget of news. Turkey has thrown off the mask, and while the Ottoman Government seems on the one hand to be levelling a threat at Egypt, two Turkish torpedo boats, on the 29th of October, sank a Russian gunboat at Odessa and fired on a French steamer, the *Portugal*; according to Bompard, this was the act of German officers and sailors. The three Allied Ambassadors in Turkey have thought it their duty to tell the Porte that, unless she showed the door at once to foreign soldiers and sailors, she would *ipso facto* assume responsibility for the act of war which they had just perpetrated. Delcassé, agreeably with Sir Edward Grey, has approved this diplomatic declaration, but, before conferring with us, Sazonoff ordered his Ambassador to ask for his passports. He then proposed that we should send a trenchant collective Note insisting that the German Mission should be sent away within twenty-four hours. As a matter of fact, the Grand Vizier was left in ignorance of what the Germans were going to do, while Enver Pasha was fully informed. The German attacks, carried out under a Turkish flag, have been renewed at Theodorie and Sebastopol, and this is the upshot of all the intrigues woven by Wilhelm at Constantinople ever since Liman von Sanders was sent there. The Russian Government, however, is very cool-headed as to the complications which may ensue : " Not a man ", Sazonoff has said to

Paléologue, " will be deflected from the German front ; before all things we must beat Germany, whose defeat will involve the ruin of Turkey ; Russia will reduce to a minimum
the defence to be put up against Turkish attacks by land or
sea." On the evening of the 30th of October the Supreme
Council, over which the Grand Vizier presided, plumped
unanimously for preserving peace with the Triple Entente
and decided to send a Note to the Russian Ambassador to
advise him of this and to ask that the happenings on the
Black Sea should be adjusted either in a friendly spirit or by
arbitration. Djavid Bey was detailed to deal with the three
Ambassadors, to make the necessary arrangements, but Bompard simply said that no arrangement was possible so long
as German forces, military or naval, were kept in Turkey.
Djavid Bey had to admit there was no chance of getting rid
of the German troops, or anyhow that the Turkish Government was unable to order their dismissal and even less able
to enforce it. The three Ambassadors have asked the Grand
Vizier for their passports.

Notwithstanding the rupture with Turkey, Sir Edward
Grey still feels sure that Bulgaria will remain neutral ; the
Bulgarian Government has promised both Panafieu and the
Russian Minister that they will not seize this opportunity to
take up arms, while they quite understand that if they cease
to be neutral they may have to deal with Roumania. But
if the Foreign Office has so far no anxiety about Bulgaria,
they have no further idea of parleying with the Sublime
Porte ; Turkey stands condemned in the eyes of England and
can no longer remain the guardian of the Narrows.

Now that Great Britain will be officially at war with
Turkey, she will proclaim her Protectorate over Egypt and
dethrone the Khedive, whose behaviour has become more and
more equivocal. The British Cabinet lets us know what is
going to be done, and we ask in return that they will recognise our Protectorate in Morocco, to which they have not consented since 1912—despite our agreement of April 1904—
because they bound up with such recognition a definite ruling
on the question of Turkey. Now the British willingly agree to
our Protectorate of Morocco while they set up theirs in Egypt.

M. Klobukowski has telegraphed from Havre :

" M. de Brocqueville confirms the deep and most salutary impression made at the Belgian headquarters by the visit of the President of the Republic to the King and Queen."

This visit was from every point of view obligatory for me, and my only regret was that it should have been so long delayed ; I could do no less than tell the King openly that France's fate was bound up with that of Belgium.

The Grand Duke Nicholas telegraphs to-day to Joffre in a message brimming with confidence and goodwill :

" As a sequel to our success on the Vistula our troops have won a real victory. The Austrians are in flight all along the Galician front, and the manœuvre of which I told you at the beginning has thus been happily accomplished and has certainly crowned the most important success on our side since the beginning of the war. . . ."

7th November.—At our daily Council Delcassé tells us that Grey has notified him officially of a British annexation of Cyprus. As a matter of fact the English have occupied this island since 1878 and have often expressed their intention of returning it to Greece, but the inhabitants, who for the most part are Greeks, can never know what fate is in store for them, and very likely England has taken them over in order to protect them against Turkey.

Millerand, who has gone to visit the armies of the Est, telegraphs from Verdun :

" From your country of the Meuse, devastated as it is by the enemy, but illumined every day by the heroism of our soldiers, I send you—together with my own—the affectionate duty of your compatriots and of the army. I have begged the Governor to convey your congratulations, at the same time as my own, to Sergeant Maginot, who has been awarded the Military Medal for his splendid conduct in face of the enemy, and for the part he took yesterday in carrying a wooded position and two villages north of Verdun.

8th November.—Again I urge that the Government shall return to Paris quickly. But the Ministers are divided in their opinion and for the moment favour a transaction which

does not please me at all. The idea is for Viviani and Briand
to return to Paris while the Government will remain at Bordeaux until the Generalissimo considers they can return. In
other words, the Ministers for Foreign Affairs and War will
remain at Bordeaux, where the Councils will have to be held,
and if I am to preside over them I must remain there also.

9th November.—In my absence Delcassé has, like Sazonoff,
been too free and easy in asking at Nish and Athens for concessions in favour of Bulgaria which neither Serbia nor Greece
were disposed to grant, and which would have done nothing
to modify the attitude of King Ferdinand. This morning
telegrams from Panafieu, Boppé and Deville leave no illusion
as to the fate of these transactions, and Sazonoff himself is
obliged to give up this particular game, anyhow for the
moment.

10th November.—Caillaux has definitely accepted the
mission that has been offered to him, and I can only repeat
that public opinion will scarcely appreciate the usefulness
of this journey to South America. But the majority of the
Council favour the notion, less from the point of view of em-
ploying Caillaux's talents than of getting rid of his irritating
opposition. Marcel Sembat laughingly says : " Although
Caillaux has no luck when he is in power, he has quicksilver
in his brains when he is out of office, and he thinks himself
predestined to be Minister of Finance because he imagines
that this quicksilver will enable him to find the real metal ".

M. Salomon, our Special Messenger to Russia, has just
arrived from Petrograd and tells us that the too famous, if
not infamous, Rasputin has been at least twice to see the
Empress while the Emperor is with the armies, and Salomon
thinks that this extraordinary individual may have some
secret understanding with M. de Witte and may be intriguing
for a separate peace ; Rasputin has been in disgrace since the
affair of his wound, but pushed out of the front door, he is
trying to return by the back entrance. Salomon had a long
talk with M. de Witte, who pleaded the German cause, was
very sceptical as to the atrocities committed by the enemy
armies, but, however Germanophile he may be, he thinks that
victory will rest with the Triple Entente.

Although we are at war with Turkey, the Government here does not wish to visit this rupture on the Turkish subjects resident in France, and *permis de séjour* are being granted, not only to Maronites, Catholic Greeks and Syrians, Armenians and Orthodox Greeks, but also to Arabs and Turks who are political refugees. One does not want to mix up the officials in power at Constantinople with the people with whom we have always had such cordial relations.

11th November.—Yesterday we had to give up Dixmude, and Augagneur reports that the Marine Fusiliers are worn out and need rest very badly.[1] And from a German wireless it would seem that 2000 of our cavalry have been made prisoners in Belgium.

Fighting is still very bitter in Lorraine, especially round St. Mihiel. I told Joffre that I would not put off my visit to the Est after Sunday, but he urges me not to come for the moment so as not to interfere with the operations which are to take place. He insists on this in two telegrams addressed to Millerand, and M. Dubost and M. Deschanel, who had asked to come with me, are, *a fortiori*, begged to stay away.

12th November.—The enemy has been repulsed in a night attack made from Dixmude, but nevertheless Germans have crossed the Yser at several points and are occupying part of the left bank.

M. de Panafieu notifies the efforts which Germany and Austria are now making to drag Bulgaria into war alongside of Turkey ; Sir Edward Grey has decided—and we are in agreement with him—to accept Sazonoff's advice to offer the Enos-Midia line to Bulgaria if she remains neutral.

13th November.—M. Paschitch complains also about his country being poverty-stricken in the matter of munitions. Poor as we are ourselves in this respect, we have already sent 20,000 rounds to Serbia, and we are sending 20,000 more, which is the utmost we can do. If the Serbian army is reduced to impotence, the Austrian army will have the road open and will try to join hands with Turkey across Bulgaria. The Serbian headquarters have retired from Valiévo to Kraguiévatz. The heavy reinforcements which the Austrians

[1] Le Goffic, *Dixmude, un chapitre de l'histoire des fusiliers marins.*

have received, and the activities which are afoot along the
Save and the Danube, lead Paschitch to fear that Austria
may be about to make a supreme effort, after having crushed
Serbia, to cut the communications between Russia and
Roumania with Western Europe.

Colonel Pénélon says that the resumption of the German
offensive in Flanders came as a real surprise for G.H.Q., who
thought that the enemy was for the moment exhausted.
Reinforcements are being hurried up to Dixmude and Ypres,
but our 32nd Corps has been decimated, and the English
are reduced from 100,000 to 45,000 men; the latter, however,
with their new divisions, will soon be able to put 60,000 men
into the line, and we have sent thirty battalions to Belgium
which we have picked up here and there along the front.
Joffre thinks, therefore, that we shall be able to put up a
good resistance, and congratulates himself on not having
taken the defensive on the Yser, which would have meant
using up the 20th Corps and other forces which have been,
and will still be, necessary to hold the enemy off, as we have
no more Reserves available.

14th November.—Viviani has returned from the Departments of the Est, where I alone seem to be forbidden to go,
and is staying on in Paris, although at Joffre's request he is
keeping the seat of Government at Bordeaux. The German
activity is as great as ever ; they have attacked our bridge-
head at Nieuport and renewed their attempts to the east
and south-east of Ypres ; day by day and night by night
they give us no peace in the regions of Lassigny and the
Aisne as far as Berry-au-Bac, and they have resumed the
struggle in the Argonne and round Verdun. We have resisted everywhere, but it is everywhere the Germans who
take the initiative and choose the battle-ground.

M. Bratiano has told the Russian Minister at Bucharest
that Roumania is ready to take up arms at once against
Austria if the three Allied Powers will guarantee her against
the consequences of a possible Bulgarian attack, and if they
will help her to obtain from America a considerable amount
of military equipment. " Just wait for a moment," Sazonoff
says, " and I will propose to you what we shall answer."

His suggestion gives no guarantee to Bratiano and embodies new promises in favour of Bulgaria, and we consider the suggestion to be wholly " wanting ".

15th November. — Bad news from Morocco. General Lyautey telegraphs that on the 13th, Colonel Leverdure's detachment was attacked by 500 rebels near Kenifra and practically annihilated, with loss of a battery of guns. Colonel Duplessis has started from Tadla to try and rescue the little garrison at Kenifra, and General Henrys is doing likewise, but even if Kenifra should hold out until reinforcements arrive, the situation has suddenly become critical, and General Lyautey fears that this serious happening may have a sinister effect on the minds of the natives. He wants his artillery reconstituted, and as he has no more men in Morocco available for the field, he must keep the African battalion which he had hoped to send just now to France.

Viviani only returns from Paris this evening and Briand has already gone there to replace him ; Guesde and Sembat have also repaired to the capital for the monthly meeting of the Socialist Party, while Fernand David is on a tour of agricultural inspection. The Government is scattered and it looks as if I might soon be condemned to represent it by myself at Bordeaux.

It would seem that the chief political personages in Cairo are opposed to a British Protectorate which would leave the Egyptians their Turkish nationality and would prefer annexation with some such regime as the Mussulmans enjoy in India. The British Government tells us that they may agree to this solution and that they would raise no objection if we were to decide to annex Tunis and Morocco. But in this respect we have no reason to imitate our English friends, as neither in Morocco nor in Tunis do we suffer from native sovereigns, nor would we give to quite loyal people the impression that their status is at our mercy ; moreover, it would be dangerous to displease the Mussulmans who live under the protection of the French flag just when we are about to be at war with Turkey.

At Petrograd they still continue to sell the skin of the bear. Gorémykine, in the course of a long talk with

Paléologue, has said that the general terms of peace will have to be decided on between the Allied Powers and will then be dictated to Germany and Austria, and that there should be no Congress or Conference except to settle questions of secondary importance.

The battle is dying down in Flanders and the enemy seem unwilling to start it again. The Kaiser, who had come somewhere near the battle area, and who in his mind's eye already saw himself shaking his fist at England across the Channel, has left his observation post and gone westwards, as angry as he is disillusioned.

16th November.—Viviani returned to Bordeaux last night rubbing his hands over the talks which he had in Paris with the Prefects, the Senators, the Deputies, and the Municipal officials; his vehement pronouncement that we must prosecute the war until decisive victory has been achieved was unanimously approved, and with equal unanimity it was urged on him that the next Parliamentary Session—which must be held before the end of the month to vote the 1915 Budget—should take place at Paris and not at Bordeaux, as Millerand wanted. Galliéni, according to Viviani, thinks there may very likely be a great attack on Paris by aeroplanes and Zeppelins, and he complains that he has not received the troops he requires for his garrison; the troops, however, are in the firing-line.

In the evening that loyal and charming, but too impressionable, personage, the President of the Council, comes to my room again and, point-blank, tenders his resignation or rather tells me that M. Briand has shown him the door Viviani flourishes a copy of the Matin, in which I read:

" M. Aristide Briand will remain in Paris for a week, and during that time will definitely decide the different questions which have lately been submitted to M. Viviani. These questions concern Paris and its outskirts, as well as the invaded Departments . . . yesterday M. Briand had several interviews with political and military authorities."

" Well, what then ? " I said. " I have telephoned to Briand," was the reply, " who denies having inspired this interview, but he must certainly have done something to bring it about. I have had enough of this sort of thing, and I hand you my resignation." "I don't accept it ; at a moment like this it is for you and your colleagues to give an example of unity." For a full hour by the clock Viviani continued to pour out complaints of Briand. " He leaves no stone unturned ", he exclaims, " to push himself into the front rank and to belittle the conduct of his colleagues." In vain I try to calm my friend, who only repeats that he will bring the incident before the Council to-morrow.

17th November.—Viviani is himself once more and is all smiles ; he has telephoned to Briand again, who has assured him that he knew nothing whatever of the paragraph which appeared in the *Matin,* and has promised him to issue a contradiction. All is well that ends well, and perhaps, with the life we are leading, it is only natural that some of the Ministers should have their nerves on edge.

Several of the Paris newspapers, despite the censorship, have made rather unpleasant remarks about the Government as to Caillaux's mission to Brazil. A large part of the criticism is of course levelled at myself, and I am always held responsible for what happens, and especially for what happens in spite of myself. What matter if only France be saved.

But we are a very long way from anything like final victory. If there is something like a quiet time in Flanders, the fighting is fiercer than ever in the Est. At St. Mihiel we have tried to push the Germans back on the right bank of the Meuse, our troops having attacked them in Chauvoncourt and established themselves in our big barracks. There has been frenzied fighting round Champigny, in the forest of Apremont, round Marbotte and Mécrin, and more than anywhere, in the usually quiet wood of Ailly which— as I could always see from my windows at Clos—so prettily crowns the slopes of the right bank.

After a long discussion with Viviani, Millerand and Ribot to adjust the troublesome matter of the Army Postal Service, as to which there are many complaints, we are confronted with further disappointment as regards munitions. The factories have not yielded what they promised, and the delay is explained by the difficulties of getting to work. A number of sub-contractors had to be brought in who knew very little of the business, and some of the more important leading establishments have not sufficiently spurred these sub-contractors to activity. Most of the manufacturers complain also of the belated arrival of workmen on whom they had relied, and some of these could only be traced with their units after a very considerable time had elapsed. As the information furnished on these points seems wholly insufficient, I am asking the Director of Artillery either to come and talk to me himself or to send one of his subordinates; Millerand asks me not to communicate with any of the artillery officers without reference to himself, and, strictly speaking, he is quite right, as he alone is responsible. But I tell him that we are at war, that I am very incompletely informed, and that I propose to leave no stone unturned to get better knowledge of the situation.

Sir George Buchanan has been instructed to tell Sazonoff that, owing to the conduct of Turkey in this European crisis, Great Britain has determined to consider that the question of the Narrows and of Constantinople must be resolved agreeably with the wishes of Russia. Sazonoff has received this bit of intelligence " with the liveliest satisfaction ". No doubt. But we can hardly share in this satisfaction, and we do not quite understand why England, without consulting us, has given carte blanche to Russia in a matter which affects all the Allies and which the Russians have never approached without having something in the back of their minds.

18th November.—General Hirschauer, Director of Aviation, furnishes us with new information as to the defence of Paris by aircraft. The central post at Bourget now comprises thirteen aeroplanes armed with machine-guns or automatic rifles, twenty pilots and forty men; there are look-out posts in all the stations, linked up by telephone with the military administration, as with the armies, the supply stations and the forts. In a fortnight Bourget will have twenty-five aeroplanes, but this is not nearly enough. Joffre and Galliéni think that the Germans are building a large fleet of Zeppelins ; in Belgium they have improved the existing aerodromes and put up others ; their three objectives will be Paris, London and the British fleet. As the armies are now placed, the enemy dirigibles could, with very little détour, by taking the triangle Laon, La Fère and Noyon as their line of direction, make their way to Paris by a course which would present little danger, and they would be able to travel by day ; they would only have about 100 kilometres to fly over our lines by night. The only defence against these machines must be with projectors and guns ; our aeroplanes are valueless in a night attack ; we must reconnoitre and open fire well beyond Paris. The searchlights which sweep the Paris sky will have the serious disadvantage of offering the enemy a point of direction, and an attack by guns overhead would be very dangerous for Parisians. We shall have to put in hand artillery with vertical fire and projectors, the whole thing on motor-cars.

Our attacks on Chauvoncourt and St. Mihiel seem to have been very unlucky, and we have been unable to keep possession of the barracks, where we had established ourselves, besides incurring very heavy losses. Some mines and time fuses had been hidden by the enemy in one of the buildings we entered, and there was a great explosion at the very moment when we were congratulating ourselves on success ; many of our men fell victims to this odious war trick.

General Florentin, Grand Chancellor of the Legion of Honour, says that the Council of the Order is very much disturbed as to the violations of rights of nations and their consequences, of which the enemy armies are guilty, and that this reflects on the Legionaries who are of German nationality. " Germany ", he says, " had agreed to the international conventions which determined the rights of belligerents ; she has disregarded her obligations and thus has forfeited her honour. In this respect her army, her authors, her artists and all the subjects of the Empire have shown themselves of one mind ; thus the Council thinks these people ought to be excluded from an Order which has for its motto the very word ' Honour '." The Grand

Chancellor adds that of course exception should be made
as regards Alsatians and Lorrainers, who have become
German subjects unwillingly, and the Ministers agree that
German names should be struck off the Roll by decree.
The Government has to consider closely the English proposals
regarding the political régime of Egypt and our own African
Protectorates, and the annexation of Morocco and Tunis do
not seem to offer us any particular advantage.   Delcassé
will therefore ask England not to come to any decision
regarding Egypt while the war lasts, as to-day Germany
would certainly pretend that England, from now onwards,
is garnering her own fruits of victory, and would thereby
try and sow dissension between the Allies.

   19th November.—Our Military Attaché in London,
Colonel de la Panouse, tells us that a new division, the 27th,
will land in France the first days of December, and another,
the 28th, a month later ; the Canadian contingent will join
up with the British army in February.   That will be all for
the moment, but Lord Kitchener, with his marvellous and
methodical organisation, is building up a great new army
composed of twenty-four divisions, about 600,000 men ; he
then intends to form twelve divisions more to take the field.
Of course these new troops will at the beginning be short of
officers and munitions and will not be ready for the firing-
line till June 1915, so we must make ready to carry on for
ourselves for some time longer.

   General Laguiche, our Military Attaché in Russia, has
been for a tour of the Eastern front and reports that the
Russian army is moving forward eagerly, but that the enemy
is retiring as he pleases and can at any moment turn round
and counter-attack.

   Once more M. Radoslavoff has told the Governments of
the Triple Entente that, after the most careful consideration,
the Bulgarian Cabinet has decided to keep " strict and
loyal neutrality ".   So poor Sazonoff is once more bowed
out of his attempts to coax Sofia.

   20th November.—The British Government inform us that
they have given up the idea of annexing Egypt and the
Protectorate will stand.

The pretty village of Lacroix-sur-Meuse has been bombarded and largely destroyed, and there is brisk fighting in the Argonne ; my native country continues to be the victim of cruel Fate.

21st November.—Along the remainder of the front the fighting is languid, and the German attacks appear to have broken down.   Since the beginning of the war the enemy has stuck to the strategy laid down and cried up by military writers : to crush the French army before swinging round against the Russian army, and, in order to finish us off, to envelop our left ; a single end to a single means.   Our first reply to the German assault was the victory of the Marne, which, from the 6th to the 12th of September, not only arrested the movement intended to swamp us, but also, by threatening the German right, brought about a German retreat.   Our second reply has been found on the Flanders battle-ground.   Once more the German Staff doggedly attempted to encircle the Allied armies, and once more their attempt has failed.   Far from gaining, the Germans have lost, ground, and their futile efforts have resulted in fearful losses.   To secure their object and overwhelm our left the Germans have, between the beginning of October and the middle of November, set going nearly twelve army corps in the region of the Nord between the Lys and the Côte, and these at the beginning of November were reinforced by a division of Marine Fusiliers and a reserve division from the 5th Corps.   The first week in October Prince Rupprecht of Bavaria, in a windy proclamation, exhorted his troops to " make the decisive effort against the French left wing ", and " thus to determine the issue of the great battle begun some weeks ago ".   The Kaiser himself tiptoed to Thielt and Courtrai to encourage his troops by his presence, and the German Press, allowing the wish to be father to the thought, entitled this struggle the battle of Calais.   To seize Ypres, round which the fighting has raged, would have been to cut our left in two, and to reach Calais would have spelt for it destruction ; further, this would have meant contact with the sea and a menace to Great Britain, not only in the matter of supplying her Expeditionary Force, but as to her own insular safety ; this was the German plan as conceived, prepared and proclaimed ; thank God it has failed.

The German failure has been largely due to our armies of the North, which, on the 4th of October, came under the orders of Foch ; the Germans have failed in spite of the fall of Antwerp, in spite of the forced retreat of the Belgian army and of the delay in the concentration of the English troops, and, moreover, in spite of the insufficiency of our own armed forces. Between the 23rd of October and the 13th of November our danger at Ypres was at its greatest, while fighting was scarcely less bitter from Nieuport to Dixmude than from Dixmude to the north of Ypres and from Ypres to the Lys. British and Belgians have, in this frenzied struggle, given us an admirable earnest alike of their indomitable spirit and their staying powers. With the breakdown of the German plan the Kaiser must have relinquished his idea of a sharp, short and joyous campaign, and it is all to no purpose that he has tried to terrorise us by murderous methods. We still stand steady on our feet confronting Germany.

22nd November.—General Laguiche made no mistake in suspecting that the retreat of the German armies is a snare and delusion ; the Germans have to-day launched a new offensive on Warsaw. And nearer home Lord Kitchener warns us that, according to information he has received from his Intelligence service, the enemy is preparing a desperate attack to break our lines between La Bassée and the sea. The Kaiser, so the story runs, has given orders that our front line must be forced at any cost in order to reach Calais ; a hundred thousand men are mentioned as reinforcements, and it is said that an attack will be launched in a few days and will be worse than anything we have yet undergone. Joffre does not think this information correct, and is of opinion that, for the moment anyhow, we have set a term to the German offensive.

23rd November.—At last I am allowed to get away, and to-morrow I start for Paris and for the armies of the East. Joffre does not think the prophecies of the British Intelligence will be realised, and has removed his veto ; I shall therefore go to Romilly and present him with his Military

Medal. Viviani, however, rather wants us to postpone our actual return to Paris and would like to put back the meeting of Parliament.

24th November.—The Grand Duchess Anastasie Michaïl-ovna, widow of the Grand Duke of Mecklenburg-Schwerin and our former neighbour of the Eze, writes me pages from Milan, and asks if she cannot be treated in France as she is in Russia ; in other words, she wants to be regarded as a Russian Grand Duchess, and not as the widow of a German prince, and also to be allowed to return to the Riviera, where she always passes the winter. Although she is the mother-in-law of the Crown Prince of Germany, the Government agree to give her a *laissez-passer*, which I send her, but it may be well to take care that she does not unwittingly send information to her son-in-law as to what is happening in France.

M. Bratiano has told M. Blondel that he is quite certain that from now onwards there is a secret agreement between Bulgaria and Austria, and he adduces as proof of this Bulgaria's purchase of an Austrian flotilla on the Danube. This flotilla will for the future fly the Bulgarian flag and will carry supplies and munitions from Austria to Bulgaria and no doubt also to Turkey. Bratiano thinks this is very much the same trick as letting the *Goeben* and the *Breslau* join the Turkish navy.

CHAPTER X

25th November.—It is cold and snowy when we arrive in
Paris at 8 A.M. to find the Minister of the Interior, the Prefects and Galliéni awaiting us at the station, but no newspaper
has announced our arrival, as the Censor has forbidden my
visit to the armies of the Est to be mentioned. Our rooms
at the Élysée have been re-arranged in some measure for us,
but my own room, the library, the only one in which I feel
really comfortable, is empty, and the books which are my
personal property have been moved to the Garde Meubles.
I wonder if I must ask General Headquarters if I may have
them back.

Mr. Herrick, who is on the eve of leaving the American
Embassy, writes to express once more his keen sympathy
for our country. " It is with deep regret ", he says, " that
I leave France just when her people whom I so quickly
learnt to love, are in agony and mourning." He thanks one
warmly for the kindly and constant attentions which have
been paid him during his stay here, and he ends with : " The
irresistible attraction which France has for all my compatriots,
no less than the claims of friendship, will in the future bring
me back again and again to Paris ". I am certain that
Herrick will be a staunch champion of the French cause in
America, and not one of us can see him leave without a pang
of regret.

26th November.—An early start in a closed motor with the
President of the Senate, who has shed his sourness—which
was never more than skin-deep—and is his own frank, loyal

and energetic self again ; the safety of France is the para-
mount, if not the only, thought of a man to whom the
present war is only the continuation of what he himself
lived through in 1870. Deschanel, on the other hand, who
follows in the next car with Viviani, is rather gloomy, and
complains that his post is a sinecure, forgetting that he refused
all the responsible posts I offered him ; both he and his
companions seem rather nerve-wracked with the horrors of
the war.

Our first visit is to Romilly, whence Joffre is about to
shift his headquarters to Chantilly, and in the courtyard of
the schoolhouse I affix the Military Medal to the Generalissimo's broad breast and pay him the tribute of praise he
so richly deserves.[1]

[1] " Mon cher Général, il m'est très agréable de vous remettre
aujourd'hui, en présence de MM. les Présidents des Chambres, de M. le Président du Conseil et de M. le Ministre de la Guerre, cette simple et glorieuse
médaille qui est l'emblème des plus hautes vertus militaires et que portent
avec la même fierté généraux illustres et modestes soldats.

" Veuillez voir dans cette distinction symbolique un témoignage de la
reconnaissance nationale.

" Depuis le jour où s'est si remarquablement réalisée, sous votre direction, la concentration des forces françaises, vous avez montré, dans la
conduite de nos armées, des qualités qui ne se sont pas un instant démenties :
un esprit d'organisation, d'ordre et de méthode, dont les bienfaisants effets
se sont étendus de la stratégie à la tactique, une sagesse froide et avisée, qui
sait toujours parer à l'imprévu, une force d'âme que rien n'ébranle, une
sérénité dont l'exemple salutaire répand partout la confiance et l'espoir.

" Je répondrai, j'en suis sûr, à vos désirs intimes en ne séparant pas de
vous, dans mes félicitations, vos fidèles collaborateurs du grand quartier
général, appelés à préparer, sous votre commandement suprême, les opérations de chaque jour et absorbés, comme vous, dans leur tâche sacrée.
Mais, par delà les officiers et les hommes qui m'entourent en ce moment, ma
pensée va rejoindre sur toute la ligne de front, des Vosges à la mer du Nord,
les admirables troupes auxquelles je dois rendre, demain et les jours suivants,
une nouvelle visite, et je traduirai certainement, mon cher Général, votre
propre sentiment, si je reporte sur l'ensemble des armées une part de
l'honneur que nous avez mérité.

" Dans les rudes semaines que vous venez de passer, vous avez consolidé
et prolongé, par la défense des Flandres, la brillante victoire de la Marne ;
et grâce à l'heureuse impulsion que vous avez su donner autour de vous,
tout a conspiré à nous assurer de nouveaux succès : une parfaite unité de
vues dans le commandement, une solidarité active entre les armées alliées, un
judicieux emploi des formations, une coordination rationnelle des différentes
armes ; mais, ce qui a plus particulièrement servi vos nobles desseins, c'est
cette incomparable énergie morale qui se dégage de l'âme française et qui
met en mouvement tous les ressorts de l'armée.

" Irrésistible force d'idéal, qui, depuis le début de la campagne, a
permis à nos troupes de développer leurs qualités acquises et d'en gagner de

General Belin, the Deputy Chief of the Staff, has then to be invested with the cravate of the Legion of Honour, after which there is an opportunity for a long talk with Joffre and Foch, who has come expressly from Cassel. Both are quite confident as to the future, and say that, whether the war be long or short, we are sure to win it, and that the Germans have already lost the game which they have planned. Nor is Joffre particularly put about by further miscalculations with regard to our munitions, as he is obliged anyhow to wait for another fortnight or three weeks until he can get the

---

nouvelles, de s'adapter à la pratique de l'organisation défensive sans perdre leur mordant, de résister également à la fatigue des combats ininterrompus et à la courbature des longues immobilités, de se perfectionner, en un mot, sous le feu de l'ennemi, tout en conservant, au milieu des mille nouveautés de la guerre, leur entrain, leur fougue et leur bravoure.

" Le jour où il deviendra possible de passer en revue quelques-uns des actes de dévouement et de courage qui s'accomplissent quotidiennement parmi vous, il sera démontré par les faits que jamais, au cours des siècles, la France n'a eu une armée plus belle et plus consciente de ses devoirs. Cette armée, d'ailleurs, ne se confond-elle pas avec la France elle-même ? et n'est-ce pas la France, la France tout entière, sans acception de partis ou de conditions sociales, qui s'est levée, à l'appel du Gouvernement de la République, pour repousser une agression perfidement préméditée ? Tous les citoyens groupés sous les drapeaux, n'ont plus qu'un cœur et qu'un esprit ; et les vies individuelles sont prêtes à s'anéantir devant l'intérêt général. Dans ce sublime élan d'un peuple libre, les représentants du pays n'ont pas été les moins jaloux de payer leur dette à la patrie ; et les Présidents qui sont venus offrir aujourd'hui à l'armée les vœux des deux assemblées souffriront que je me joigne à eux pour envoyer d'ici un souvenir ému aux membres du Parlement tombés, morts ou blessés, sur les champs de bataille.

" Les deuils et les horreurs de cette guerre sanglante n'attiédiront pas l'enthousiasme des troupes ; les pertes douloureuses que subit la nation ne troubleront pas sa constance et ne feront pas chanceler sa volonté. La France a épuisé tous les moyens pour épargner à l'humanité une catastrophe sans précédent : elle sait que, pour en éviter le retour, elle doit, d'accord avec ses alliés, en abolir définitivement les causes ; elle sait que les générations actuelles portent en elles, avec le legs du passé, la responsabilité de l'avenir ; elle sait qu'un peuple ne tient pas tout entier dans une minute, si tragique soit-elle, de son existence collective et que, sous peine de désavouer toute notre histoire, nous n'avons pas le droit de répudier notre mission séculaire de civilisation et de liberté.

" Une victoire indécise et une paix précaire exposeraient demain le génie français à de nouvelles insultes de cette barbarie raffinée qui prend le masque de la science pour mieux assouvir ses instincts dominateurs. La France poursuivra jusqu'au bout, par l'inviolable union de tous ses enfants, et avec le persévérant concours de ses alliés, l'œuvre de libération européenne qui est commencée, et lorsqu'elle l'aura couronnée, elle trouvera, sous les auspices de ses morts, une vie plus intense dans la gloire, la concorde et la sécurité."

newly invented engines of war which are to destroy wire entanglements and blow up trenches.

A so-called "pot-luck" breakfast in the villa where Joffre nightly sleeps the sleep of Condé, and then we set off for Châlons-sur-Marne, where we meet General de Langle de Cary, who commands the Fourth Army, and General Dalstein, who is in charge of the 6th District, and who is as youthful-looking and as beautifully groomed as when I knew him twenty years ago at the Élysée. De Langle de Cary—who was shot in the chest forty-three years ago at the battle of Buzenval—is also a fine-looking officer, who had just been placed on the Reserve when the war broke out and was at once recalled to command an army. He stands very high in Joffre's esteem, and tells me he has no anxiety as to his front, which he considers invulnerable, but he is just a little anxious with regard to the Argonne side, where the Germans are more aggressive than elsewhere ; without any set speech, I give him the Grand Cordon in the presence of the troops.

At dusk our little cortège of cars makes its way at top speed to the camp where the Territorials from Montauban are lodged in huge sheds, very feebly lighted with tallow candles ; some of the men are doing their cooking in the mud by torchlight, but in reply to inquiries as to their health and their rations they say they are perfectly satisfied, and perhaps, whatever their privations, they are too proud to say otherwise.

The wounded in the field and town hospitals are in good spirits, though many of them are grievously hurt, but unhappily cases of typhoid fever have occurred, and the epidemic is difficult to check.

27th November.—Last night we heard by telephone that the battle of Lodz was still going on, that the Russians were doing well and had taken an enormous number of German prisoners. This morning de Langle de Cary, who—unlike Joffre—thinks that the Germans are going to try another throw, comes with us to the Argonne. We pass through Valmy, where the son-in-law of Dubost is in charge of an ambulance ; the President of the Senate did not like to ask me to stop here, but when I proposed it to him his good-

humour became positive gaiety, and I foresee the moment
when he will be treating me to a story of the battle of Valmy,
explaining to me of Dumouriez and Kellermann and pointing
out to me that it would be dangerous to-day to lead troops
across open country waving their hats on the points of their
swords. Anyhow I have to be reminded that Goethe said
of Valmy : " Here and to-day there begins a new era for
the history of the world ". " Perfectly true," says Dubost
in cheerful tones, " and a hundred and twenty-two years
later Goethe would be well able to say the same thing." We
make a halt at General Gerard's headquarters to invest him
with the Star of Grand Officer. Gerard, who was Galliéni's
Chief of the Staff in Madagascar, has had charge of the
2nd Corps, with which he fought the battle of Mangiennes,
and in September he was told to defend the Argonne and
has been fighting almost every day in this Thermopylæ of
France. He goes with us through the beautiful wooded
country, so much of which is familiar ground to me, and
takes us to where the men are quartered in wooden huts
furnished with sleeping berths, tables and wooden stools.
The batteries of 90's and 105's are well concealed under the
beeches and oaks ; the gun-fire seems to be continuous, and
the General tells us that the Germans daily bite off a bit of
our Argonne front ; at this rate they absorb about 100 metres
a month, and their dogged advance in one direction suggests
that they have by no means given up the idea of investing
Verdun.

In the commune of Islettes, where General Sarrail is
awaiting us and where the people are living under the
enemy's constant threat, I am welcomed indeed as the
former Senator for the Meuse much more than as the President of the Republic. Alas ! Clermont in Argonne, the
favourite resort of my dear parents, is little more than a
heap of burnt-down houses, the Würtemberg soldiers and
Prince Wittgenstein's Uhlans having set the little town on
fire on the 5th of September. The hospital is about the
only building left, and this is due to Sister Gabrielle, who
went straight to the German General, who was surrounded
by his staff, and bluntly said to him : " Your officers gave

me their word the hospital should be spared, and they are going back on it ; you will never find a French officer behaving like that ". The General was furiously angry at first with the good nun, but eventually relented and gave orders that the hospital should not be burnt.[1] " I did no more than my duty, M. le Président," is Sister Gabrielle's simple reply to my hearty congratulations ; she shall have the Cross of the Legion of Honour next time I am here.

Through villages such as Récicourt and Regret, which I know by heart, and where the people, who are all mixed up with the soldiers, wave friendly greetings, we make our way to Verdun, which is swarming with officers and soldiers. So far the place is unmolested, and the people are walking about quite unconcernedly, shops are open, the Cathedral stands serene, the beautiful façades of the Bishop's Palace and the Museum are intact, and it seems unthinkable that the enemy is already laying siege to the fortress and making his maleficent plans to invest the town. Ever since the battle of the Marne the Crown Prince, who commands the Fifth German Army and has his headquarters at Stenay, has tried to push his way across the wooded and broken ground of the Argonne ; he wants to seize the railway line from St. Menehould to Verdun, and for this purpose he has been given several *corps d'élite*, including the 16th Metz Corps, which is chiefly composed of the sturdy miners of the Sarre. The Crown Prince is faced by our 5th Corps under General Michelet and General Gerard's 2nd Corps, and about two months ago we still held the dominating point of the forest ; but little by little the enemy has gained ground, has attacked the 2nd Corps round La Gruerie, and is trying to wrest from the 5th Corps the slopes 263 and 295, the Fille Morte (the real name of which was originally the Feuille Morte), Bolante and the Haut Jardinet.

Despite the growing peril Verdun has all its pre-war appearance, and we breakfast quietly at the Sous-Préfecture with some of the deputies who are now under arms, and with Sarrail, who has succeeded General Ruffey in the

---

[1] See *La Guerre de 1914-18 dans la Meuse*, par Ch. Aimond, chanoine honoraire de Verdun.

command of the Third Army. Sarrail has let his white
beard grow, but with his tall, upright and well-knit figure,
he looks younger than his years, and the blue eyes, which
at one moment seem to pierce your thoughts and the next
moment to be lost in contemplation, suggest a character
temperamental almost to the edge of fanaticism. Sarrail by
no means minces his words and is more disposed to criticise
than to praise ; he regrets very much the attack on the
barracks at Chauvoncourt, which resulted so murderously
for ourselves, and he puts much of the blame for the unhappy
affair of the Hauts de Meuse and the capture of St. Mihiel
on the General who commanded the 75th Reserve Division
and who was wounded, but he says the chief fault was
moving the 8th Corps, for which he was in no way responsible.

In the afternoon we go to the Douaumont fort, the only
one which so far bears the German marks ; the bombardment,
whatever people may say, has done a great deal of damage
here, but Douaumont could still hold out for a good many
days against enemy assaults. Sarrail agrees with Galliéni
that it will not be possible to secure the defence of a place,
whether under the shelter of the city walls or from the
interior of the fort, and that a whole system of field fortifications must be organised. He is not anxious about Verdun,
and his troops are moving forward in the Wœvre from the
Étain and Fresnes sides, and he is pushing his advance lines
out as far as possible. At nightfall we move on to Bar-le-Duc,
where the hospitals are sheltering a great number of typhoid
cases as well as the wounded ; the fever has already claimed
many victims, and if the epidemic continues it may be very
serious, but the doctors still think they will find a serum
to deal with the disease. The sight of the house where I
was born brings back many thoughts of childhood and dim
memories of the war and enemy occupation which over-
shadowed that childhood.

28th November.—Before leaving Bar-le-Duc, where the
people have got to know of my presence and have given
many signs of their goodwill, I visit the unhappy refugees
from the invaded communes who have been lodged in a
house in the Rue de la Banque, where they are sleeping on

camp-beds or straw, and are in a pitiful plight, though not one utters a single complaint.

At Commercy we are welcomed by General Dubail, who commands the First Army, and General Mondésir, who is in charge of the 8th Corps, and we hear from them that very severe fighting has been going on the last three days round Apremont La Forët.

General Dubail, a simple, modest soldier, as gentle in manner as he is resolute in action, tells us very clearly what happened to his army. On Wednesday last, under the first snowfall of the year, the 8th Corps was attacked on one of the salients in the Louvière wood, and a Minnenwerfer bombardment, which our artillery was unable to silence, forced our troops to evacuate part of their trenches,[1] and our counter-strokes failed to recover the ground lost ; yesterday the right of the 8th Corps was heavily shelled from the redoubt of the Bois brûlée, and we have had to give up another trench. Dubail is much worried about these repeated reverses, especially as the Germans, all through last night, tried to exploit their gains, and have redoubled their attacks this morning ; the General, just before our arrival, sent word to General Mondésir that he must hold on at any cost to the redoubt which is being attacked and that at the first possible moment he must himself attack the crest-line west of the Bois brûlée so as to force the enemy to split up his attacks.

The dear little village of Commercy, the cradle of my parliamentary life, is full of refugees from the neighbouring communes which are in the hands of the Germans. In the Woëvre and in the valley of the Meuse the inhabitants had to pack up and leave hearth and home at a moment's notice, and this was a sort of dumb resignation, just as if they were doing what their forebears have periodically been called upon to do. When talking to them they utter no complaint and only thank one for what is being done for them ; the least one can do oneself is to give them what little pecuniary help

---

[1] See *Quatre années de commandement*, par le Général Dubail. (" J'expose au Président la situation de la Ière armée. Je vois qu'il est parfaitement au courant des opérations : il s'y intéresse d'une façon toute particulière.")

one can. The factories in Commercy are not closed, though of course the work there is very much reduced, as a large proportion of the workmen are at the front.

After breakfast with the Mayor, who is an old friend and who is showing hospitality to many of my relations, we take the Gironville road and stop for a little while this side of the crest of the Hauts de Meuse, to the left of the fort. It is a fairly clear day, and one can easily take stock of the front occupied by our troops ; the batteries from the Liouville fort are firing on the redoubt in the wood, but of course there is neither a horseman nor a footman in sight ; thousands are burrowing in the ground, and the immense plain which stretches at our feet seems absolutely deserted. As the Gironville fort was heavily fired on on the 31st October, Dubail thinks that a string of motor-cars may induce another bombardment, and I arrange to go to it alone with Dubost and the General, being particularly anxious to see my gardener who is serving in the fort. We then make our way to Toul by Gironville and Corniéville, the motor-cars keeping at a respectful distance from one another so as not to attract the attention of the enemy. General Rémy, the Governor of Toul, shows us all the advance defence posts on the hills and in the woods, as well as the works constructed at the outbreak of hostilities to replace the permanent forts, which are no match for the German heavy guns. For the moment Toul has only to fear assaults from the air, and is not disturbed by the enemy guns ; the place we regarded as one of our chief guardians and as the most exposed point on our frontier of the Est is now sheltered from enemy attacks, while Maubeuge, which was under the protection of Belgian neutrality, is in the enemy's hands. We arrive at Nancy late in the afternoon and are greeted at the Prefecture by M. Mirman, his wife and daughters, who, these last weeks, have set a noble example of courage to the Lorraine folk. The fair town of Stanislaus has recovered from the alarm she underwent during the battle of the Grand Couronné, and has only to put up with aeroplane raids and gun-fire at very long range ; normal life has been resumed, and the streets seem as animated as in time of peace

29th November.—Dubail, who has picked us up at Nancy, takes Dubost, Deschanel and myself to the principal positions of the Grand Couronné and over the battlefields of August and September, and I can see once more the familiar country of my youth, and the waste ground where I so often drilled with the 26th Regiment. We are taken to Champenoux, which was the centre point of the battle, and to Crévic, which is almost entirely destroyed ; the Mayor of the latter commune tells us that the Germans deliberately and without any reason whatever set the houses on fire and started with General Lyautey's home. "And these ruffians", the worthy Mayor exclaimed, "were mere lads, mere lads!" He seemed to be more irritated by their immaturity than their brutality.

We push on northwards nearly to the frontier, and leaving the motor-cars go on foot across the forest, and on the farther side find our advance posts, where the men have made trenches and underground shelters under the trees ; at Brin there is an advanced platoon, and on the other side of the Seille the Germans are in the villages within sight. To-day everything is quite quiet ; there is no fighting in this sector, and the opponents are simply facing one another.

From Nancy we make our way through Lunéville to the poor town which was once Gerbéviller but of which nothing remains now but some blackened walls and a mass of debris, with the clock tower of the old church, eviscerated by German shells, still standing and making, as it were, a final protest against a horrible outrage. M. Mirman asks me to give the Cross of the Legion of Honour to Sister Julie, the Superior of the hospital, who, with the help of four other Sisters, has worked untiringly to heal the wounded and help the poor people who are threatened alike by fire and hunger. Dubost says that he has heard some murmur in the crowd against this decoration, and he supposes that the malcontents are politically inspired, but Mirman on the contrary assures us that everyone is agreed as to the splendid part Sister Julie has played, and that the only people opposed to any honour being paid her are some women who think that they have been rather neglected in the way of rations.[1]

At Neuves Maisons we wish good-bye to Dubail, leaving him at his headquarters to get ready the attack the 8th Corps is going to launch to-morrow on Vaux Féry, the 31st Corps making for the Sonnard wood, and the 73rd Division the Mort-Mare forest. After dinner with the senators and deputies of Meurthe and Moselle and with the painter Guinand de Scevola, who is now serving as an Artillery Brigadier, we take train from Toul, to be pulled up every minute on our journey to Paris by military transports.

30th November.—A heap of papers has accumulated for me even during my short absence, of which the most important, perhaps, is a confidential note from London. Sir Edward Grey has said to Paul Cambon :

" Austria and Prussia have representatives at the Vatican, who exercise constant influence over the Catholic world against the Triple Entente. These emissaries keep on saying that the war is essentially a conflict between the three Powers—England, who is an enemy of Holy Church, schismatic Russia with atheist France —and the two Powers who hold Catholicism in deepest reverence. This assertion is being made in every Catholic country, in Spain and America, and as it may have the most regrettable effect on general opinion, the British Government has decided to be represented in Rome at the Holy See. Nothing is actually settled as to the character and composition of the Mission, but this will be decided in a few days."

Sir Edward ended up by saying to Cambon : " It would be a very good thing if France were to do the same as us '. Sir Edward is perfectly right, and it is really ridiculous for us, in time of war, to stand aloof from an observation post as important as the Vatican. But can the French Government be persuaded to understand this ?

According to another telegram the British Chargé d'Affaires in Cairo thinks that his Government will very soon put out a proclamation announcing the deposition of the Khedive, with Prince Hussein to replace him, and will declare a British Protectorate.

---

[1] See L'Âme française et la guerre. Les Saints de la France, par Maurice Barrès.

Sazonoff is busy again, and now says that he has good reason to think Bulgaria could be set against Austria if the three Powers would guarantee her Thrace as far as the Enos-Midia line, and the share of Macedonia as laid down in the agreement of 1912. Sazonoff is still following his will-o'-the-wisps, and he suggests that anyhow, considering the importance which Greece and Serbia attach to the contiguity of their frontiers, we ought to maintain this even at the expense of Albania. Delcassé says we must certainly pour a little cold water on our friend's heated imagination.

Paléologue telegraphs :

" I have such difficulty in getting any precise information about the battle of Lodz that I cannot help fearing the Russian victory is less decisive than the Russian General Staff at first supposed ; anyhow the battle is still going on."

Russia is treating us more and more to alternate hopes and disappointments, and it is quite likely that the Russian Government knows very little more what is going on at their front than we do.

From Serbia the news is even less comforting, and one hears of signs of discouragement in the troops of their First Army, and that the young recruits who have just joined up have been stricken with little less than panic. The Prince Regent remains at the front doing all he can to restore confidence to the soldiers and setting them an admirable example of courage and devotion.

Delcassé telegraphs that the King of England is coming to France to see his troops, and Viviani agrees with me that I ought to go and greet His Majesty ; Colonel Pénélon, who has come back with us from the Est, is telephoning to the British Headquarters to arrange a meeting between the King and myself to-morrow at Merville.

Cardinal Amette has handed to Jules Cambon a letter from Cardinal Gasparri. The Pope wants the belligerent Powers to agree to a truce for Christmas Day, but the Holy Father does not wish to give expression to this thought unless it is likely to be well received, and he has desired

the Archbishop to sound the authorities.   Jules Cambon has
told the Cardinal that he is not in a position to express any
opinion, but that the French Government could certainly
only do the same as the Allies, and they would of course
have to consult the military authorities.   Cambon asks me
what I think about the matter, and I can only tell him that it
may be very difficult to give effect to the wishes of the Holy
See, the more so as the Russians do not keep Christmas on
the same day as ourselves ; nor can anyone say now whether
the military situation on the 25th December would admit of
any break off.   The Holy Father's thought is very generous,
but one fears it may be a little shadowy, and I can only tell
Cambon to refer the matter to the Government at Bordeaux.

1st December.—We arrive—Viviani General Duparge,
Colonel Pénélon and myself—at one o'clock at St. Omer,
where Joffre is waiting at the station to take us to Merville.
One of the British divisions has its headquarters here, and
we find King George in a private house which has been
requisitioned by the troops.   The King, who is in service kit,
thanks me for having been kind enough to have come, presents some of his officers and asks me to go with him in an
open car to inspect some of the troops.   The men, many of
whom have come from the trenches, are lined up facing one
another on each side of the road, and we pass at a foot's pace
between their ranks, the soldiers standing like statues while
the officers salute, and then, unlike our own people, cheering
lustily.   In Hazebroucke, Estaire and other places through
which we pass, there is a hearty welcome from the groups of
people standing about, and the King in his usual friendly
manner talks about the troubles which have beset us these
last months.   What seems to give him the greatest pleasure
is that the Germans were baulked in their effort to get to
Calais.   " It was their great game," he says, " and their
disappointment must have been all the greater because they
laid themselves out for it."   King George is also greatly
pleased that the Allied Governments should have pledged
themselves not to sign any separate peace.   " I have always
thought myself ", he says to me, " that England ought to
take the field against Germany if Germany should attack

France, but I was obliged to be very careful in my reply to your letter because my Government had not made up its mind on the matter, and because public opinion was not prepared for any intervention on our part. I told Grey that it was for him to let the country know the rights and wrongs of the situation, and the people would then certainly understand that England could not remain aloof ; as a matter of fact Grey had very little difficulty in opening the eyes of the large majority of our people." The King seems horrified by the fearful ravages the Germans have committed, and draws my attention again and again to houses which have been burned down, and to damage done by shells, and he seems keenly alive to the fact that people who are fighting on their own soil have very much the worst of it. Visits have to be paid to two headquarters and cavalry, artillery and infantry are inspected before we return latish in the afternoon to St. Omer, which has all the appearance of an English town, while the British officers and soldiers are on the very best terms with the townsfolk.

At eight o'clock dinner with Sir John French, but at the invitation of the King, who considers himself at home in the midst of his armies although he is on French territory. The only guests at dinner are the Prince of Wales—who looks nearly as young as he did when he was staying with the Marquis de Breteuil—two British officers, General Duparge, Colonel Pénélon and Colonel Huguet, sometime Military Attaché in London, and now our chief liaison officer at British Headquarters. The King does not mince his words when he speaks of Caillaux, whom Sir Francis Bertie[1] has represented to him in a none too favourable light ; " Anyhow," His Majesty says, " he is off to Brazil, which is a relief " ; he also tells me that he is heart and soul with his Government in wishing to prosecute the war until the system of Prussianism has been crushed, and he hopes to be able to greet his cousin King Albert either at Furnes or La Panne before going back to England.

2nd December.—A night journey brings us to Paris, and I have hardly said good-bye to Viviani before he is back at the

[1] Diary of Lord Bertie.

Élysée ; Briand has telephoned to him that the Cabinet at
Bordeaux has replied to England to the effect that France
does not see her way to send a representative to the Holy
See, and it would seem that the Ministers went so far as to
suggest that the British Government was acting too hurriedly
in nominating someone on their own behalf.   Surely this is
a wretched policy of ours to sacrifice blindly our national
interests to party politics.   Viviani seems to have resigned
himself to this unhappy reply, but why on earth did not
Delcassé and Briand arrange to await our return to Bordeaux
before registering a decision ?   All the belligerent Powers
will now have a representative at the Vatican except ourselves, and it is nonsense to think that the separation between
Church and State forbids our having diplomatic relations
with the Holy See, or that we have the right to hold ourselves
aloof from what is happening at the Vatican.

Viviani has also received from Millerand, as I have done,
a copy of a letter from Joffre regarding the defence of Paris :

" The experience of the war ", the Generalissimo writes,
" goes to show that one cannot rely with certainty on the resistance of fortifications, whether permanent or improvised, nor
on the Territorial troops, which—with some honourable excep-
tions—have proved to be of rather poor military stuff.   And
should Paris be threatened—which seems now less and less likely
—the defence of the town should be undertaken by a Field Army,
composed of trained men and organised in the theatre of war,
which should be as far as possible from the place into which the
enemy must not be allowed again to intrude.   I have already
taken care to set afoot this organisation on the Beauvais-Villers-
Cotterets front, and I shall have to detail the troops for this line.
Thus the existing state of things, when the Military Governor of
Paris can dispose of four Territorial divisions to defend in different
sectors a line only a few kilometres away from the exterior forts
does not in any way correspond to the exigencies of the situation.'

The Generalissimo now makes certain proposals, the
inevitable effect of which would be to belittle a position conferred on the Military Governor of Paris by the decree of the
26th of August.   Joffre foresees that Galliéni could scarcely
accept duties thus diminished, and suggests replacing him by
General Maunoury, but does not like to take any decision as

the whole question is bound up with the return, even if provisional, of the Government to the capital in view of the imminent meeting of Parliament. This, Joffre adds, would necessitate the fortified system of Paris being, up to the line of exterior forts, outside the zone of the armies.

Joffre therefore does not see any immediate—or final—necessity for the Government to return to Paris, and Viviani himself thinks this might well be put off till January. I can only tell him again that I think these perpetual postponements are quite unjustifiable, but I agree that it is not easy to reduce Galliéni's command without finding some post which is really worthy of him. A telephone message is sent to Millerand to beg the Council not to come to any decision on this point in our absence.

During the day I have a visit from Barthou, whose responsibility for the Three Years' Service would more than justify his return to office in time of war, but presumably it is the recollection of the Fabre trial [1] which is preventing Viviani from including him even in an enlarged Cabinet. Barthou is dying to be employed, and it is certainly most unfortunate he should not be so ; he says he would gladly preside over a Committee for organising supplies in Alsace Lorraine, and this Viviani has proposed to him. Something must certainly be done at once to regulate matters in the Communes which are occupied by our troops. I point out to Barthou that while a Commission, which seems rather to have sprung up by itself, is already functioning, General Headquarters has also taken local measures. Dubail even said to me the other day openly that he was remunerating the priests in Alsace and promising the people that their cloth should be respected. Barthou is quite agreeable to this, and only says that the work of the military and civil authorities should be co-ordinated, and that as President of a General Committee he could do this.

Jules Cambon, after talking on the telephone with Delcassé, has seen Cardinal Amette again and pointed out the objections to a truce on Christmas Day. General Headquarters fears it would be dangerous to suspend operations

[1] L'Union Sacrée.

even for twenty-four hours; the Cardinal perfectly understands Joffre's motive, and he also thinks that the good faith
of the German army is far too suspect for us to rely on any
promises they may make. This he will represent to the
Vatican.

3rd December.—Once more at Bordeaux, where, among
important questions for decision, is the one concerning the
Military Governor of Paris. Millerand sees eye to eye with
Joffre as to replacing Galliéni by Maunoury and giving the
former, by way of compensation, the command of the troops
of the interior. Viviani would prefer that Galliéni, with
whom he had a talk yesterday, should have command of a
group of armies, but, according to Pénélon, this idea does not
commend itself to Joffre; Galliéni was Joffre's superior officer
in the Colonies, and the latter thinks the position might be
difficult if Galliéni were now brought under his immediate
orders. Viviani takes the same view as Joffre and Millerand
as to our remaining at Bordeaux for the present, his chief
anxiety being lest Parliament, with the Ministers once more
settled in Paris, might claim to sit from January to the end of
June, as usual next year, which constitutionally they can do.
My answer is that at the present moment political considerations are of quite secondary importance. " The military
authorities ", I urge, " have already led the Government into
a bad blunder when they imposed on us the necessity of
leaving Paris forthwith. If we had only hung on for forty-
eight hours as I wanted to do, we should never have left at
all. It would be a fresh, and a worse, blunder if we allow
the garrison to be reduced and the Military Governor to be
replaced before showing, by our own presence in the town,
that Paris is henceforward perfectly safe." I say also that
personally I would like to return at once, and that anyhow
there should be an official return to Paris even if some
Ministers wished themselves to delay, and that the Corps
Diplomatique should be asked to come back, and that when
everyone was settled in, satisfactory arrangements might be
made with Galliéni. What would be inadmissible would be
to deprive France of the services of so great a man.

After a somewhat lengthy discussion, the Cabinet comes

round to my opinion, and it is settled that no definite steps shall be taken before our return to Paris next week.

The Serbian Government has decided that they must give up Belgrade, and they want England, Russia and ourselves to insist on Greece sending 80,000 men to help them ; they also beg for a further advance of 110 millions. Venizelos is inclined to do as Paschitch wants, but on condition that the Triple Entente should guarantee Greece against an attack from Bulgaria ; it is rather difficult to see how the Triple Entente could do anything of the sort.

While I have been away, Sazonoff's fertile brain has again been active, and Paul Cambon has felt himself bound to warn Delcassé against the rather random suggestions of the Russian Minister.

" I am sure ", he telegraphs, " that if the representatives of France and England were to put forward their own observations and discuss the new schemes which he is always evolving without awaiting the result of their predecessors, he would quite understand, for he is as intelligent as he is well intentioned."

Perhaps this very just surmise will prevent Delcassé from being led by the nose by Sazonoff.

4th December.—The new American Ambassador, Mr. William Sharp, presents his letters of credence and makes me a speech in English, being as blissfully ignorant as his predecessors of the language of the country where he is accredited ; it really seems as if America makes a point of sending us diplomatists who do not know a word of French. Mr. Sharp expresses the wish that " the trials of the present hour may soon issue in the benefits of a long and happy peace ". I reply with a few amiable platitudes and thanks for the good wishes that " a long and happy peace " may be restored. " If it had depended on the French Government," I add, " peace would never have been disturbed ; we only countered a brutal attack with the patriotism and courage to which you have been good enough to pay tribute. We are determined to fulfil to the uttermost the duty which has been imposed on us, and if peace is to be long and happy, and not merely trumped-up and ephemeral, it must be guaranteed by a complete reparation of rights which have been violated, and must be guarded against future attacks."

Pénélon brings me a Note from Joffre which runs :

"General Joffre thinks that after the battle of Flanders Paris is wholly free from danger, and that the German army is no longer able to take the offensive. He has therefore transferred his headquarters to a place between the capital and the enemy's troops in order to be near the area where he will, at the given moment, resume the offensive. The General therefore thinks that it would be wholly advantageous to place Paris outside the zone of the armies, and only to leave there such troops as are necessary to maintain order and police the town ; he thinks also that it would be well for the Government now to return to Paris in order to make it clear to Europe that the first phase of the campaign, that of the German offensive, is over. General Joffre intends to form the divisions drawn from Paris into a force under command of General d'Amade ; and as the special duties entrusted to General Galliéni in Paris are over, the Commander-in-Chief would like to place him in command of all the depots, and to entrust him with the organisation of the units which will be sent to the front as soon as they are properly trained."

Joffre has therefore changed his mind as to the opportuneness of our return to Paris, but as regards Galliéni, his proposal is scarcely likely to be acceptable. The Note is read out in Council, but Millerand still sticks to his wish to remain where he is ; it would be inconvenient to move his office, he says, and so forth. The upshot is that the War Minister will stay here until further orders, except for occasional visits to Paris, but Viviani, Delcassé and I will repair to the capital next week, and the question of the Military Government of Paris can be settled on the spot.

Bad news from Russia. The Grand Duke Nicholas declares that he has in front of him large forces who have been brought from west to east, and that if these enemy reinforcements continue, he will be obliged to give up his present tactics and adopt the system of trench warfare, which is in vogue on the Franco-Belgian Front. The Grand Duke wants to know if Joffre is going to make a move soon, and while he seems not to take into account the difficulties which we are encountering, it is quite possible that we scarcely appreciate those with which he is confronted. Joffre, however, is certain that, with the exception of some cavalry, no German troops that were opposite us have been sent to Russia.

Serbia is also apparently in a bad way ; a new Cabinet has just been formed under Paschitch, but the military situation is no better, while as regards Greece, Venizelos continues to clamour for quite impossible guarantees against Bulgaria.

5th December.—Joffre sends word to me by Commandant Herbillon that the question of the garrison and the military government of Paris must be settled at once, and it looks as if the relations between the staffs of the two big soldiers are more and more acidulated. I can only say to Herbillon what I have said to Pénélon. " The Government must first get back to Paris, resume the authority which has been partly lost, and give the impression that the safety of the town is again assured. Until this has been done, Paris must not be shorn of her garrison nor deprived of the man she regards as her saviour."

It is now finally arranged that the Ministers may, from to-morrow, return as they please to Paris. Briand is already there, Viviani and I will go on Tuesday evening, and Millerand will join us next day and arrange a meeting between Joffre —whom he will see on Thursday at Chantilly—and Galliéni as early as possible on Friday. The meeting of the Council does not pass over without one or two incidents. Viviani not only thinks aloud but, so to speak, he feels aloud, and much upset by the bad news from Russia, he gives vent to a spasm of acute pessimism. There is only one way, he protests, of saving France—we must at any cost get Japan to come in and pay whatever price they like to ask, even, if necessary, Indo-China itself.

Delcassé puts the thing into its proper focus ; he describes our negotiations with Japan, the difficulties we encountered, the hesitations of the Government at Tokio ; he does not think that Japan covets Indo-China, but that the Japanese want their colonial relations with our Colony to be under the same conventions as with France, and so far he is authorised to promise. The Foreign Minister thinks that Japan wants some financial help to improve Manchuria and Korea, and this again we might do. But it is primarily necessary that Russia should agree to sign a treaty of alliance with Japan and should recognise certain Japanese spheres of influence in China. So Delcassé is to try and persuade Russia and England of the necessity of making certain compensations to the Japanese Government in order, if it be in any way possible, to contract an alliance *à quatre*.

Millerand, who is more depressed than I have ever seen him, discourses to me about the telegrams from Russia, which are indeed more and more disquieting, and the Russian General Staff seems to be trying to make us responsible for their reverses. Why is the Russian army, with its great numerical superiority so impotent, and how can the Grand Duke Nicholas contemplate standing on the defensive ? Millerand will reply that we shall continue to bear the brunt of the German army's weight, and that we have seen no sign of troops having been taken away from the front here, and that we shall keep on attacking so as to keep the enemy forces pinned down in front of us.

Prince Bülow has been appointed German Ambassador in Rome ; he is married to an Italian, and evidently his Government want to avail themselves of the former Chancellor's brain and activities—as well as of the numerous relations and friends he has in every phase of Roman society —so as to try and stem the feeling which, throughout Italy, is flowing more and more towards laying claim to Italy's " natural frontiers ".

6th December.—Madame Poincaré has seen Maurice Barrès, who is very unhappy about the misunderstandings in Haute Alsace and has alluded to them in an article, under the title " Pour Ehrmann et pour Colette ", which the *Écho de Paris* published two days ago.

" Many people ", he writes, " shut their eyes to the fact that, mixed up with the actual natives of Alsace Lorraine, are many who have come from across the line since 1870 and who hate France. Our soldiers, having had experience of this hatred, often lay the blame by mistake on our own folk. . . . In this respect we have no cause to blame ourselves. We have often watched, understood and admired the young man yonder who has been obliged to serve his time in Germany, and the girl who has had to repel the attentions of some heavy German. We were not always believed, and it was thought that we were going rather far. Yet to-day Paul Ehrmann is considered by many Frenchmen as a real enemy."

Barrès also protests, not unreasonably, against the extreme facility with which Alsatian men and women have been taken to concentration camps, and says that for the last four months women have been lying on straw huddled together under disgusting conditions. He winds up with :

" Winter is upon us, and for Christmas fare Colette is cold and hungry ; and this is in France. I do not want money for these poor folk, and I should not know how to use it, but I most respectfully beg Madame Poincaré to see what can be done to help our compatriots in Lorraine and their friends, our sisters, in Alsace."

My wife will do what she can to relieve the most necessitous cases, but obviously the Government must arrange for regular inspections in the concentration camps and for Alsatians of known origin to be set free. For this one might well employ men like Laugel, Wetterlé, Blumenthal and other refugees, whose French feelings are beyond doubt.

Day after day my bulging post-bag contains letters from men at the front, which are delightful to read, and to-day there is one which touches me particularly. A lieutenant and two non-commissioned officers of the 6th Corps—all three totally unknown to me—send me from the village of the Meuse Nubécourt a charming note, together with two water-colour drawings of the little family burial-ground which has been desecrated by the Germans, and also some verses which the outrage provoked one of them to write. One only wishes one could tell these good fellows how deeply one feels their kindly thought just now when life is so full of pain.

7th December.—M. Giolitti made a very sensational statement in the Italian Parliament yesterday. He explained how his Government had refused, on the 9th of August 1913, to join in a premeditated Austrian attack against Serbia ;

Austria having conceived the idea of crushing Serbia long before the Serajevo murder. Thus Italy's attitude at the beginning of the present hostilities could not have come as anything of a surprise to the Central Empires, the Cabinet in Rome having already, a year earlier, refused to become their accomplice ; it is quite impossible to pretend that the conduct of M. Salandra and his colleagues this year was in any way tinged with disloyalty.

Colonel Pénélon reports that at General Headquarters the question is acute as to whether the Russian army will be able to resume the offensive, and Joffre has begged Millerand and Delcassé to telegraph to the Grand Duke Nicholas to this effect :

" I do not believe in any important transport of German troops from France to Russia. The Russians say that this has happened in the case of the 13th, 18th (Reserve) and 20th (Reserve) Corps, but during the last week we have been able to ascertain, by the killed and wounded, that all these units are still in front of us except the 26th Division of the 13th Corps, and the 21st Division of the 18th Corps. These two divisions may actually be in Russia, as also the 48th Reserve Division, but except for these three divisions no important unit has been moved from our front and we have still fifty Army Corps facing us. If our offensive has been suspended for the moment it is in spite of our wishes and simply because the Germans have entrenched themselves from the sea to Belfort and the Swiss frontier, and we have been obliged to get together a whole mass of material absolutely necessary for the regular trench warfare with which we have to deal. It seems unthinkable that, in the vast territories where the Russian armies are operating, the Germans can ever be able to put up the same continuous line of defence."

8th December.—Millerand now informs us that Joffre, without prejudice to the question of the military government of Paris, wants to have at once, behind the front line but well in front of Paris, three divisions and a Territorial Brigade drawn from the Paris fort. The War Minister thinks that this is a matter wholly within the discretion of the Generalissimo, and is allowing him to do as he wishes, but it means a very considerable diminution of the Paris garrison, and it might have been better to talk the matter over to-morrow with Joffre and Galliéni ; this haste on the part of G.H.Q. points to increasing tension between the two Commands.

The Pope has asked the Russian Government as well as ourselves whether they will agree to a truce on Christmas Day. Russia, while thanking the Holy Father for his compassionate thought, has been unable to agree to an armistice, partly because the Orthodox and Catholic Christmases do not coincide and partly because they could not trust Germany to keep to the agreement. The Russian troops, therefore, do not think of taking a rest, but for fear they should make our inaction a pretext for interrupting their own offensive, Joffre has issued a very important general order to his armies. He sets out that the reconstitution of our units and our supplies of munitions are well on their way, and that there is good ground to think the Germans have sent some of their forces to Poland.

" The moment has therefore come ", he says, " to renew the offensive so as to push the enemy north-eastwards and arrange to attack a little later his communications. This offensive will take shape in two principal attacks to be developed where the situation seems most favourable. One of these attacks will be made from Arras towards Cambrai and Douai by the Tenth Army, while the other will be entrusted to the Fourth Army and have Attigny for its objective. The Generalissimo foresees also that there will be a good many minor actions on various parts of the front, and he hopes that the whole effect will be, not only to push the enemy towards the north-east, but to cut his communications with Germany."

But one cannot help wondering how this " siege warfare " of which Joffre spoke yesterday when he was addressing the Grand Duke Nicholas is going to be transformed so quickly into a war of movement.

Whatever happens we are really off this time without any idea of return, and we shall only leave behind us Millerand and his officials, who, notwithstanding Joffre's permission, have not yet made up their minds to go back to Paris. Viviani will go in my train this evening, and we shall again discuss the unhappy difference between Joffre and Galliéni, which seems now to be pretty sharp. Viviani, like myself, would prefer that the Military Governor should not be obliged to leave his post, and this difficulty spoils my satisfaction in getting nearer to the armies. But anyhow we shall be able to see men and matters from a nearer angle, and the change of vision cannot be other than useful.

CHAPTER XI

9th December.—Here I am back in Paris in the Élysée, which
I never thought I should regret to leave ; it has anyhow the
merit of being much nearer than Bordeaux to the men in the
firing-line and the invaded districts.   The front looks like
being stabilised throughout ; we have moved forward two or
three hundred metres near Quesnoy and Andechy, less than
that in the Aisne and Champagne, and practically only a few
inches in the Argonne and at Vauquois.   At this pace centuries
will elapse before France is free from the invader, but however great the difficulties to be overcome, I refuse to be dis-
couraged.   To think oneself beaten is to be beaten.   And
surely our situation, uncertain and uncomfortable though it
be, is really better than that of the enemy.   The basic plan
of the German General Staff has failed once and for all.   They
had promised themselves to crush France with one smashing
blow and in a few weeks to render us impotent.   This is just
where Germany has not succeeded.   Our army has been tried
as gold is tried in the fire, but it has been built up again ;
the men have entire confidence in their leaders and are
absolutely certain that victory will finally rest with France.
Germany, failing to secure the immediate and decisive conquest which she expected, has sought to obtain minor advantages in the various and more limited operations which
she has set afoot.   She has been no happier in this respect.
During the three days which followed the declaration of war,
the German General Staff massed large forces facing Nancy
with the evident intention of breaking our lines at once by a

sudden onrush. This idea had to be abandoned because the
reinforcements for our covering troops, rendered possible by
the Three Years' Service, and the organised defence of the
Grand Couronné, begun early this year, denied the enemy an
enterprise which, however possible before the military re-
forms of 1913, had since become a very risky one to undertake.
Baulked of Nancy, the Germans then sought, by every means
in their power, to envelop our left, which would have enabled them to invest Paris. Vain hope. Our left was not
enveloped, and Paris suffered no siege; and the German army
must save its own threatened communications by a precipitate retreat in the second week of September. Then came
the desperate effort of the German Staff—unable to tell the
people that they had been defeated—to try and make up for
the unhealthy moral effect of a forced retirement by piercing
our centre in the plains of Champagne. Once more failure
and once more a hurried retreat. Then, in the month of
October with a wider and more sweeping movement, our
foemen again tried to turn our left. But to the shores of the
North Sea we had barred the way, and the enemy, with all
his massed forces in Belgium, failed utterly to reach our naval
bases; he then sought, but again vainly sought, to break
through south of Ypres; the Allied line, bruised and bleeding,
stood firm. In a word, the enemy since the beginning of the
war—besides the breakdown of the general plan—has had
to record seven distinct set-backs. The attack on Nancy, the
rapid march on Paris, the envelopment of our left in August,
the piercing of our centre in September, the coastal attack
on Dunkirk and Calais, the new attempt to envelop our left
wing in November, the assault of Ypres, have all been doomed
to failure. The German army, powerful and admirably
equipped though it be, has scored no definite advantage at
any point. Joffre, on the other hand, tells us that he is sure
of the real improvement in our army; moral improvement,
for the men feel now their own worth and their powers of
resistance; technical improvement, because the troops have
learnt their war lesson on the field of battle; they know now
how to make use of ground, and know much better than
they did how to act on the defensive. Nor is their physical

improvement any less marked; the physique of the troops is much better, their bodies are braced and hardened by a new experience, perhaps as severe an experience as humanity has known; nor can the improvement in material be disregarded, although, truth to tell, there is still much headway to make for our requirements. The High Command itself has been able to reap no little profit from initial mistakes ; they have served an apprenticeship which has been far from valueless ; they have shed some preconceived ideas which were difficult to put into practice ; they have adapted themselves to circumstances which scarcely any human being could foresee. Thus we have the right to hope that, with goodwill and dogged perseverance, victory will remain for us. Anyhow, my own duty is perfectly clear: to hold on and try and strengthen the weak-hearted, and to substitute utter confidence for despondency, if any despondency still exists.

10th December.—Millerand is to go to Chantilly to-day and try and arrange with Joffre the matter which affects alike the military regime of Paris and the future of Galliéni. He tells me that Sir Francis Bertie has been to see him to ask, on behalf of Lord Kitchener, whether it would be possible for the British armies to be posted on the extreme left of the line, so that their flank may rest on the sea ; at present we are keeping our own troops on the left of the Belgian army, and the British are posted on their right. The Ambassador, when conveying this request, took upon himself to say that Kitchener had probably acted without consulting French, that the Secretary of State was not behaving with correctitude in this matter, and that he was interfering with what was not his own business ; but Sir John French is certainly no less anxious than Kitchener to get to the sea. Millerand simply replied that he would consult Joffre, but that the latter was scarcely likely to view with favour a shuffling of places at the moment.

M. Augagneur comes to talk over with me several questions affecting his Department, and incidentally remarks that he does not think Joffre at all wishful to hand over an army to Galliéni. He thinks that the best way of getting over the difficulty, without annoying Galliéni or offending

Parisian opinion, would be to give the Military Governor temporary charge of our Embassy at the Quirinal, and for Barrère, who has not been at all well recently, to take a holiday for the sake of his health. " This ", he says, " would be a pendant to Bülow's mission to Rome, and Galliéni is intelligent, clever and a diplomat to his fingers' ends." Augagneur backs his suggestion by showing me a copy of *Le Petit Marseillais*, in which there is a letter to the Milanese composer, Vanzo, signed *Galliéni, Francese, ma anche Italiano*. I can only say that, however ingenious the idea, Barrère doesn't seem to me to be unwell enough to leave Rome, where, by the way, he has made a great name for himself.

The Japanese continue to turn a deaf ear when we ask them to send troops to Europe, and Sir Edward Grey has told Paul Cambon that he has already sounded the Government of Tokio on this point, and has had to put up with a refusal, nor does he think that any new attempt in this direction will be successful.

Germany, Great Britain and Belgium have informed the Holy See that they are, in principle, in favour of a truce on Christmas Day, but that it is unlikely the Orthodox countries will agree.

By a rare return of fortune the Serbian army has pulled itself together, just when the enemy thought they were down and out. It would seem that this miracle is largely due to the old King Peter himself, who has gone about among the troops, and by words—some of which have become proverbial—and actions has restored courage among the men and re-established the authority of the commanders. Serbia has resumed the offensive, and has recently made 17,000 prisoners and taken twenty-seven field guns, fourteen mountain guns, besides some machine guns and ammunition waggons.

11th December.—Millerand did not fix up anything definite with Joffre at Chantilly, and he brings him to-day to the Élysée so that we three can talk things over. The Generalissimo again emphasises the undesirability of tying to the Paris garrison Territorial troops, who would be much

more useful nearer the front, and Galliéni himself quite
recognises this.   As a result of moving these men, Galliéni's
command would be greatly diminished and his post would
then scarcely be worthy of so important an officer.   Contrary to what Augagneur feared, Joffre would not object to
give Galliéni the command of an army in the Vosges or in
Alsace, and he would be very glad, he confides to us, if circumstances were to cause Galliéni to dissolve his civilian
Cabinet.   He tells us that Doumer recently went to see
Foch at Cassel, and said to him : " If I become Minister for
War I shall remove Joffre, who is incapable, and I shall
make Galliéni Commander-in-Chief ".   Joffre is pretty sure
why Doumer has a grudge against him.   " I refused ", he
says, " to give the command of an army corps to General
Nicolas, whom Doumer enthusiastically recommended, but
whom I did not think equal to the place.   I may have been
right or wrong, but it seems to me unthinkable that the
Military Governor of Paris should have civilian allies who
busy themselves in belittling the Commander-in-Chief to
his Assistant General."   Joffre next tells us that he is going
to start some little local attacks from next Wednesday onwards ; he does not expect to suck any great advantages,
especially as the siege guns are not yet ready, but he fears
that, if he folds his arms any longer, the Germans, being
left to their own devices, will draw off considerable forces
from our front and send them eastwards, where they may
do heavy damage to the Russians.   Our attacks will be
made south of Ypres, north and south of Arras and west of
Argonne, and Joffre will be quite satisfied if at certain points
he can push the Germans back twenty or thirty kilometres.
I am rather nervous myself about these attacks, and fear
that we may find them very costly if our men, without
sufficient heavy guns, are up against impregnable entrenchments ; I don't conceal my fears from Joffre, but he does not
think that we can leave the Russians exposed to too formidable an attack.

For the first time for many weeks the Ministerial Council
is held in the Élysée in the same room as usual.   Millerand
has spoken to Joffre about Kitchener's wish to shift the

British army seawards, but Joffre, while having no radical
objection, wants to postpone the move for the moment.
Kitchener is especially anxious to give some satisfaction to
his compatriots, who, not unreasonably, will better understand that the British army is fighting for Great Britain if
that army is not far from the coast.   Joffre, without being
convinced by this sort of argument, has good-naturedly
allowed it to be thought that the next offensive will pave
the way to place the English troops where England would
like to see them.

Galliéni is raising no objection to sending three and a
half of his Territorial divisions to Joffre, and Joffre does
not object to Galliéni remaining for the present Military
Governor of Paris, while Maunoury will continue, till further
orders, to command his army.   We must then wait until
Galliéni himself, finding his post less important, asks for
more active employment, when Joffre will offer him the
command of the army of the Vosges and Alsace ; meanwhile
Paris will remain in the zone of the armies, but Galliéni
will at once break up his civil Cabinet, which, with the return
of the Government to Paris, has no more *raison d'être*.   " It
seems to require a good deal of diplomacy ", Viviani says,
" to arrange military matters."

12*th December.*—The Serbian troops have retaken Valiévo
and Ouchitze, and I am telegraphing my congratulations to
the Prince Regent.

At two o'clock I start with only General Duparge, my
chief military officer.   I have decided for the future to visit
the armies without the War Minister or any other member
of the Government.   This is a new departure, which may
provoke some murmurs of disapproval, but I think that I
ought to go as often as possible among the troops and the
folk who have suffered so cruelly at German hands.   There
will be no newspaper correspondent, and no account of any
visit which I pay ; there will be no speeches of any sort, but
the soldiers and the inhabitants of the devastated districts
will know that the Chief of the State is heart and soul with
them.   I have therefore arranged with the Prefect of the
Marne to go to Rheims to-morrow.

At the Prefecture of Châlons, where I stay for the night, General de Langle de Cary, commanding the Fourth Army, tells me that Joffre came to see him this morning and asked him if he would be ready to take the offensive on Friday or Saturday (the 19th or 20th) ; however keen de Langle de Cary may be, the idea does not appeal to him ; and he thinks it will be much better to mark time for a little longer, as he badly wants the siege guns which we are just beginning to make and also unlimited discretion as to the expenditure of " 75 " shells. Nor does he pin his hopes to any special results from the offensive, as he thinks the Germans are far too strongly entrenched for us to secure any decision like that of the battle of the Marne ; when, so he says, we ought to have pursued the enemy straight on instead of giving twenty-four hours' rest to our troops. In a word, the General very quietly and tactfully has some observations to make with regard to the past and the present which entirely agree with my own. But we must not think only of the French front ; the Russians must be reckoned with, for if they were to taste of real disaster, the Germans would swing back and bring all their weight to bear on us.

13th December.—After a very early breakfast we start for Rheims, passing through the rich Champagne district, where the vineyards this year have been ruined by the fighting, through Veuve, the Grandes-Loges and Petites-Loges, and then, so as to avoid the back lines, through Verzy. Suddenly, under a lowering sky but on a fairly clear day, the martyred town comes in view ; now and again a column of black smoke, the herald of a gun burst, rises over the houses, and denotes a German shell fired from the batteries either of Brimont or Nogent l'Abbesse.

The Prefect has asked the Mayor and other municipal officials who have remained at Rheims, in spite of the daily danger which they run, to come at noon to the Hôtel de Ville, merely telling them that an important military authority will be there to meet them. Through the faubourgs, still fairly busy, though most of the shops are shut, we make our way to the Hôtel de Ville, and as soon as the Place Louis XV. is reached there is seen a hideous example of ruin and desolation. The Mayor is an old friend, Dr. Langlet, and is delighted to see me again, as well as to receive my congratulations on his own and his colleagues' courage in continuing to carry on their duties in a bombarded town. The Prefect is a little afraid that the espionage, so successfully exercised, may enable the Germans to hear of my visit and pay us extra attention in the matter of shelling, and he wants only Langlet to accompany us to the Cathedral; I shall not even see Cardinal Luçon, whom I hope, however, to decorate next time I come here.

The sight of the glorious building enables one to have some idea of the barbarous method of this fearful war, and one is pulled up short in dismay before the ruined façade. The damage done is even worse than one was led to believe from the photographs; the great West Door is horribly injured, the windows are shattered; the groups of sculpture have crumbled into dust; the statues—the Queen of Saba, St. Clothilde, St. Thierry and the image of the Christ—are frightfully mutilated; the roof has collapsed, and the blackened and smouldering stonework is in pieces. Dumb with horror, one remains transfixed gazing at this magnificent and mournful skeleton. A few paces off the Archbishop's house has been completely burnt down, while on the other side of the Cathedral precincts the famous Lion d'Or Hôtel is three parts destroyed. Paul Dubois' Joan of Arc alone remains imperturbable on her bronze charger and seems to defy the devouring flames. The last shell which fell on the Cathedral was on the 4th of December and destroyed the Clock Tower, while others, a week earlier, had struck the buttress of the nave and the point of the bell turret on the Assumption Tower. One can check from day to day what has happened since the beginning of September; for over three months the savage bombardment has gone on uninterruptedly, and it is as likely as not to begin again to-morrow, if not to-day. Every inhabitant of Rheims declares that the pretexts put forward by the German General Staff to justify a cynical violation of the right of nations are pure invention. There has never been a single anti-aircraft machine gun, and à fortiori no heavy gun, mounted on the top of the Cathedral as was alleged in the Wolff Agency communiqué ; there has never been any assembly of men or any depot of war material either in or near the Cathderal, nor has the Cathedral ever served as a military observation post. The attack, renewed again and again with fresh fury, is wholly without excuse.[1]

One is so upset by the terrible sight that it is difficult to tear oneself away from it, but time is passing and one must have a few words with as many of the inhabitants as possible, and also give what material help one can. The evening closes in, and, however regretfully, I must leave the unhappy town, once the theatre of royal coronations, and return to Paris by Château Thierry and Meaux. On reaching the Élysée I hear that German shells have fallen on Commercy, so Lorraine, like Champagne, has her large share of the ills which are besetting the country.

14th December.—General von der Goltz, on his way to Constantinople, as if on his way to a German colony, has stopped for a couple of days at Sofia, as if he were paying a visit to another Imperial property. He is the bearer of an autograph letter from the Kaiser to King Ferdinand, who, having read it, felt himself obliged to grant the General an audience, a thing he had originally neither wished nor dared to do. Nothing has leaked out as to what happened at the interview, but it is easy to guess what theme was discussed and to foresee the issue.

Without worrying themselves about these intrigues, the Serbians fight on, and have just attacked towards Belgrade and turned the enemy out of more than one important position.

We hear that the Sovereigns of the three Scandinavian kingdoms are to meet in Sweden before the Christmas holidays to consult as to how to maintain neutrality in their respective countries. This is evidently the best that we can hope for.

15th December.—Colonel Pénélon telephones from headquarters that young Max Barthou, only son of the former President of the Council, has been killed in the streets of Thann by a German shell. The boy had joined up as a

[1] See *La Cathédrale de Reims*, par Mgr. Landrieux, évêque de Dijon. 1919.

volunteer a few weeks ago, and, at his request, had been
lately sent to the front at Alsace.   He was spoiling for a
fight, and so far had had no opportunity ; now he has been
struck down in the spring of life without having himself
been able to strike a blow for his country.   I hurry off to
see his father, whom I find overwhelmed with grief.   " My
boy ", he tells me, " insisted on going, and said that the son
of the Frenchman who was responsible for the Three Years'
Service must be the first to set an example to other boys.
Of course I was obliged to let him go, but I knew that I was
giving him for France."

In the evening there come to dinner, together with
Viviani, Delcassé and Ribot, the three Belgian Ministers who
have come to treat with the French Government of a very
important question.   M. de Brocqueville has for his companions the Minister of the Interior and the Minister for
Finance, who urgently ask for a loan of seven or eight
million francs to feed the civil population in the invaded
portion of Belgium.   A very difficult dilemma : to give the
necessary credit is to do for the Belgians what we cannot
do for our own compatriots in the occupied regions, and,
moreover, it may mean provisioning the German army itself ;
to refuse is to disoblige a people who are our friends and to
whom we owe a large debt of gratitude.   Ribot thinks that
the first reason outweighs the second, but the Belgian
Ministers tell him that they have obtained the consent of
England and of Joffre, and that King Albert is anxiously
awaiting our decision.   We must do what we can to solve
this delicate problem, and anyhow, French civilians must be
helped and a neutral Commission appointed to superintend
the distribution of foodstuffs in the invaded districts.

16th December.—Yesterday morning old King Peter, with
the Prince Regent and Prince George, rode triumphantly, at
the head of his troops, into his own capital, and proceeded
at once to the Cathedral, where a religious service was held
The only Austrian soldiers in Serbia between the Dwina and
the Save are the 60,000 prisoners whom the Serbians have
taken, and M. Paschitch, when M. Boppé congratulated
him on the heroism of the Serbian peasant soldier, replied

that much of the Serbian success was due to the French guns.

17th December.—Joffre has to-day vigorously attacked the German lines at one or two points, notably at Nôtre Dame de Lorette and in Argonne, and has used every variety of gun he possesses for the purpose ; we have gained a few yards here and there and lost a great many men in doing so. The offensive in Champagne is to take place in a few days, and one can hardly look for any better results ; we must resign ourselves to regarding a war of movement as impossible for some time to come, and it is no longer Paris which is under threat of investment, but France herself from Switzerland to the sea ; must we, as Franchet d'Esperey thinks, seek another theatre of war in the Near East ?

After scoring his signal success, King Peter has said good-bye to his soldiers and retired into seclusion.

The Foreign Office tells us that the British Protectorate over Egypt will be solemnly proclaimed in Cairo to-morrow. Tittoni is evidently keeping a sharp eye on what is happening in the Balkans, and has said to Delcassé : " My country quite understands how eager the Serbians are not to be land-locked ; they cannot get access to the Black Sea with the Roumanians and the Bulgarians established on the shores, and the same applies to the Aegean, as the Greeks are in Salonika. There remains the Adriatic, and it may well be a question of life and death for them to be able to have an issue there. But, on the other hand, no one can deny the importance of Italian interests in the Adriatic, which is for us just what the Western Mediterranean is for you, and we hope that the Triple Entente will not settle any questions affecting these waters without consulting us." Delcassé told the Ambassador that Italy had only to come in with us in order to see at once that we entertain no sinister designs against her, to which Tittoni replied : " Foreign policy ought to draw us more and more together ".

18th December.—In Russia, things seem to be going from bad to worse, and heavy losses of men, together with lack of munitions, have all along the line, except in Eastern Russia, resulted in failure and retreat ; to reorganise and refit, the armies must take up positions farther back.

The French Government recognises the British Protectorate in Egypt, and, in return, the British Government agrees at last to the Franco-Moroccan Treaty of 30th March 1912.   If England and ourselves were not now at war with Turkey, we might possibly still have to wait for this agreement ; the delay in registering it has been a little unhappy.

19th December.—I proposed to go with Madame Poincaré on Christmas Day to take some presents to the children in the Alsatian districts occupied by our troops, but Joffre and General Pütz, who commands the army of the Vosges, have begged me to put off this visit, as they think it might stir up the Germans to further viciousness in Haute Alsace.   As a matter of fact, since Joffre went the other day to Thann and the newspapers spoke of his being there, the enemy has massed troops about Mulhouse and seems to be preparing a fresh offensive.   But, curiously enough, just when the military authorities are ordering me to stay away from the zone of the armies, the *Bulletin des Armées* is vocal this morning about the installation of a French judge at Thann, a step which is reported to have been taken by the local commander " in the name of the French people ".   The Ministers not unreasonably think that some officers at G.H.Q. are too prone to ignore altogether the civil power, and Millerand is to remind the General Staff that there is in existence a Government.

The news from Russia is more precise ; the casualties, heavy though they be, can be made good fairly soon, as there are plenty of soldiers at the depots.   The serious shortage is in rifles, of which hundreds of thousands are needed, while the factories are only turning out a hundred thousand per month.   The expenditure of projectiles has surpassed anything that was foreseen or dreamt of, and in four months of fighting six million shells have been fired off.   There can be no question of any big battle being delivered until the middle of April, and one fears lest the Germans, being left alone in the east, may swoop down on our front, which would be the converse of what Joffre anticipated a little while ago. Anyhow, in the Russian as well as in our own theatre of war, hostilities will be protracted for many a long day yet.

20th December.—From Vosges to Nieuport we keep on losing or winning a few trenches, and gradually opinion here is being reconciled to the knowledge that finality is still far out of sight.

Madame Poincaré and I spend a good deal of our time in visiting—and taking our gifts to—the hospitals and other institutes which are rendering real service to the soldiers and their families. Private enterprise is admirably reinforcing what is being done officially, and people in every class of life are setting a wonderful example of generosity and devotion. This hideous scourge of war is provoking not only acts of heroism but marvels of goodness and self-sacrifice.

Isvolsky has handed in another Note from Sazonoff. The Russian Minister—who continues to give birth to an idea every morning and strangle it every evening—has now a fortieth or fiftieth suggestion, as infallible as the predecessors, as to reconstituting the Balkan " bloc " and winning over Bulgaria with territorial concessions. It is a question of urging Bratiano to enter into *pourparlers* with Belgrade and Sofia, but Delcassé is to remind Russia that M. Paschitch will not give anything in Macedonia to Bulgaria until Serbia, by extending her own frontiers, can realise her national unity. To bring pressure to bear would be to run the risk of hurting sensitive feelings without any chance of success. As to Roumania, she is hanging back, and to try and extract an immediate answer from Bratiano would only be to increase his unwillingness to form an alliance with Serbia. We seem to be making passionate and tearful advances to the little Powers, who, for the moment, have no wish to embrace us, but only to flirt with us, and we forget that they are not concerned with our interests, but only with their own ; it is really pitiful to keep on taking little steps which are as ridiculous as they are resultless. And while Bulgaria is perhaps no longer independent, Roumania, who is no doubt much more favourably disposed towards us, should be left to choose her own moment. It is in France, and on our own front, as also on the Russian front—and not in the Chanceries—that we must gain new Allies.[1]

M. Carton de Wiart, Belgian Minister of Justice—with Briand and Delcassé—dines at the Élysée and is no less anxious than M. de Brocqueville as to supplying the civil population in the invaded parts of Belgium, and for this loans are required from France and England. The United States, he thinks, will undertake the distribution of material or will anyhow allow one of their people to regulate and control it ; with all one's heart one wishes that something like this could be arranged, but it will anyhow need some time.

Russia is celebrating just now with all solemnity the twentieth anniversary of the Czar's accession, and the accounts of the festivities bring back vividly to me two recollections. I see the Czar arriving for the first time in Paris in 1896, very pale, very nervous and very much embarrassed by his Imperial inexperience, and I remember no less clearly our last conversations in August in which he seemed so sure that a solid peace would be maintained. In my telegram of congratulation I tell the Czar how much I hope that the next anniversary will be coloured with the victory of our arms. He replies that for himself he has entire confidence that the Allied armies will be wholly successful, but unfortunately our mutual assurances do nothing to supply the Russians with the munitions which, according to General Laguiche, are entirely lacking.

The same lack of material has prevented Joffre from making the two big attacks which his instructions of the 8th of December prescribed, but the Fourth Army's offensive in Champagne is not cancelled. De Langle de Cary says that this army has been reinforced and equipped as thoroughly as possible ; the operations will have been set afoot to-day by the 17th Corps and the Colonial Corps on either side of Perte and at La Main de Massiges, with heavy fighting and little result.

[1] Delcassé to Paléologue. There will be found in the Russian diplomatic documents (*Éditions d'État Moscou Pétrograd*, 1922) the telegrams from Sazonoff to the Ambassadors and Ministers in the Balkans. The impression gained confirms what the French Government and Paul Cambon felt in 1914.

21st December.—Parliament will meet to-morrow, when Viviani will read in the Chamber and Briand in the Senate a Ministerial Declaration which we have carefully revised. Parliamentary gossip is already rife, and Clemenceau, whose impish whims are inexhaustible, is especially anxious to foment a little revolt of the Commission de l'Armée. Millerand is to appear this afternoon before this Areopagus and will be questioned as to materials of war and supplies. Doumer, who, rightly or wrongly, is supposed to reflect Galliéni's mind and who anyhow has very definite military ideas, intends to give the Minister for War rather a bad time. Millerand, according to a *mot*, bandied about erecting a statue to Joffre in order to place himself in a niche of the pedestal ; in other words, he is said to give too free a hand to the General-in-Chief, General Headquarters and the Military Department. Anyhow, he would be complained of very much more, and much more reasonably, if he were so foolish as to try to override them, and everyone would then say that he was substituting his own incompetence for the competence of experts.

Our Military Attaché in Serbia tells us that the infantry divisions there are mere skeletons, with only 7000 or 8000 men to each, and Serbia does not seem to have more than about 120,000 men altogether available. The 1915 Class has just been called up, and when trained will provide 40,000 recruits ; munitions are again running very short, but the feeling that they have won battles is still giving the Serbian army considerable moral force. Moral force is what I see largely in France, in England, in Serbia and in Russia, but one cannot help remembering that Germany finds an invaluable stimulant in her material strength.

22nd December.—Parliament has met to-day in special Session ; the places occupied by the three deputies who have fallen in the fight were draped in black, and Dubost in the Senate and Deschanel in the Chamber have made admirable speeches, while Viviani in the Ministerial Declaration said : " For the moment there is only one policy : to fight on until the freedom of Europe is established and guaranteed by a victorious peace. This was the cry which is on every lip when, on the 4th of August, there was founded, as M. le Président de la République so well said, the Union Sacrée which will be written for honour in the pages of our history." The Government then submitted once more to Parliament what was the origin of, and whose are the responsibilities for, the war.

" On the first day of hostilities Germany denied the Right and appealed to Might ; poured contempt on history and, in order to violate the neutrality of Belgium, she invoked the law of self-interest. A little later her Government, realising that they must reckon with the opinion of the world, tried again to justify the German attitude by throwing on the Allies the responsibility for the war. But Truth shines out from the clumsy lies which do not even deceive those who might like to be deceived. All the documents published by the nations interested, and yesterday the sensational speech of a highly distinguished Italian, go to prove that for a long time past our enemies had decided upon a trial of strength. If needs be, a single one of these documents would suffice to enlighten the world ; when, at the suggestion of the British Government, all the nations concerned were entreated to suspend their military preparations and negotiate in London on the 31st July 1914, France and Russia agreed to the proposal : peace would have been saved, even at this eleventh hour, if Germany had followed suit. But Germany brushed aside the idea, and on the 1st of August declared war on Russia and rendered inevitable an appeal to arms. . . . Since France and her Allies, clinging as they did to peace, have been forced into war, they will prosecute that war to the end. France will be loyal to the signature which she subscribed to the Treaty of the 4th of September when she pledged her honour—which is the same as pledging her life. In accord with her Allies, she will never lay down her arms until the rights of nations have been avenged, until she has bound to herself again the provinces which were torn from her side, and restored heroic Belgium to the fullness of her substance and political independence, and until, moreover, she has broken down the system of Prussian militarism so as to build up again on the foundations of justice a Europe finally regenerated."

This Declaration, which all the Ministers, Socialist as well as others, entirely approved and which defined clearly our conditions of peace, was received with enthusiasm, and after laying on the table a certain number of Bills, the Session was adjourned till to-morrow.

While Parliament was giving this fine example of patriotism, our troops and those of Sir John French were trying in vain to get forward ; we seem to have made scarcely any progress anywhere.

23rd December.—As Joffre asks me to postpone my trip to Alsace, I shall not have the pleasure of distributing my Christmas gifts among the children in the districts where our troops are stationed, but anyhow, Madame Poincaré and I console ourselves with sending sweetmeats and toys to 3000 little Alsatian scholars.

Parliament, which met yesterday, closes to-day, as everyone feels this is no time for talking. The Senate and the Chamber have unanimously and without discussion accepted the proposals of the Government, and provisional credits, amounting to over nine milliards of francs, have been voted for the first half of next year. The application of a general Income Tax has *nem. con.* been postponed till the 1st of January 1916, while death duties have been abolished in the cases of successors, descendants and widows of soldiers killed on the field of battle, and of all who have met their death at the hands of the enemy.

The battle continues along the whole front with very little progress ; we have gone forward 150 metres between the sea and the Nieuport-Ostend road, and with the help of the English we have retaken Givenchy. Near the Perthes-les-Hurlus mill we have painfully secured 800 metres, and in the Grurie wood about twice that amount. Nothing more.

24th December.—A sad Christmas Eve, and it is finally decided that the troops will not have for their Christmas Day the truce which the Pope suggested ; neither our orthodox Allies nor our own General Staff could agree to this, the latter thinking it impossible to interrupt movements of attack.

We sample the " wireless " between Lyons and Moscow, and the Czar telegraphs :

" Accept, together with the expression of my friendliest feelings, my best wishes for your Christmas festivities."

The waves reach me without being at all confused ; but the festivities, where are they ?

Brieux, burning with patriotism, has gone to America to defend our cause there and to represent the Academy at the Assembly organised by the American Academy of Arts and Letters.   He is the bearer of a letter to President Wilson renewing my regrets at being unable myself to attend the occasion, and the President, in the course of his friendly reply, says :

" The relations between our two peoples have always been so friendly, so cordial and so spontaneous that I am specially happy, as the official representative of the American people, to send you, as the distinguished representative of France, the assurance of my warmest feelings for the citizens of the great French Republic."

25th December.—The submarine which bears the splendid name of *Curie* has been sunk at Pola by coast guns and the Austrian steamboats which were patrolling the Roads, and the Commander and twenty-five of the crew have been made prisoners.   This unhappy happening brings back the memory of Pierre Curie and of the fatal accident which gave such a shock to Paris eight years ago.   Destiny will try in vain to embitter that memory, and can do nothing to prevent us remembering that in France the great gift of radium was discovered.   There comes another little shock in the news that the *Jean Bart*, which escorted us to Russia, has been torpedoed by an Austrian submarine, but although dreadfully knocked about, the gallant ship has been able to make its limping way to Malta.

On our front our offensives, which were to proceed on Christmas Day, have already given way to something like a very painful defensive.   Between Berry-au-Bac and Bray-en-Laonnois we have been repeatedly attacked by the enemy infantry, and in the Ailly wood we have only just been able to stem a violent onrush.   In Argonne we have had to stand up against troops hurling themselves on St. Hubert, Bagatelle and the Grurie wood, and the same thing has been happening in the Perthes and Ménil-les-Hurlus districts, and north of Sapigneul.   Blood is flowing everywhere and the roar of the cannon drowns the Christmas bells. But there must be no giving way.

26th December.—Despite all our efforts to secure Japanese help, Clemenceau, who never leaves us alone, and his friend Stephen Pichon, who, roughly handled as he was last year by his old Chief, has now slipped back into the Tiger's claws, are daily declaiming against the Cabinet of Tokio, the one in the *Homme Enchaîné* and the other in *Le Petit Journal.* The Japanese Government have met with every obstacle in Parliament in the matter of intervention in the war, and as a result have been placed in a minority on a question of internal politics ; so there is every reason to fear that Clemenceau's oriental dream will not come true.

Dubost and Bérard tell me that the Commission des Finances du Sénat is by no means pleased with some of the war contracts, which have been entered into without sufficient care.

27th December.—The King of Italy telegraphs that the Queen has just given birth to a Princess, and I duly send my congratulations ; but as yet the King and the Queen of Italy are only unknown Sovereigns to a friendly country, and one can only hope that war will do what peace has not been able to do, and give us the pleasure of receiving them officially in Paris. Meanwhile Italy is not wasting her time and is doing her best to reap profit from her neutrality, as M. de Fonteney telegraphs from Durazzo that she has just occupied Vallona.

The Germans are spreading a story in Copenhagen that they have gained a great success in Poland.

As the last paragraph in Mr. Wilson's letter was addressed to the French people, I have asked Delcassé if it may be read to the Academy, and the President of the United States willingly consents, and, so Jusserand reports, says also that he entertains the liveliest feelings of friendship and admiration for the President of the French Republic in the midst of this terrible struggle. Mr. Wilson questioned Jusserand at length as to the state of our country and the spirits of the troops and of the public, and our Ambassador told him how deeply touched France was by the kindly feeling which Americans of all classes were showing, and by the generosity with which they were helping the wounded, the refugees and all our sufferers in the war.

28th December.—Besides letters of grateful acknowledgement from the Mayors of Thann, Saint Amarin and Massevaux, messages of thanks pour in from the little Alsatian scholars themselves to whom we sent Christmas gifts, and many of these are couched in most touching terms. Poor children, they scarcely know whether to-morrow they will find themselves French or German, but meanwhile they look confidingly toward us. How can we afford to disappoint them ?

M. Lebrun, Deputy for Meurthe and Moselle, who was Colonial Minister in my Cabinet of 1912 and who is one of the most level-headed men I know, pays me a little visit before going back to Verdun, where he is serving as an officer in the artillery. He declares that General Headquarters are still very insufficiently informed as to what goes on at the front, and that they hug themselves more and more with a quite unjustifiable optimism, while they conceal from the Government and the public many little set-backs mostly due to over-rash attacks. The initial blunders, such as the foolish offensive in the Ardennes and Charleroi, the shutting their eyes to the value of trenches, the premature respite given to the troops three days after the battle of the Marne, all these, instead of serving as object-lessons, are already forgotten, and, should occasion arise, the same sort of imprudences, according to my friend, are likely to be again committed. I agree with him that although the Government ought not to intrude by a hair's-breadth into the arena of operations, they ought to exercise some control over the High Command, but the difficulty is how, and how far that control should be exercised ; time and experience may show us.

Augagneur is very anxious that the Marine Fusiliers, who fought so splendidly round Dixmude, should enjoy a flag like every military unit, and that this flag should be presented to them by myself ; I gladly accept the suggestion and say that the sooner it is carried out the better.

The Roumanian Minister sends me one of his compatriots, a M. Diamandy, who has just come from Sofia, where

Radoslavoff told him that Bulgaria would never, never take up arms against the Triple Entente, but that she might well move forwards towards the Enos - Midia line as soon as Turkey has retired some of her troops from there. Diamandy also is sure—I wish I could be equally sure—that Roumania will come in at the end of February ; my energetic visitor had also been to Nish and declares that the Serbian victory was due not only to Serbian pluck but to an Austrian rout, the result of the Slav regiments surrendering.

29th December.—The Ministers are a little fretful because Millerand remains at Bordeaux, and Viviani, Ribot and Sembat accuse him of showing fine contempt for Parliament, of allowing it to be said that it does not much matter what Parliament thinks, and of taking it too easily that the General Staff exhibits entire independence of the civil power.

In a long *tête-à-tête* I ask Galliéni to tell me frankly what his personal wishes are for the future. He would like to be made an Army Commander, as Joffre has proposed to him, preferably in Alsace, but he thinks there may be some delay as to this, because Joffre cannot for the present have sufficient men available to organise a separate Alsace army. As is only natural, Galliéni would not accept a Command other than an important one, and he sees no immediate vacancy ; he speaks somewhat bitterly, but with perfect correctitude, of the false situation in which he is placed, and I can only promise to do everything in my power to find some post worthy of him. Galliéni thinks it will be extremely difficult to pierce the enemy front, and does not look for much result from the current offensives now afoot, which have broken down completely near Arras and do not seem to be any more successful under de Langle de Cary.

Kindly telegrams from the Kings of Spain and Italy have already come in, but the New Year wishes which they convey are addressed to myself and not to France. Neutrality has her claims, and I suppose it would be difficult to send good wishes for the New Year to France without seeming to wish the converse to Germany.

30th December.—The Prince Regent of Serbia urgently asks for more munitions and says that without three more

mountain batteries it will be difficult to resume any offensive
in Bosnia ; he is very nervous as to a possible fresh Austrian
attack, and thinks that the appointment of an Archduke to
the command of the army detailed to march on Serbia shows
that Austria has set her teeth and is determined to wipe out
her recent defeat. Whichever way we look, the New Year
seems to be wrapped in impenetrable fog.

Tittoni has exhausted all his resources in his attempts
to justify the occupation of Vallona in Delcassé's eyes, and
he says that Essad Pasha, who has been bitterly opposed
by the combined efforts of Turks and Austrians in Tirana
(his own fief), finds himself in a highly awkward position.
Delcassé asked the Ambassador what would happen if Essad
Pasha were to beckon for help. " We should not move a
finger," was Tittoni's reply. " I have said, and repeated at
Rome, that our detachment of Marines must not go beyond
gunshot of the squadron ; in Albania circumstances are
very threatening, and we must not enlist ourselves on the
one side just when our own interests may enjoin us to enlist
ourselves on the other."

We have again attacked in Champagne, and the attacks
have been as costly and as unfruitful as on the 20th and 21st
of December ; all along the line we seem to be up against
an impregnable fortress.

31st December. — Malvy tells me that the Censor this
morning cut out half of an article which Clemenceau devoted
entirely to myself. In the first paragraphs, which were not
blue pencilled, my indefatigable antagonist relates that, at
my request, Millerand has brought Dragoons from the front,
so that I shall have an escort for my New Year visit to the
two Presidents. In the latter part of the article, which was
struck out, Clemenceau alleged that I had dared to ask for
my emoluments to be increased at a moment when unhappy
people are dying of hunger. Inured as one is to the whims
of a man who despises humanity because once and for all
he has represented humanity to himself as despicable, one
bitterly resents the double accusation which, at a moment
like this, is levelled at the citizen who, anyhow, is supposed
to represent France in the eyes of the men fighting for their

country as well as the rest of the world. I wrote at once to Clemenceau :

"M. le Président, I hear this morning that the Censorship has been applied in part to a paragraph in which you lodge two charges against me. I have of course no idea of offering you explanations on this point, but having been informed as to what the blue pencilled article contained, I cannot let pass your double imputation without a personal reply. You are a Senator, you have been Prime Minister, you are Georges Clemenceau ; I have to-day to exercise an office of the State in the presence of the enemy, and it shall never be said that I have neglected any occasion to avert civilian controversy. You have been the victim of a twofold hoax. The idea has never even occurred to me to bring back troops from the front for my visit to-morrow to the Houses of Parliament ; had I wished to have the usual cavalry escort, it would have been easy to call upon the mounted men who are in garrison here. But ten days ago I agreed with M. Dubost and M. Deschanel that the Ministers and I would go to-morrow without any display whatever. Thus no single Dragoon has been taken from any of the armies.

"Nor have I ever entertained the criminal thought of asking for any increase of my emoluments, and I should hold in utter contempt a President who, in this present stress, could conceive any such idea or who would not employ the last penny he could afford in helping the unfortunate. When the arrangement as to twelfths was set out, it was in conformity with the usual practice ; as the Presidential expenses were payable in advance and quarterly, the Exchequer allocated, according to custom and without my knowledge, one portion in excess of the six-twelfths for these expenses. This has always been done every time that the twelfths were voted, but, of course, the quarter's advance does not constitute any increase, but is subsequently deducted from the total annual allotment. Whether rightly or wrongly this procedure has been followed ever since 1875, and even gave rise a few years ago to an exchange of views in the Senate between M. Delahaye and the then Under-Secretary for Finance.

"At the last Session Parliament voted the twelfths without offering any objection to the figures which were attached to the draft, but having noticed later the figures proposed for the Presidential costs, I at once made inquiries of Ribot and, in spite of the explanation which he gave me and of which I now remind you, I asked him to depart from the usual custom, which, in my opinion, is scarcely justifiable, and only to credit me with the six-twelfths ; this is precisely what has been done. Thus, not only has nobody entertained the atrocious idea that you have attributed to me, but I have myself, and of my own accord, put a term to a practice which might lead to misunderstanding. I am aghast at your habit of lightly accepting the most absurd rumours so long as those rumours echo your own suspicions; what you said to me in our last interview bore witness to your strange errors of psychology when at any time you have *a priori* discredited someone. All the same, you might remind yourself that, unless he be a coward or a lunatic, a man who is charged with certain functions should be morally and physically incapable of yielding, in circumstances like these, to any personal considerations. If you really are unable to understand this, I can only pity you for being so utterly blinded by hatred and contempt.''

It seems almost unthinkable that the President of the Republic should in time of war have thus to justify himself for the good pleasure of M. Clemenceau ; there will of course be no reply to my letter, but I did give some relief to my feelings in writing it.

It is pleasant to turn from the articles of the *Homme Enchaîné* to the New Year wishes which flow into the Élysée : good wishes from the King of England, the King of the Belgians, the Belgian Government, the King of Serbia and his Prince Regent, General Joffre and the army, to mention no others ; everywhere the same expressions of confidence, everywhere the same determination to fight to a glorious finish.

Certainly the old year does not go out with a hymn of triumph. The enemy has failed in his big attempt and has tasted defeat at Nancy, the Marne and in Flanders ; he is brought to a standstill everywhere, but we are not the less so, and much of our land is still at the mercy of the invader. Each effort we make to break down the wall in front of us has been hideously costly, and has itself been broken against a resistance we can do nothing to diminish. We were unable to pierce either the centre or the wings of the enemy's lines ; we forbid that enemy any further passage, but we are in a sense bound hand and foot by him. There really seems no reason why the Germans and ourselves should not stand facing one another for all eternity.

Yet for every thoughtful and cool-headed Frenchman

the old year leaves behind it the promise of success ; I do
not say that time is on our side ; time only helps those who
help themselves, but in this respect we are going to be helped.
The material of war so grievously lacking we shall be able
to manufacture or buy ; the seas are open to us and we
can communicate freely, not only with our Allies, but with
America, while our enemy, on the other hand, is almost
under blockade. England and the Dominions are preparing
the armies which Lord Kitchener has told us we may look
for in 1915 ; in our midst youth is being trained, and is
impatient to rejoin its elders ; and soon our Allies and
ourselves will have fresh troops, better armed and better
equipped than ever. Surely we may lean with some trust
on the future. Circumstance wholly forbids us to despair.
For myself, if any doubt of the final issue were to intrude
itself, I should ask France herself to sustain and cheer me.
Day and night my country is in my thoughts. The more
she suffers the more she seems to me a living creature with
the features one knows so well. I see her before me, erect,
still bearing in her side the wounds of 1870, but calm, proud,
resolute. I hear her say, in tones which admit of no reply,
" As it is I who have bestowed on you the post which you
have accepted at my hands, it is for you to set the right
example. Remain at your post and be faithful to the end."

INDEX

Abd el Aziz, deposed Sultan of Morocco, received by Poincaré, 188-189

Académie Française, Poincaré's visit to, 219; Brieux represents in U.S.A., 289

Adriatic Fleet at Antivari, 179-180

Aeroplanes, French deficiency in, 187

Aisne, German stand on, 179-180, 183

Albert, Duke of Wurtemberg, 84

Albert, King of the Belgians, takes command of Belgian Army, 6; gratitude of, for help by Sordet and Mangin, 16; conversation with Berthelot on Belgian resistance, 18; offered and accepts French Military Medal, 21, 30; letter to Poincaré, 38; explains retirement on Antwerp, 68-69; praises Joffre and the Marne victory, 158, 162; on the Kaiser and Crown Prince's feeling against Belgium, 165-166; confidence of, 186; to leave Antwerp for Ghent, 204; French hospitality offered to, 208, 209; at the evacuation of Antwerp, 213; Poincaré visits, at La Panne and Furnes, 216, 226, 228, 233; to meet George V., 260; anxiety of, for Belgian civil population, 281; New Year greetings from, 295

Aldebert, Colonel, letter brought to Poincaré from King of Belgians by, 38; letter of, criticising Belgian retreat, 67-69; removed from Belgium, 69

Alfonso, King of Spain, offers to mediate, 58; and proposed sale of Spanish rifles, 135, 150; recalls Marquis de Villa-Urrutia, 142-143;

sympathy of, for France, 212-213; New Year's greetings from, 292

Algiers, loyal spirit of, 26

Almeyreda, M., 10

Alsace, French enter, 17; and advance in, 24; German offensive in, 27; French give way, 37-38, and 7th Corps evacuates, 45; Joffre's dispositions in, 59 *et seq.*; Guesde's interview with Poincaré on, 46; attitude of, to France, 70; commission to study administration of, 73; evacuation of, 90, 91, and becomes a secondary theatre, 110; German advance on Belfort, 112; organisation of supplies in, 262; Maurice Barrès on misunderstandings in, 267-268; proposed Christmas visit by Poincaré to, 283, 288, 291. *See also under* Lorraine

Altkirch, French take, 17, 37, 58

Amade, General d', at Lille, 73 and his evacuation of the town, 89, 101 161; on left of British at Mons, 86; no news of, 145, but found, 148, and proceeds to Beauvais, 149; inaction of, 155; his army re-formed and given to Brugère, 174; to take divisions drawn from Paris, 265

Amette, Cardinal, Archbishop of Paris, Jules Cambon confers with, on election of Pope, 72, 83; invites Poincaré to Memorial Mass for Pope Pius X., 73-74; letter to Poincaré from, enclosing letter from Pope Benedict XV., 170 and reply to and criticism of, 171-172 and *n.*; confers with Jules Cambon on Pope's wishes for Christmas Day truce, 258-259, 262-263

297

inof

Bourgeois, Léon, appointed on Commission Assistance and Supplies, 11, and is President, 111 ; conversation with Poincaré on loss of Mulhouse, 37 ; against Government leaving Paris, 121

Bourget, Air station at, 241

Bratiano, M., attitude to Sazonoff's proposals, 48, 55-56 ; favours Roumanian intervention, 178, 181 ; offers alliance, 237-238 ; on relations between Bulgaria and Austria, 246 ; hesitates, 284

Bréménil, German excesses at, 60

Breslau, see under *Goeben*

Breteuil, Marquis de, 260

Breux, German excesses at, 52

Briand, M. Aristide, 135, 150, 232, 261, 266 ; demands broadening of Cabinet, 10, 11 ; accuses Ministers of inefficiency, 89 ; offered Cabinet seat, 93, 94, and becomes Minister of Justice, 98 ; Clemenceau's opposition to, 103 ; concern for Delcassé, 145 ; goes to Paris, 150, 157, returns and reports on Galliéni and the populace, 164 ; visits the Est and Verdun, 214, 216 ; in Paris, 238, and statement in *Matin* regarding, 239-240 ; reads ministerial declaration in the Senate, 286-287

Bridoux, General, replaces Sordet, 157

Brieux, Eugène, represents the French Academy in U.S.A., 219, 289

Briey, Germans occupy, 23-24, 45 ; action at, 67

Brocqueville, Baron de, Belgian Prime Minister, conversation with Berthelot on Belgian resistance, 18 ; on Vandervelde's invaluable services, 43 ; conversation with Klobukowski on Belgian retirement to Antwerp, 67 ; confidence of, 186 ; asks aid for defence of Antwerp, 189 ; note of, desiring French hospitality for Belgian Army, 207-208 ; goes to Havre, 210 ; at evacuation of Antwerp, 213 ; at Dunkirk, 222 ; Poincaré's meeting with and impression of, 225-226 ; on Poincaré's visit to King and Queen of the Belgians,

234 ; asks for French loan for Belgium, 281, 285

Bruay, Poincaré at, 230

Brugère, General, takes over d'Amade's army, 174, and moves on Cambrai, 179

Brussels, German movement towards, 6, and preparations for protection of, 18 ; German entry into, 63, 74 ; occupation of, 87 ; arrest of M. Max at, 189

Bryan, Mr., Bernstorff's conversation with, 151

Buchanan, Sir George, British Ambassador at Petrograd, warns Sazonoff of need for Russian offensive, 45, 49 ; note to Sazonoff on final goal before peace, 177 ; asks for information of Russian movements, 213 ; on English attitude to the Narrows question, 241

Bujonchet, Colonel, Poincaré gives Cross of Legion of Honour to, 228

Bulgaria, relations with Russia, 25 ; mobilisation in, 37 ; Austrian overtures to, 41 ; promises neutrality, 44, 243, 292 ; sympathies with Austria, 82 ; attitude to Serbia and Greece, 83 ; violation of neutrality by, 115 ; effect of military and political events in Galicia, Roumania, and Turkey on, 154, 233 ; Allies' offer for neutrality of, 236 ; Sazonoff's proposals regarding, 238, 257, 284 ; Bratiano on secret agreement of Austria and, 246

Bülow, General von, in Charleroi region, 86 ; between Sambre and Meuse, 109 ; in Battle of the Marne, 151, 155 ; at Epernay, 200

Bülow, Prince, appointed German Ambassador in Rome, 276

Caillaux, M., in the Army Pay Department, 107-108, but name removed from Army List, 216 ; is given mission to Brazil, 232, 235, 240 ; George V. on, 260

Calais, Battle of, 244, 245, 273

Cambon, M. Jules, on German propaganda in Norway and Denmark, 48 ; on his journey from Germany, 70-71 ; confers with Cardinal

186 ; help planned for defence of Antwerp, 190 *et seq.* ; declares Protectorate over Egypt, 233, 238, 257, 282 ; annexes Cyprus, 234 ; policy of, regarding the Narrows, 241 ; new army trained by, 243, 296 ; representation of, at the Vatican, 257, 261 ; attitude of, to Christmas truce, 275 ; agrees to Franco-Moroccan Treaty, 1912, 283. *See also under* Grey, Sir Edward, *and* Expeditionary Force

Entente Cordiale, 2

Enver Pasha, 26, 41, 232

Epernay, Poincaré at, 200

Esperey, General Franchet d', 87, 209, 282 ; replaces Lanrezac, 137, 138 ; in Battle of the Marne, 144, 156 ; defeats Bülow, 151, and helps Foch, 152 ; Poincaré's visit to, and impression of, 200-201

Essad Pasha, Italian attitude to, 293

Expeditionary Force, first drafts sent, 20 ; Joffre on importance of, 22 ; General Wilson and transport of, 31 ; advance party at Rouen, 31 ; delay in reaching front line, 51 ; arrival of, 54 ; position of, 59 ; at Le Cateau, 61, 68; delay of, deplored, 73 ; takes up position near Mons, 86, 87 ; retires on Valenciennes-Maubeuge line, 96, and to Cambrai-Le Cateau line, 100 ; praised by Joffre, 104, 105 ; retreat before Von Klück, 110 ; splendid turn-out of, 113 ; Joffre's desire for slowing-up of, in retreat from Mons, 121, 122 ; plan of, to entrench at Meaux, 127, 128 ; in action and retreat to Marne, 128 ; to act with French troops, 133 and *n.* ; collaborates with Joffre on Marne, 136, 138, 140, 141, 143, 144, 146, 150, 155 ; attacked on the Aisne, 176 ; Joffre on movements and position of, 197 ; Joffre, Foch, and Kitchener confer on, 222-223; Foch's praise of, 224-225; losses in Flanders, 237 ; in the Battle of Calais, 244-245 ; Kitchener desires to be near the sea, 274, 275-276 ; Givenchy retaken by, 288. *See also under* French, Sir John

Fabre trial, the, 262

Fagolde, Captain, 133

Fashoda incident, the, 14

Ferdinand I., King of Bulgaria, Russian offers and demands to, 18, 19-20 ; intentions towards Serbia and Roumania, 25 ; distrusts Russia, 82 ; vacillating attitude of, 154, 235 ; von der Goltz visits, 280

Ferdinand, King of Roumania, announces death of King Carol, 206 ; takes the oath to Parliament, 210

Fère Champenoise, German looting at, 157

Fère-en-Tardenois, British G.H.Q., Poincaré visits, 199

Ferrata, Monsignor, candidate for Papacy, 72, 83 ; elected Secretary of State to Benedict XV., 170

Flanders, German offensive in, 211, 213, 223 *et seq.*, 236, 237, 239, 244-245, 273, 295

Florentin, General, Grand Chancellor of Legion of Honour, recommends excluding Germans from the Order, 242-243

Foch, General, in charge 20th Corps, 59, and retirement of, 72 ; Ninth Army constituted under, 137, 141 ; successful action in St. Gond marshes, 152 ; takes up offensive on the Marne, 156 ; Doumergue's praise of, 181 ; Joffre desires as assistant C.-in-C. with succession, 181-182, 183, and is appointed, 198 ; at Ypres, 215 ; reinforced, 219 ; plans to co-ordinate Allied troops in Flanders, 223 ; describes German attack on Yser, 223-224 ; Poincaré's visit to, and impressions of, at Cassel, 228-229; happy relations of, with Sir John French, 229 ; confers with Joffre and Poincaré at Romilly, 249 ; Doumer's conversation with, on Joffre, 276

France, relations of, with England and Russia at outbreak of war, 1-2 ; preparedness for war, 2-3 ; relations with Austria, 5, 6, and Russian proposals regarding Italy and Roumania, 9 ; note on state of war with Austria sent, 38-39 ; secrecy regarding setbacks, 42 ; Turkish policy of, 57-58; economic